T0385596

The Open
Sanctuary

The Open
Sanctuary

Access to God and the Heavenly Temple
in the New Testament

NICHOLAS J. MOORE

Baker Academic
a division of Baker Publishing Group
Grand Rapids, Michigan

Published by Baker Academic
a division of Baker Publishing Group
Grand Rapids, Michigan
www.bakeracademic.com

Printed in the United States of America

Library of Congress Cataloging-in-Publication Data
Names: Moore, Nicholas J. (Nicholas James), 1984– author.
Title: The open sanctuary : access to God and the heavenly temple in the New Testament / Nicholas J. Moore.
Description: Grand Rapids, Michigan : Baker Academic, a division of Baker Publishing Group, [2024] | Includes bibliographical references and index.
Identifiers: LCCN 2023049239 | ISBN 9781540965493 (cloth) | ISBN 9781493444496 (ebook) | ISBN 9781493444502 (pdf)
Subjects: LCSH: Heaven—History of doctrines. | Temples—History. | Bible. New Testament—Criticism, interpretation, etc.
Classification: LCC BT846.3 .M65 2024 | DDC 236/.24—dc23/eng/20240117
LC record available at https://lccn.loc.gov/2023049239

Temple image (as reconstructed by Charles Chipiez), Lebrecht History, Bridgeman Images

Baker Publishing Group publications use paper produced from sustainable forestry practices and postconsumer waste whenever possible.

24 25 26 27 28 29 30   7 6 5 4 3 2 1

For my parents

If a man should ascend alone into heaven and behold clearly the structure of the universe and the beauty of the stars, there would be no pleasure for him in the awe-inspiring sight, which would have filled him with delight if he had had someone to whom he could describe what he had seen.

Cicero, *On Friendship*

What kind of a person is he that can fully understand the activities of heaven, so that he can see a soul, or even perhaps a spirit—or, even if he ascended into the heavens and saw all these heavenly beings and their wings and contemplated them; or, even if he can do what the heavenly beings do—and is able to live?

1 Enoch 93.12

Even the Holy of Holies was broken open.
The deep darkness vanished into ordinary daylight,
and the mystery of God was only made more splendid.

Marilynne Robinson, *Gilead*

Contents

Preface

If there is wisdom in counting the cost of a building project before embarking on it (Luke 14:28–30), it is also fitting to look back with thanksgiving upon its completion (1 Kings 8:15–21). The foundations for this particular project were laid during my postgraduate work on Hebrews when I began to read and think about the concept of a heavenly tabernacle. In subsequent writing on Hebrews, I found myself returning again and again to cosmology. The plans for the book began to take shape in 2019, in part in connection with a paper I presented at the annual meeting of the Society of Biblical Literature in San Diego, and the initial scaffold was set up in a keynote lecture to the Doctor of Theology and Ministry residential school in Durham in January 2020. Construction began in presentations given at the Acts and Revelation seminars of the British New Testament Society in 2020, which took place online due to the coronavirus pandemic. Work continued in earnest in 2021 during a term of study leave, for which I am grateful to colleagues at St. John's College, Durham, and Cranmer Hall, the theological college nestled within St. John's. Special thanks are due to Philip Plyming, then warden of Cranmer Hall and now dean of Durham Cathedral, for his support in guarding and nurturing time for writing as part of our wider vocation to teaching and formation. My (now former) colleagues Richard Briggs and Andy Byers provided particularly helpful advice on the book proposal, in addition to their wisdom, encouragement, and humor over the years. Bryan Dyer, Wells Turner, and all at Baker Academic have been a wonderful combination of professional and personable throughout.

During 2022 a series of further presentations enabled me to test and reinforce the emerging edifice, at the Later Epistles seminar of the British New Testament Society in St. Andrews, the Tyndale Fellowship Biblical Theology Study Group, the Durham New Testament and Early Christianity and the Ancient Judaism research seminars, and the Oxford New Testament seminar. I am grateful to the convenors and participants at all these presentations. During the project, I have written several freestanding articles, festival booths to this tabernacle: one of these is essentially reproduced with minor changes as chapter 2,[1] and sections of two others are incorporated in chapters 3 and 6.[2] I record here my thanks for the open access agreements and (in one case) publisher's permission that have enabled me to reproduce them.

No undertaking like this is achieved without the collaboration of others, and I wish to express my thanks to a number of willing colaborers who graciously read and commented on sections of the manuscript or papers that preceded it: Andy Angel, Andy Byers, Philip Church, Kylie Crabbe, Rachel Danley, Will Foulger, Ian Galloway, Judson Greene, Lizzie Hare, Robert Hayward, Luke Irwin, Scott Mackie, Sarah Millican Jones, Lucas Mix, Walter Moberly, Geoff Moore, James Morgan, Philip Plyming, and Seb Rab. I am also grateful to Chris de Stigter, who provided invaluable assistance with the production of the ancient sources index. Any faults that remain, whether of design or execution, are mine alone.

Alongside the academic setting, our church and home have been invaluable contexts for the writing of this book, not least for reminding me why it all matters. My wife, Bekah, has been unstinting in her support for the project and (more importantly) her belief in and love for me. I am grateful to our sons, Simeon and Francis, for keeping me grounded, whether by watching films together or in teatime conversations. One particularly memorable exchange started with the question "Where is the garden of Eden?" After listening to me postulate and stumble on for several minutes, one of the boys cut in and asked, "Is it heaven?" Questions like that go to the heart of my topic more directly and incisively than I do here! I also record our shared memory of our third son, Phoenix, whose knowledge of heaven already far surpasses mine.

1. "Heaven and Temple in the Second Temple Period: A Taxonomy," *Journal for the Study of the Pseudepigrapha* 33, no. 1 (2023): 75–93, reproduced under a CC BY 4.0 license.

2. Chapter 3: "'God's Sanctuary in Heaven Was Opened': Judgment, Salvation, and Cosmic Cultus in Revelation," *Neotestamentica* 55, no. 2 (2021): 409–30, reproduced with permission. Chapter 6: "'He Saw Heaven Opened': Heavenly Temple and Universal Mission in Luke-Acts," *New Testament Studies* 68, no. 1 (2022): 38–51, reproduced under a CC BY 4.0 license.

My parents, Alison and Geoff, taught me what living as if heaven were real looks like, and they continue to model it. As a mark of my love and thanks, this book is dedicated to them. Finally, all this reading, thinking, and writing has been an imperfect offering of worship to Christ our high priest, through whom "we gaze into the heights of the heavens" (1 Clem. 36.2 LCL).

Durham, UK
Holy Week 2023

Abbreviations

General and Bibliographic

//	indicates a parallel Scripture passage
AAR	American Academy of Religion
AD	*anno Domini*, after the birth of Christ
ANF	*The Ante-Nicene Fathers*. Edited by Alexander Roberts and James Donaldson. 10 vols. New York: Christian Literature, 1885–96. Reprint, Grand Rapids: Eerdmans, 1950–51.
AT	author's translation
BC	before the birth of Christ
BDAG	Walter Bauer, Frederick W. Danker, William F. Arndt, and F. Wilbur Gingrich. *A Greek-English Lexicon of the New Testament and Other Early Christian Literature*. 3rd ed. Chicago: University of Chicago Press, 2000.
ca.	*circa*, about
chap(s).	chapter(s)
col(s).	column(s)
e.g.	*exempli gratia*, for example
esp.	especially
ET	English translation
KJV	King James Version
LCL	Loeb Classical Library
lit.	literally
LSJ	Henry George Liddell, Robert Scott, and Henry Stuart Jones. *A Greek-English Lexicon*. 9th ed. with revised supplement. Oxford: Clarendon, 1996.
LXX	Septuagint, Greek Old Testament
MT	Masoretic Text
NASB	New American Standard Bible
NIV	New International Version
NRSV	New Revised Standard Version
NRSVue	New Revisded Standard Version Updated Edition
NT	New Testament
OT	Old Testament

OTP   *Old Testament Pseudepigrapha*. Edited by James H. Charlesworth. 2 vols. New York: Doubleday, 1983–85.
ref(s). reference(s)
RSV   Revised Standard Version
SBL   Society of Biblical Literature
TDNT   *Theological Dictionary of the New Testament*. Edited by Gerhard Kittel and Gerhard Friedrich. Translated and edited by Geoffrey W. Bromiley. 10 vols. Grand Rapids: Eerdmans, 1964–76.

Old Testament

Gen.	Genesis	Song	Song of Songs
Exod.	Exodus	Isa.	Isaiah
Lev.	Leviticus	Jer.	Jeremiah
Num.	Numbers	Lam.	Lamentations
Deut.	Deuteronomy	Ezek.	Ezekiel
Josh.	Joshua	Dan.	Daniel
Judg.	Judges	Hosea	Hosea
Ruth	Ruth	Joel	Joel
1–2 Sam.	1–2 Samuel	Amos	Amos
1–2 Kings	1–2 Kings	Obad.	Obadiah
1–2 Chron.	1–2 Chronicles	Jon.	Jonah
Ezra	Ezra	Mic.	Micah
Neh.	Nehemiah	Nah.	Nahum
Esther	Esther	Hab.	Habakkuk
Job	Job	Zeph.	Zephaniah
Ps(s).	Psalm(s)	Hag.	Haggai
Prov.	Proverbs	Zech.	Zechariah
Eccles.	Ecclesiastes	Mal.	Malachi

New Testament

Matt.	Matthew	1–2 Thess.	1–2 Thessalonians
Mark	Mark	1–2 Tim.	1–2 Timothy
Luke	Luke	Titus	Titus
John	John	Philem.	Philemon
Acts	Acts	Heb.	Hebrews
Rom.	Romans	James	James
1–2 Cor.	1–2 Corinthians	1–2 Pet.	1–2 Peter
Gal.	Galatians	1–3 John	1–3 John
Eph.	Ephesians	Jude	Jude
Phil.	Philippians	Rev.	Revelation
Col.	Colossians		

Old Testament Apocrypha and Pseudepigrapha

Apoc. Ab.	Apocalypse of Abraham	Apoc. Zeph.	Apocalypse of Zephaniah
Apoc. Mos.	Apocalypse of Moses	Bar.	Baruch

2 Bar.	2 Baruch (Syriac Apocalypse)	Mart. Ascen.	Martyrdom and
3 Bar.	3 Baruch (Greek Apocalypse)	Isa.	Ascension of Isaiah
1–3 En.	1–3 Enoch	Sib. Or.	Sibylline Oracles
2 Esd.	2 Esdras	Sir.	Sirach
Jub.	Jubilees	Tob.	Tobit
Jdt.	Judith		
LAB	Liber antiquitatum biblicarum	T. Dan	Testament of Dan
Let. Aris.	Letter of Aristeas	T. Levi	Testament of Levi
1–4 Macc.	1–4 Maccabees	Wis.	Wisdom (of Solomon)

New Testament Apocrypha and Pseudepigrapha

| Apoc. Paul | Apocalypse of Paul | Ep. Ap. | Epistula Apostolorum |

Jewish Hellenistic and Rabbinic Works

Josephus

| Ant. | *Jewish Antiquities* | J.W. | *Jewish War* |

Philo

Alleg. Interp.	*Allegorical Interpretation*	Moses	*On the Life of Moses*
Decalogue	*On the Decalogue*	QE	*Questions and Answers on*
Dreams	*On Dreams*		*Exodus*
Drunkenness	*On Drunkenness*	QG	*Questions and Answers on*
Heir	*Who Is the Heir?*		*Genesis*
Embassy	*On the Embassy to Gaius*		
Migration	*On the Migration of*	Spec. Laws	*On the Special Laws*
	Abraham	Unchangeable	*That God Is Unchangeable*

Rabbinic Works

Abbreviations appear before tractate names to indicate the following sources: Mishnah (m.), Tosefta (t.), Babylonian Talmud (b.), and Jerusalem/Palestinian Talmud (y.).

| Gen. Rab. | Genesis Rabbah | Pesiq. Rab. | Pesiqta Rabbati |
| Num. Rab. | Numbers Rabbah | Tg. Ps.-J. | Targum Pseudo-Jonathan |

Dead Sea Scrolls

| 1QS | Rule of the Community | 4Q430 | Hodayot |
| 4Q174 | Florilegium | 11QT^a | Temple Scroll |

Apostolic Fathers

Barn.	Letter of Barnabas	Diogn.	Letter to Diognetus
1–2 Clem.	1–2 Clement	Herm.	Shepherd of Hermas,
Did.	Didache	Mand.	Mandate(s)

Herm. Sim.   Shepherd of Hermas,   Herm. Vis.   Shepherd of Hermas,
               Similitude(s)   Vision(s)
                                             Mart. Pol.   Martyrdom of Polycarp

Ignatius

Eph.   To the Ephesians   Phld.   To the Philadelphians
Magn.   To the Magnesians   Pol.   To Polycarp

Polycarp

Phil.   To the Philippians

Classical and Patristic Sources

Clement of Alexandria   ### Irenaeus

Strom.   Stromateis   Haer.   Against Heresies

Diodorus Siculus   ### Livy

Lib. Hist.   Library of History   Hist.   History of Rome

Diogenes Laertius   ### Origen

Lives   Lives and Opinions of Eminent   Cels.   Against Celsus
        Philosophers
                                             ### Pseudo-Heraclitus

Epiphanius   Ep.   Epistle

Pan.   Panarion

Introduction

This book is about heaven and also about the temple. This combination would not have raised any eyebrows in the ancient world, where a temple reflected heaven, and heaven was a temple. Both were dwelling places for gods. The idea is not present everywhere, but it is widespread. It was found across the ancient Near East, including ancient Israel, and (though in more fleeting fashion) in Greek and Roman thought. It is also not everywhere the same. There are many variations on the basic theme. The earliest followers of Jesus shared this notion with their wider cultural context, and especially with the Jewish milieu of the Second Temple period that they inhabited. Consequently, the idea's presence in many of the texts that would in time come to form the New Testament (NT) should come as no surprise. In this book, I explore notions of a heavenly temple in NT texts, both where it is evident, as in Hebrews and Revelation, and also where it is less obvious, as in the Gospels and Acts. I hope to show that heavenly temple language is not merely a figurative way of speaking about God's location and making sense of Jesus's ministry, death, resurrection, and ascension. Rather, it reflects an understanding of how the universe actually is and how God relates to human beings on earth. Early Christians drew on understandings of heaven and temple to make sense of what had happened in Jesus—or, better, they sought to place their experience of Jesus into what they already knew about the universe and its relation to the temple. That is to say, this study is interested not just in the heavenly temple but in the particular intersection of cosmos, cultus, and Christ. Early Christians affirmed that the heavenly temple had a bearing on Jesus's earthly ministry and that it became the setting for his ministry after his ascension. They also believed that he did not leave heaven unchanged. Thus, the heavenly temple both shaped and was shaped by the good news as they understood and articulated it, the very gospel that Jesus embodied and had entrusted to them.

Heavens, Temples, and the Setting of Early Christianity

In this introduction, I locate my topic in the context of studies of space and place and provide a plan of the book. Before that, we need to set the scene and define some terms. The English word "heaven(s)" reflects an ambiguity that ancient languages also knew. The heavens can refer to the sky or to the realm of God. We need some context to know whether the expression "the heavens opened" refers to a revelation from the divine throne or a torrential downpour of rain. "Heaven(s)" can indicate the visible skies, higher parts of the created order beyond them, or the uncreated realm where God is. In ancient cosmology, the universe is divided into three parts: heaven, earth, and sea.[1] Heaven is what lies above the solid firmament, or dome of the skies. The earth is a flat disc of land, surrounded by water and supported either as a raft on the waters or by subterranean pillars. And the sea is the waters around and below the earth. In the ancient Near East, gods could dwell in any of these three tiers, though they tended to make their home in the lower or upper regions. Ancient Israel's deity dwelt in the upper tier. Over time, we find recognition that as this heaven above the firmament was itself created, the Creator God must also have an uncreated dwelling place beyond it.

Astronomical observations in ancient Greece began to change the three-tier picture, solidifying in Aristotelian cosmology in the fourth century BC and refinements made by Ptolemy in the second century AD. The idea that the earth was spherical began to emerge, and the heavens were divided into the seven planetary spheres conceived as concentric circles (one each for the sun and moon, plus the five planets from Mercury to Saturn), with the fixed sphere of the stars above them. Beyond this lay the Empyrean, the realm of the element of fire and the unmoved mover, which Jews and Christians readily identified with God. For all the advances in the accuracy of astronomical predictions, this picture did not radically challenge ancient cosmology but only qualified it. In both systems, the earth lay at the center; it remained fixed and surrounded by waters. The planetary spheres simply added layers and distinctions within the third, heavenly tier. Thus we find writers in the Hellenistic and Second Temple periods happily using both threes and sevens (and other numbers as well) in their division of the universe or the heavens.

---

1. For accessible introductions to ancient cosmology, see Parry, *Biblical Cosmos*; Greenwood, *Scripture and Cosmology*.

This picture would remain intact until the Copernican revolution of the sixteenth century, which decentered the earth and identified it as another planet orbiting the sun. In this book, I use the term "heaven(s)" to refer to the upper part(s) of the created order and also occasionally to the uncreated realm of God. "Cosmos" and "universe" are used as synonyms for the whole created order. As we shall see, our texts sometimes speak of heaven, parts of it, a place or building within it, or multiple heavens as a temple or temple chamber. At other times, they connect the temple with the whole cosmos or with a primeval, central, representative part of it, such as the garden of paradise or the cosmic mountain.[2]

The practice of religion in the ancient world involved holy places, ritual processes, and specific personnel.[3] This threefold distinction is nicely represented in the final form of the Pentateuch, where divine command directs the Israelites to provide for each in turn: the holy place of the tabernacle (Exod. 25–40), the ritual process of the sacrifices (Lev. 1–7), and the religious personnel of the priests, specifically Aaron's family (Lev. 8–9). Priests oversaw the performance of religious rites and tended to holy places. Sacrifices were of animals, cereals, or libations of water, wine, or other liquid. These could be offered to a god in a number of ways, including by consumption, burning, pouring out, ritual application to altars or other items, or some combination of these. Along with the terms "priest" and "sacrifice," I make wide use of the noun "cult" (or sometimes "cultus") and the adjective "cultic" in their technical sense to refer to involvement or association with ritual process. Place, process, and personnel together, rightly observed, ensured good relations with the gods or a specific god and facilitated good cosmic order, including by influencing weather and disasters. The interest of this study is primarily in holy places, but the integral part played by all three in the practice of religion means that my discussion will frequently encompass religious personnel and processes as well. Because of the focus on place, below I engage the work of spatial theorists to help situate my discussion.

Our word "temple" derives from the Latin *templum*, which originally meant a portion of the skies marked out for divination by augury. It came to refer to a place set apart as holy and by extension to any shrine or building within it. For the most part, I use the term "temple" interchangeably with

---

2. As will become clear in chaps. 1 and 2, these motifs are important but are not pursued in their own right except insofar as they demonstrably intersect with temple in the texts at hand. On the garden motif, see Bockmuehl and Stroumsa, *Paradise in Antiquity*.

3. Menahem Haran (*Temples and Temple-Service*, 1) separates out time or occasion as a fourth "dimension" of cultic activity. My use of the term "process" is intended to incorporate temporal aspects of the cult.

"sanctuary" (derived from the Latin *sanctus*, meaning "holy," via Old French) to refer to a structure set apart for the worship and service of a deity. At times it is important to distinguish between the wider precinct, which may have contained various buildings and furnishings, and the central building itself. On these occasions, I reserve "temple" for the former and "sanctuary" for the latter, and where the difference is particularly significant I make the distinction even clearer (for example, by referring to the "temple complex" in contradistinction to the "temple proper," "temple building," or similar). Likewise, where temples had inner divisions, these are denoted either using the terminology of the text under discussion or with terms such as "chamber" or "compartment."

For the intersection of these domains—the cultic and the cosmic—I use "heavenly temple" as a convenient catch-all term, with occasional substitution of equivalent terms (for example, "cosmic sanctuary") for stylistic variety. The variation in specific conceptualizations across antiquity and in the early Christian texts of interest here will become apparent throughout the book, and in chapter 2 I introduce a more precise taxonomy and terminology to help distinguish four key points on the spectrum of possibilities. At all points the near context will clarify what I am referring to, allowing for the fact that in many cases the precise construal of a heavenly temple is underdetermined or ambivalent, at points perhaps deliberately so. In identifying relevant texts where a heavenly temple is not explicit or immediately obvious, I have sought out places where one of the two poles (heaven or temple) is evident, and from there have worked toward the other. The inclusion of a text indicates that I believe (and in my discussion, aim to show) that a sufficient case can be made for the presence of the other pole. That is, the texts treated here (particularly in chaps. 5–8) are either about heaven, with indications that they should be construed cultically, or about the temple, with indications that they should be construed cosmically. As ever, the proof of this particular pudding is in the eating.

We turn now to the specific setting of early Christianity. Religious places for the offering of sacrifice were ubiquitous in the ancient world, though buildings were not always required. It was possible to conceive of portable or temporary shrine structures, as with the Israelite tabernacle or sanctuaries at Shiloh and Gibeon. On the whole, however, where temple buildings were constructed, they were expensive and permanent edifices of stone or other solid materials, a token of their social, cultural, religious, and political importance. Ancient Israel was unusual—not for having a temple building for its patron deity, which was expected in the ancient Near East—but for insisting (with greater and lesser degrees of emphasis and success) on having no cult statue in the temple and on worshiping this god alone by sacrificing in this place alone. There is ample evidence of shrines, high places, and temples to other gods within Israel's borders during its history and also records of other Jewish temples, notably at Elephantine and Leontopolis in Egypt as well as the Samaritan temple at Mount Gerizim. However, through the centralizing reforms of kings such as Hezekiah and Josiah, the mainstream of Jewish thought and observance through and after the exile came to hold that there was only one legitimate temple, the one on Mount Zion in the holy city of Jerusalem, the place that YHWH had chosen for his name to dwell.[4] Having one temple was held to be a fitting reflection of the oneness of Israel's God and his universal sovereignty.

At this holy place, a temple was built by King Solomon, rebuilt after the exile, and renovated and extended by King Herod the Great at the turn of the eras. This final version was the temple Jesus and his early followers knew and frequented. Its centrality for Jewish national identity and religious, political, and economic practice is reflected in many of the Jewish texts that survive from the Second Temple period, including texts by those who rejected its current status or leadership as impure or corrupt. The NT also witnesses to this centrality in a number of ways. The Jerusalem temple is prominent in the Gospels and Acts, and cultic language is applied to the practice of ministry in Paul and 1 Peter. John's Gospel depicts Jesus as a temple, and Paul describes the community of his followers as a temple, a feature that has parallels in the Qumran community's self-understanding as reflected in the Dead Sea Scrolls. Both the NT's treatment of the Jerusalem temple and its extension of temple language to Jesus, ministry, and church have been widely noted and studied. In this light, it is surprising that the extensive association of temple with *heaven* in the NT has often been overlooked or downplayed, and it is the intention of this book to redress that balance. In the conclusion, I will return to this question and explore possible reasons for the neglect.

Heaven, Temple, and Spatial Theory

Given this study's primary interest in place and space, it will be useful at the outset to situate my discussion in the context of spatial theory (sometimes referred to as "critical spatiality"). In the humanities and social sciences, reflecting broader philosophical trends, time has had the upper hand against

4. Like the idea of paradise or Eden, the city of Jerusalem cannot be treated in detail here but is touched on only in connection with the temple; see further Walker, *Jesus and the Holy City*.

space. In response to the privileging or even hegemony of time and history over against space and geography, a number of spatial theorists in recent decades have contested the conceptualization of space as time's negative opposite.[5] This is often referred to as a "spatial turn." An example of the privileging of time is found in the work of the philosopher Henri Bergson, who saw space as a sphere for the representation and domination of time and therefore associated it with fixity, stasis, and closure. By contrast, the geographer Doreen Massey affirms that space is as "equally lively and equally challenging" as temporality.[6] Within biblical studies, an example of the prioritization of time over space can be seen in the way that "apocalyptic" (as both genre and worldview) has often been taken to mean simply "eschatological," treating the end of the present age and the beginning of the age to come.[7] Such a view has led in some biblical scholarship to the automatic classification of spatial elements as Platonist or Hellenistic. In reality, however, many apocalypses and apocalyptic texts incorporate spatial aspects as well as temporal ones, as we shall see recurrently in the following pages.

A distinction is often drawn between *space*, as something abstract and general, and *place*, as "space to which meaning has been ascribed."[8] This helpfully draws attention both to the existence of designated spaces and to the processes by which spaces are set apart as meaningful places. In relation to temples, meaning is ascribed by the demarcation of the physical location, the gathering of resources, the work of construction, the rites of consecration and inauguration, and by ongoing cultic service. In the case of the Israelite tabernacle, the nation's holy place was mobile within the wilderness, able to constitute any space as a holy place when it was set up. Yet it was also fixed in relation to the camp, located always at the center of the twelve tribes and therefore giving meaning to the wider national space. We should nevertheless exercise caution about the space-place distinction, for at its worst, like the space-time antithesis, it uses space only as a negative foil. Massey objects that the "global is just as concrete as the local place." This is not to devalue place: "My argument is not that place is not concrete, grounded, real, lived etc. etc. It is that space is too."[9] This is an important point: the temple-cosmos

---

5. A key study expressing this critique is Soja, *Postmodern Geographies*.

6. Massey, *For Space*, 14. For her critique of Bergson, see 20–30.

7. This despite the fact that the oft-quoted definition from the SBL Genre Project gives equal weight to both: apocalyptic is "both temporal, insofar as it envisages eschatological salvation, and spatial insofar as it involves another, supernatural world" (J. Collins, *Apocalypse*, 9). For a critique of the overemphasis on eschatology, see Rowland, *Open Heaven*, 23–48.

8. Carter, Donald, and Squires, *Space and Place*, xii.

9. Massey, *For Space*, 184–85. See also 101–3, 140–41.

connection in some ways constitutes the entire universe as a holy place and therefore meaningful; yet even when construed as space the cosmos remains concrete and real.

Dissatisfied with binary construals of space, a number of thinkers have utilized a threefold division. Henri Lefebvre identifies three dimensions, which are taken up by David Harvey.[10] He speaks of "material space" (or experience) as the location for physical interactions in space, "representations of space" (or perception) as the ways in which we understand and talk about material space, and "spaces of representation" (or imagination) as ways that we "imagine new meanings and possibilities for spatial practices."[11] In recent work, Loïc Wacquant has identified a "trialectic" of space in the thought of sociologist Pierre Bourdieu.[12] Wacquant's three categories of "physical space," "symbolic space," and "social space" do not map directly onto Harvey's, but they encapsulate some of the same concerns. In particular, Bourdieu highlights the constant renegotiation of space through struggles of power.[13] Even physical or material space is not simply static but is a place for encounter: all space is "the product of interrelations . . . constituted through interactions, from the immensity of the global to the intimately tiny."[14]

The work of Edward Soja has been especially influential in promoting a threefold categorization, building on the work of Lefebvre and Harvey but introducing the terminology of "firstspace," "secondspace," and "thirdspace."[15] Firstspace is material, physical, and objective, the world as we experience it. We inhabit firstspace and, as well as moving through it, might seek physically to circumscribe and appropriate it. Secondspace is space as it is mentally conceived and articulated or projected; it is space in the abstract, a conceptual, cognitive, and symbolic world. Secondspace involves the projection or production of knowledge through discourse or practice and thus is often a way of attempting to impose fixity and order on the encountered reality of firstspace. It is not, however, necessarily derivative of or dependent on firstspace but has its own integrity and even, arguably, dominance.[16] Thirdspace is lived space, an unpredictable other that disrupts the binary

10. Lefebvre, *Production of Space*; Harvey, *Condition of Postmodernity*, 201–323.
11. Harvey, *Condition of Postmodernity*, 218–22.
12. Wacquant, "Rethinking the City."
13. Wacquant ("Rethinking the City," 820–21) identifies symbolic space as molding how we think and act and thus informing our *habitus*, whereas social space is the parent category for Bourdieu's concept of *field*.
14. Massey, *For Space*, 9, and 117–25.
15. Soja, *Journeys*.
16. Soja, "Expanding the Scope," 266.

relation between space-as-it-is and space-as-we-construe-it.[17] Soja describes thirdspace as

> an-Other world, a meta-space of radical openness where everything can be found, where the possibilities for new discoveries and political strategies are endless, but where one must always be restlessly and self-critically moving on to new sites and insights, never confined by past journeys and accomplishments, always searching for differences, an Otherness, a strategic and heretical space "beyond" what is presently known and taken for granted.[18]

As Soja articulates it, thirdspace is a "*lived space as a strategic location* from which to encompass, understand, and potentially transform all spaces simultaneously."[19] It is, therefore, a disruptive space but also a constructive one in which new understandings are forged: it "seeks to disorder, deconstruct and tentatively reconstitute in a different form the entire dialectical sequence and logic."[20] In many ways, Soja's thirdspace is simply a more acute or intensive form of Harvey's "spaces of representation," which are mental constructs for the reimagination of space.[21]

Spatial theory, especially but not only in Soja's terms, has been found generative for reading biblical texts.[22] Here I will elucidate the notions of cosmos and temple in the spatial terms outlined above. In the chapters that follow, spatial theory is not engaged explicitly; rather, the argument proceeds using the usual tools of historical and philological exegesis, and I will return briefly to spatial theory in the conclusion.

The firstspace of a temple is its physical and geographical location and the space circumscribed by its precincts, walls, and chambers. Already here, however, we see the interaction between firstspace and secondspace. For example, the firstspace of Herod's temple instantiated the secondspatial mapping of the Jew-gentile distinction in the perimeter wall with its inscription warning

17. Thirdspace seeks "to break out from the constraining Big Dichotomy by introducing an-Other" (Soja, "Expanding the Scope," 268).
18. Soja, *Journeys*, 34.
19. Soja, *Journeys*, 68 (emphasis original).
20. Soja, "Expanding the Scope," 269.
21. For Soja, the disruptive aspect is postmodern; for the texts studied here we might appropriately characterize it as apocalyptic.
22. Note especially the AAR/SBL seminar Constructions of Ancient Space and the five-volume *Constructions of Space* emerging from it. For useful introductions and surveys, see Stewart, "New Testament Space/Spatiality"; Schreiner, "Space, Place and Biblical Studies"; Sleeman, *Geography and the Ascension*, 22–56. Sleeman ("Critical Spatial Theory 2.0") sounds a note of caution against uncritical adoption of spatial theory in that it is not a value-neutral tool kit. I engage it as a helpful framework for elucidating findings that emerge from the ancient texts.

foreigners not to enter on pain of death (Josephus, *Ant.* 15.417). The whole cosmos is also a firstspace, including heaven. For ancient cosmology, it is "up there," above the firmament, and even when not construed in such literally vertical terms, it remains another concrete place. While most do not go there, some can and do, such as exalted humans as well as gods and angels who pass between there and earth.

Ancient Near Eastern temples are secondspaces in that they map either the heavens or the whole of the created order. In chapter 2 especially, I will trace a range of ways in which Second Temple Jews understood their sanctuaries to chart heaven or the cosmos. The relationship is reciprocal, in that understandings of the universe shape temple building and vice versa.

Ancient temples are fundamental to their people's conceptual world on the horizontal plane as well. As the omphalos, the center or navel, an ancient city-state temple such as the temple of Marduk in Babylon or the oracle at Delphi holds a structuring function for its people's national life and identity as well as for the people's understanding of geography. The Jerusalem temple determined the contours of Israel's everyday life: food and purity regulations, association with gentiles, and times of prayer. This secondspatial function reaches a particularly intense form in the teaching of the Pharisees, for whom daily life was to mirror the standards of temple purity, but this is only an extension, not an invention, of the temple's conceptual and symbolic power.

As for thirdspace, if we take this as the lived reality of space, then there is a constant and ongoing encounter with temple spaces that shapes the understanding and at times the reimagination of the other two spaces. In its more acute, Sojan form, thirdspace involves disruption. This might be planned, such as Herod's reconstruction of the temple, which sought to establish his power and reputation as king and incorporated Hellenistic architecture into the expanded temple complex. The unsettling nature of his plans is evident in the way he had to reassure the people that he had the means and not only the intent to carry them through (Josephus, *Ant.* 15.380–425). Reconfiguration can also be more abrupt, as in the destruction of the first and second temples, or in the rupture between Qumran's Teacher of Righteousness and the temple establishment's Wicked Priest. These events function thirdspatially to force a renewed conceptualization of temple, as in Ezekiel's vision or the Qumran community's self-understanding as temple and its production of the utopian Temple Scroll. In the texts to be explored in the following pages, such thirdspatial reimaginings are often prompted by heavenly visions, ascents, and angelic visitations. Supremely, they are prompted by key moments in the lifetime of Jesus: his birth, baptism, transfiguration, crucifixion, resurrection, and ascension. This imaginative work prompts the early Christian movement's reconfiguration of Second Temple secondspace both before and after the destruction of the firstspace of the Jerusalem temple in AD 70.

Plan of the Book

This book is organized into eight chapters. Chapters 1 and 2 set the scene for our study of early Christian texts. I first lay out the relation of heaven and temple in ancient Near Eastern texts, in the Old Testament (OT), and in Greco-Roman writers. All of these corpora connect temples with heaven, although already a variety of ways of relating the two can be seen. I then move to the Second Temple period, when the association becomes fuller and more fruitful, both because we have more texts to go on and because of a number of developments and elaborations of the basic idea. Here I propose a new taxonomy charting a spectrum of four main ways of relating heaven and temple that can be found in the period. These also account for the material covered in chapter 1.

Chapters 3 and 4 turn to Revelation and Hebrews, the NT books that most explicitly treat the notion of a heavenly sanctuary. Revelation begins with the already-glorified sacrificial Lamb on the throne of the heavenly sanctuary. It offers a striking conception of the temple opening for the holiness of God to emanate in judgment but also sees the temple and altar as a place of refuge for faithful martyrs. At the end of time, the heavenly temple unites with the earth in the holy city of Jerusalem, a cube-shaped most holy place whose open gates symbolize the fulfillment of eschatological peace and security. Hebrews envisages not a heavenly temple but specifically a heavenly tabernacle, which is the model for Moses's tabernacle; this in turn becomes instructive for the nature of Jesus's ministry as both priest and sacrifice on the Day of Atonement. His ascension reconfigures heavenly space by drawing aside the veil and constituting heaven as a single-chambered sanctuary that is now open to give help and assurance to believers.

In the second half of the book, we turn to the Gospels, Acts, and other early Christian literature, where the concept of a heavenly temple is more muted. Chapter 5 explores Mark and Matthew, both of which present an open heaven in temple terms. For Mark, this is integrated into his literary structure, which places baptism, transfiguration, and crucifixion in relation to one another. For Matthew, it finds expression in his presentation of heaven and earth and his exploitation of the motif of the holy mountain. In chapter 6, I show how Luke and Acts carry forward the idea of a heavenly temple through the pivotal narration of Jesus's ascension, placing him firmly in heaven, from where he continues to direct the expansion of the Way. Such expansion happens through a series of cultically framed heavenly interruptions. Chapter 7 turns to John's Gospel, where I argue that the idea of a heavenly temple is not in competition with but rather fundamental to John's distinctive temple Christology. Finally, in chapter 8 I explore other early Christian texts within and beyond the NT canon in order to trace the notion of the heavenly temple within the developing stream of early Christianity.

In the conclusion, I summarize the argument of each chapter before offering reflections on why biblical scholarship and biblical theology have tended to prioritize community-as-temple over heavenly temple and articulating the contribution of this study in terms of early Christianity's reconfigured map of the cosmos. The heavenly temple is presupposed across much of the NT, a notion shared with its wider Second Temple milieu. Yet it has a particular christological configuration, with Christ's ministry bringing about structural (and not only ritual) changes, which relate in one way or another to the openness and accessibility of the divine realm.

Antiquity

The Cosmic Center

The connection between temples and heaven is ancient and widespread. This chapter sets the context for the more detailed exploration of Second Temple and NT literature that will follow in the rest of the book, and it does so in three unequal parts. First, we explore heavenly temple notions in ancient Near Eastern literature. The association is commonplace, usually in relation to creation myths, even if underdeveloped. Second, we turn to the OT, where the presence and significance of heavenly temple motifs have been disputed. Examination of Gen. 1–3 suggests that while these chapters have an interesting intertextual relationship to the tabernacle's construction and other temple passages, they do not in themselves present either the cosmos or the garden of Eden as sanctuaries. The heaven-temple connection is nevertheless attested in a number of OT texts with various shades of emphasis. Our last stop in the OT is Ezekiel's temple vision, which reveals a heavenly temple and introduces the question of eschatology to mirror the ancient Near Eastern interest in protology. In the third and final subsection of this chapter, we briefly examine Greek and Roman cultic practice. Although many temples to various gods were found in every city, Greco-Roman religion centers on the altar and its sacred precinct, the temenos, more than on the temple. Associations of temple architecture with the cosmos are not persuasive, but there is a recurrent if fleeting "universe as temple" motif in Greek and Roman writers.

The Ancient Near East

From extant textual and archaeological remains, a striking commonality can be detected in ancient Near Eastern temple ideology.[1] Creation myths depict a god or gods establishing creation as a temple, and either deities or human kings construct the earthly temple building to reflect this cosmic reality.[2] The Sumerian Gudea cylinders, dating from the late third millennium BC, describe the building of the main temple of Girsu, which is dedicated to the god Nin-girsu. Both of these two-foot-long cylinders (labeled A and B) were installed by Gudea, ruler of Lagash, who rebuilt the temple.[3] It is "like a huge house embracing heaven," which floats "in the midst of heaven as a cloud" and fills "the space between heaven and earth like the hills" (cylinder A, 578–90).[4] Its scale is "high as a great mountain," and its foundation pegs are driven so deep into the ground they are associated with Apsu, the primordial water source (602–16). It is replete with imagery of flora, and the beams "looked like dragons of the *abzu*" (591–92). The Ekur temple in the city of Nippur was the most important temple in Sumer, the home of the leading deity Enlil, and was known as Duranki, the bond between heaven and earth. There is some evidence to suggest that the temple or its city was also considered the navel of the earth. The idea of temple/city as navel would become popular later in various Mediterranean cosmologies.[5]

The Babylonian creation epic Enuma Elish, written in Akkadian and dating to the second millennium BC, describes the cosmic battle between the chaos-monster Apsu and the god Ea. After Ea's victory, he "established his dwelling" upon Apsu. He uses the name Apsu for the "sacred chamber" in which he rests, placing shrines there: "In that same place his cult hut he founded" (1.69–77).[6] Later, Ea's son, the god Marduk, is made "patron of our sanctuaries" by the other gods after he defeats Tiamat, who was seeking to avenge Apsu. Marduk decrees the building of his temple above Apsu, as a house to receive the gods when they come up from Apsu or down from heaven (5.113–30), the name "Babylon" meaning "the houses of the great gods." In the sixth tablet, Marduk commands the lesser gods to construct Babylon

---

1. Lundquist, "Common Temple Ideology," 54. Hundley (*Gods in Dwellings*, 131n2) observes that "to the ancient Near Eastern mind, the way forward was often a return to the glorious past."

2. Kapelrud, "Temple Building"; Van Leeuwen, "Cosmos, Temple, House."

3. Kramer, "Temple in Sumerian Literature."

4. Text from the Electronic Text Corpus of Sumerian Literature, https://etcsl.orinst.ox.ac.uk/.

5. Kramer, "Temple in Sumerian Literature," 7; Burrows, "Cosmological Patterns in Babylonian Religion," 28–30.

6. Text from Pritchard, *Ancient Near Eastern Texts*.

as his throne and chamber, to be named "The Sanctuary." The scale of this temple is "as high as Apsu [is deep]" (6.47–72). Later in tablet 6, we read the instruction "Make a likeness on earth of what he [Marduk] has wrought in heaven" (6.113).

Scholars of these texts identify a number of recurrent features. First, the temple represents the cosmic mountain, a connection particularly evident in the foundation of temples on mountains and in the Mesopotamian ziggurat's multiple tiers that mimic the form of a mountain.[7] "The local sacred mountain was . . . the symbol, or representation, of the cosmos which formed the true abode of the deity whom men worshipped."[8] As such, second, it was the center of the universe, the axis mundi that bridged the cosmic span from the primordial waters of the deep (called *nun* in Egypt, *abzu* in Mesopotamia, and *tehom* in Israel) to the heights of the heavens.[9] In this vein, a temple or its setting could be identified as the primordial hillock, the first place to arise from the waters of chaos. Third, the connection with the waters of the deep also leads to an association of temples with the waters of life, represented by the springs or reservoirs found near or below them. There is a ready connection here with the use of water for purification and libations in temple ritual. Finally, temples are often associated with the tree of life, with fecund vegetation, and with a garden.[10] The various construals of the cosmos-temple relationship (imitation of creation, imitation of what has been made above, cosmic center) are not highly elaborated in their own right, and they should not be sharply distinguished.[11]

Ancient Near Eastern temples hosted a cult statue representing the deity.[12] There was acknowledgment both that the gods dwelt in their temples and at the same time that they could not be confined to a single place on earth, given

7. Clifford, "Temple and the Holy Mountain."

8. Lundquist, "Common Temple Ideology," 57; Clements, *God and Temple*, 3. For evidence relating to Mount Zaphan, the Canaanite holy mountain, and its echoes in the OT, see Clements, *God and Temple*, 6–9.

9. On the cosmic center, see Eliade, *Myth of the Eternal Return*, 6–11, 21–34. For a critical appreciation of Eliade, see J. Smith, *Map Is Not Territory*, 88–103.

10. These points are well articulated in Lundquist, "Common Temple Ideology," 60–70; Levenson, *Sinai and Zion*, 111–37. In this light, the connection between Eden and the holy mountain in Ezek. 28:11–19 is noteworthy. In defense of creational imagery here, see Strong, "Cosmic Re-creation and Ezekiel's Vocabulary," 246–49.

11. Mircea Eliade (*Sacred and the Profane*) provides a breadth of material suggesting commonality across an even wider range of ancient cultures, though he runs the risk of too readily conflating these.

12. On the nature of cultic service, see Levavi, "Sacred Bureaucracy of Neo-Babylonian Temples."

their heavenly origins and dominion over large parts of the world.[13] A particular temple might be designated the primary earthly abode of a specific god, with other temples to the same god relating to the central temple. Religious prominence was inextricably bound up with political power in this regard.[14] There could be many copies or instantiations of the one true dwelling place of the deity, and the local gods were understood as forms of the universal gods; the two could not be sharply distinguished.[15] As an imitation of the divine act of creation and as a house within which the deity dwelt, "the temple was a mixing of worlds—in effect, heaven on earth—with elements of both built into the architecture itself."[16]

The Old Testament

The cultural continuity in ancient Near Eastern temple ideology lasted into late Hellenistic times,[17] and it is therefore natural to ask whether such ideology is reflected in the OT. Shmuel Safrai is skeptical, stating that "it is doubtful whether any evidence of the heavenly Jerusalem or Temple is to be found in the Bible," though he notes that numerous texts are open to interpretation in this direction and are indeed read this way in the Second Temple period and beyond.[18] At one level, what matters for this study is the fact of a range of heavenly temple concepts manifested in a large number of texts of a variety of genres and provenances from the Second Temple period. These texts form the pertinent context for an investigation of similar ideas in the NT and are examined in some detail in chapter 2 below. Yet before we do this, it is important to ask whether and how we find such notions within the OT, given the importance of this collection of texts for Second Temple authors.[19]

13. Clements, *God and Temple*, 1–3.
14. Root, "Palace to Temple."
15. In this regard, see the recent thesis by George Heath-Whyte that Marduk denotes the god in all his roles and Bel refers to the same god specifically in his role of patron deity for Babylon and as instantiated in his cult statue. Heath-Whyte, "'Bēlu' and 'Marduk' in Neo-Assyrian Royal Inscriptions."
16. Hundley, *Gods in Dwellings*, 131.
17. Lundquist, "Common Temple Ideology," 54. On the wider points of commonality between the OT and the ancient Near East, see Stavrakopoulou, *God: An Anatomy*.
18. Safrai, "Heavenly Jerusalem," 13.
19. I do not intend to suggest a sharp delineation between OT and Second Temple texts, since many of the former reached final form or were even composed well into the Second Temple period (defined as starting with the return from exile in ca. 516 BC). Nevertheless, with the exception of Daniel, which most scholars date to the second century BC, the texts considered here are earlier than those considered in chap. 2.

Creation and Eden as Sanctuaries?

Some have seen in the creation account of Gen. 1 an Israelite version of the cosmogonic myth of a deity creating the universe as a temple in which to dwell.[20] Yet there is no explicit designation of creation as a temple or dwelling place for Elohim, in marked contrast to the language seen above in ancient Near Eastern accounts.[21] Some have argued for connections between Gen. 1:1–2:3 and the depiction of the tabernacle's construction in Exod. 25–40 (largely the work of the priestly source P). Exodus 40:2, 17 dates the tabernacle's construction to the first day of the first month. As there are six speech acts prompting the six days of creation, so there are six commands to build the tabernacle.[22] The seventh command is to observe the sabbath, just as God rests on the seventh day, and sabbath is connected with creation (Exod. 31:17). Peter Kearney seeks to establish further connections between the commands and what is made within each day.[23] His schema struggles in that the first command in Exodus is very long (25:1–30:10) and is followed by a series of relatively short ones. Some of the connections made are also tenuous, such as connecting Aaron's lamps with God's creation of light, but this same connection was observed by the rabbinic text Midrash Tanhuma (Pequde 2.3), so it is not strictly a modern scholarly observation.[24] Furthermore, the completion narratives for creation and tabernacle parallel one another, as noted by Joseph Blenkinsopp: language of finishing all the work, blessing, and making holy (compare Gen. 1:31–2:3 with Exod. 39:32, 43; 40:9–11, 33–34).[25] Other elements of Gen. 1 have suggestive connections with priestly material elsewhere in the OT. For example, the creation of the firmament to "divide" the waters above from the waters below in Gen. 1:6 uses the same verb in the hiphil stem that is used for the priests' division of holy from common in Lev. 10:10, and a wall fulfills the same function in Ezek. 42:20 (הבדיל, מבדיל). From this it is easy to see how later Jewish interpreters could identify the firmament with

20. John Walton is a prominent proponent of this idea, in an article and a monograph and also a popular book. See his "Creation in Genesis 1:1–2:3"; *Genesis 1 as Ancient Cosmology*; and his popular work, in part positioned as a rebuttal of six-day creationism, *The Lost World of Genesis One*. See also Beale, *Temple and the Church's Mission*, 60–80; Lioy, *Axis of Glory*, 5–16, 33–38.

21. For a critical response to J. Walton et al., see Jenson, "Cosmic Temple? A Skeptical Assessment."

22. Note the seven instances of "The LORD said to Moses": Exod. 25:1; 30:11, 17, 22, 34; 31:1, 12.

23. Kearney, "Creation and Liturgy," 375–78.

24. For these critiques and the similarity with Midrash Tanhuma, see Levenson, *Creation and the Persistence of Evil*, 83–84, 97–98.

25. Blenkinsopp, "The Structure of P," 280; Levenson, "Temple and the World," 287.

the temple veil, as we will see in chapter 2. None of this means creation in Gen. 1 is a sanctuary, but it shows how the editors of the Pentateuch shaped tabernacle and creation narratives in relation to one another, and it illustrates the kind of verbal connections that later writers picked up on.

Similar arguments have been raised with respect to Gen. 2–3. These chapters should not be conflated with Gen. 1, both because they derive from different sources (Gen. 1 from P; Gen. 2–3 from J or non-P) and because in relation to this question the proposals represent quite different construals of the cosmos-temple relationship. In a suggestive article, Gordon Wenham identifies a series of features of Eden that mirror the tabernacle and temple.[26] The verb used of God "walking about" in the garden elsewhere describes God's cultic presence (the hithpael stem מתהלך, Gen. 3:8; cf. Lev. 26:12; Deut. 23:15 [ET v. 14]; 2 Sam. 7:6–7); the verbs "to till and to keep" are elsewhere in the Pentateuch used together only of the Levites' duties (לעבדה ולשמרה, Gen. 2:15; cf. Num. 3:7–8; 8:26; 18:5–6); and the Gihon river, which bears the same name as the spring below the temple mount in Jerusalem (Gen. 2:13; 2 Chron. 32:30). Other connections are the cherubim at the entrance to the garden and sanctuary, both approached from the east, and the tree of life, which is like the menorah. The other suggested connections are rather weak, certainly on their own: precious jewels and the gold of Havilah (Gen. 2:12) paralleling the gold of the tabernacle furnishings and the jewels of the high priest's vesture; the knowledge of good and evil connecting with the law kept in the temple; and the fact that both Adam and the priests are clothed in "tunics" (Gen. 3:21; Exod. 28:40–41).

All of the proposed links have been subjected to scrutiny by Daniel Block, who finds them wanting. For example, "walking about" relates to God's presence with his people in general, and not specifically in the sanctuary.[27] He also raises the question of divine dwelling: whereas the ancient Near Eastern texts clearly present a god or gods establishing creation or a part thereof as their dwelling, little in OT Scripture suggests that God forms either creation or Eden for this purpose.[28] In short, while Gen. 1–3 has connections to cultic functions elsewhere in the Hebrew Scriptures, and while some of these links doubtless represent editorial work that shaped Genesis as much as the other, canonically later, texts, there is insufficient evidence to support seeing a cosmic temple or garden-temple in these texts. Block articulates it well when he notes that "the Edenic features of the tabernacle, the Jerusalem temple, and the

---

26. Wenham, "Sanctuary Symbolism." See also Beale, "Eden, the Temple, and the Church's Mission"; Beale, *Temple and the Church's Mission*, 29–122.
27. Block, "Eden: A Temple?," 5–17.
28. Block, "Eden: A Temple?," 21–27.

temple envisioned by Ezekiel are obvious. . . . However, the fact that Israel's sanctuaries were Edenic does not make Eden into a sacred shrine. At best this is a nonreciprocating equation."[29] The evidence demonstrates that Israel's sanctuaries evoke Eden,[30] but this does not entail that Eden is a sanctuary.

Connecting Heaven and Temple

In addition to the Edenic aspects of the tabernacle, Exodus contains the idea of correspondence that we noted in some ancient Near Eastern texts:

> In accordance with all that I show you concerning the pattern of the tabernacle and of all its furniture, so you shall make it. . . . See that you make them according to the pattern for them, which is being shown you on the mountain. . . . You shall erect the tabernacle according to the plan for it that you were shown on the mountain. (Exod. 25:9, 40; 26:30)

The most natural reading of "pattern" (תבנית, παράδειγμα [τύπος in 25:40]) here is that it refers to a plan or outline for the sanctuary and its furniture. What is foremost is that Moses constructs the tabernacle in exact accordance with the divine command and intent. Yet along with this primary emphasis, these verses in Exodus establish the principle of correspondence between what is above and what is below (cf. Enuma Elish 6.113). This will become very important, as we shall see in the following chapter. According to the chronicler, Solomon's temple has a similar divine validation and mirroring function: David entrusts his heir not only with raw construction materials but also with "the plan [תבנית, παράδειγμα] for the temple" (1 Chron. 28:11–12, 19) revealed to him in written form by the Lord.

Heaven is identified with God's temple in a number of texts, particularly in Psalms, where poetic parallelism conveys the idea with great economy of expression. Psalm 11:4 reads, "The Lord is in his holy temple; / the Lord's throne is in heaven [בשמים]," using a term that can refer to a temple or palace (היכל). The distinction between political and religious spaces cannot be sharply drawn in the period, and certainly not in relation to a deity whose location is always also a place of veneration. This accounts for the identification of the regal furniture of the throne with the cultic furniture of the ark, as we shall see below.[31] Psalm 150:1 similarly states, "Praise God

29. Block, "Eden: A Temple?," 21.
30. Janowski, "Tempel und Schöpfung."
31. See also Jer. 17:12, which names the throne the "shrine of our sanctuary." This is not to say that such motifs cannot occur with only political connotations. In fact, this seems to be the case in the vision of Micaiah ben Imlah in 1 Kings 22:19–22, who observes heaven as a royal

in his sanctuary [בקדשו]; / praise him in his mighty firmament [ברקיע]," using the same term for firmament as in Gen. 1:6.[32] If these texts are viewed as establishing a parallel, then they equate heaven, the space above the firmament, with God's sanctuary. Alternatively, if they are viewed as establishing a lesser-to-greater analogy, then they relate heaven to the earthly sanctuary as two centers for the divine presence.[33]

Other texts establish an analogy between the sanctuary and creation. In Ps. 78, God's election of Judah is demonstrated by his choice of Mount Zion and establishing David's dynasty. The construction of God's "sanctuary" (מקדשו) is "like the high heavens, / like the earth, which he has founded forever" (78:69).[34] The emphasis here lies on the security of the nation as demonstrated in the temple and monarchy, but the analogy suggests that the correspondence between heaven and earth is instinctive. The holy mountain and sanctuary are equated in the Song of Moses in Exod. 15:17, which suggested to later readers a correspondence between earthly and heavenly sanctuaries.[35] Zion's global significance can be seen in Ps. 65, which opens with praise to God in Zion and the temple (vv. 1–4) and moves seamlessly to describe the ends of the earth, God's control of the gateways of the morning and evening, and the abundance of creation under his sovereignty (vv. 5–13). The Psalter is full of references to God's dwelling in heaven and of worship at his temple, and at times the line between these two is blurred. For example, Ps. 29 invokes the worship of heavenly beings and affirms God's cosmic sovereignty over flames and flood; in verse 9 we read that "in his temple [בהיכלו] all say, 'Glory!'" It is not possible to say with certainty whether this temple is the earthly one or the location of the "sons of gods" in their holy attire of 29:1–2.[36]

Still other texts regard heaven and the temple as functionally connected in some way. This idea is consistent with the notion of correspondence but is not quite the same thing. In an anthropomorphic vein, the God who is enthroned on the cherubim in heaven has a "footstool" (הדם רגליו, ὑποπόδιον)

courtroom with God on his throne and the host of heaven serving as advisers and courtiers. See also Job 1:6–12; 2:1–6; and Dan. 7:9–14, 23–27, where emphasis falls on the judicial function of the royal court.

32. The word רקיע is relatively rare in the MT, occurring in Gen. 1 (9×); Pss. 19:2 [ET v. 1]; 150:1; Ezek. 1 (4×); 10:1; and Dan. 12:3.

33. Allen (Psalms 101–50, 322–24) discusses both options in Ps. 150:1 but settles on heavenly sanctuary.

34. "Heights" (רמים) here could refer to the heavens (NRSV) or to Mount Zion; see Tate, Psalms 51–100, 283.

35. On the strong resonances with 1 Kings 8, see below. For the case that the heavenly temple in Exod. 15:17 goes back to the author, see Sarna, Exodus, 82.

36. Craigie, Psalms 1–50, 248. He draws attention to the Canaanite elements of this psalm.

on earth (Ps. 99:1, 5 MT; 98:1, 5 LXX). The footstool can denote the temple or Mount Zion in general terms (e.g., Lam. 2:1) but is often identified with the ark of the covenant.[37] In 1 Chronicles, David discusses his plans to build the temple, describing it as "a house of rest for the ark of the covenant of the Lord, for the footstool of our God [הדם רגלי אלהינו]" (1 Chron. 28:2) and thus placing the ark and the footstool in direct apposition (cf. Ps. 132:7–8).[38] The ark represents the divine throne within the temple, but when designated a "footstool" the imagery is not so much of a copy or representation but rather of an additional item of cultic and regal furniture that naturally accompanies the heavenly throne. Here we might also make mention of Isaiah's vision, which takes place in the temple. He sees the Lord "sitting on a throne, high and lofty, and the hem of his robe filled the temple" (Isa. 6:1). The voices of the seraphim cause the thresholds to shake, and the house fills with smoke, much like the tabernacle and Solomon's temple did at their inaugurations. The vision is in keeping with the idea of the ark as footstool: the hem of God's robe falling to the ground and filling the temple pictures him as seated on the heavenly throne directly above the temple.

A rather different use of the footstool image is found in Isa. 66: "Heaven is my throne / and the earth is my footstool; / so what kind of house could you build for me, / what sort of place for me to rest?" (66:1 NRSVue). By expanding the scope of the throne to encompass the whole of heaven, and the footstool to encompass all the earth, this oracle emphasizes God's greatness. The sentiment could be taken as anti-temple, and it forms part of an oracle that exemplifies the so-called prophetic critique of sacrifice.[39] Yet such critique as is found in various OT prophets targets impure and insincere practice of the cult, not the cultic system per se.[40] Interpreters have often been too quick to absolutize prophetic sayings such as Hosea 6:6 ("I desire steadfast love *and not sacrifice*"), when in fact they are hyperbolic statements of relative contrasts. Isaiah 66 highlights God's transcendence and the inability of any earthly place to contain him, implying that the universe is (only just) large enough for him to sit in sovereignty.[41]

---

37. Haran (*Temples and Temple-Service*, 256) argues that "footstool" denotes the whole temple in Pss. 99:5; 132:7.

38. God's dwelling in Jerusalem is described as rest in 1 Chron. 23:25–26, and the Levites need no longer carry the tabernacle.

39. Other examples include Pss. 40:6–8; 50:5–14; 51:16–19; Isa. 1:11–17; Jer. 7:21–23; Amos 5:21–26.

40. Contra, e.g., Watts, *Isaiah 1–33*. See the astute treatment of these passages in Ullucci, *Christian Rejection of Animal Sacrifice*, 31–48; Giambrone, *Bible and the Priesthood*, 81–104.

41. J. A. Motyer (*Isaiah*, 532–33) highlights the consistency of Isa. 66 with the dedication of Solomon's temple in 1 Kings 8 and detects a certain irony in the question of v. 1, as if the temple is too small for God to see from heaven.

Isaiah's identification of the whole created order as God's dwelling place
is consistent with a number of texts that direct attention from the temple to
heaven as his actual abode. In Ps. 18:6, the psalmist cries out to God, and he
hears "from his temple" (מהיכלו, ἐκ ναοῦ ἁγίου αὐτοῦ, 18:7 MT; 17:7 LXX);
yet when help actually arrives, God "bowed the heavens [שמים]," "thundered
in the heavens [שמים]," and "reached down from on high [מרום]" (18:9, 13,
16 [18:10, 14, 17 MT]; cf. 2 Sam. 22:2–17). The same dynamic is found in Ps.
20: God is entreated to "send you help from the sanctuary" (מקדש, ἐξ ἁγίου,
20:2 [20:3 MT; 19:3 LXX]), but his answer comes "from his holy heaven"
(משמי קדשו, ἐξ οὐρανοῦ ἁγίου αὐτοῦ, 20:6 [20:7 MT; 19:7 LXX]). This is
precisely what we find in King Solomon's inauguration prayer in Kings and
Chronicles. Solomon affirms God's uniqueness and his covenant and his choice
of David and the place for the temple (1 Kings 8:15–26). He then immediately
denies that God can dwell on earth, or even within any part of the created
order: "But will God indeed dwell on the earth? Even heaven and the highest
heaven cannot contain you, much less this house that I have built!" (8:27).
The remainder of the prayer recurrently associates human prayer "toward this
place" with God hearing in heaven and responding (8:29, 30, 35; cf. 2 Chron.
6:18–42), just as we observed in the psalms above. Such expectations are also
reflected, for example, in the Levites' prayer rising to God's "holy dwelling in
heaven" during Hezekiah's Passover (2 Chron. 30:27) and in Daniel praying
toward Jerusalem (Dan. 6:10).

Ezekiel's Temple Vision

The most prominent depiction of a heavenly temple in the OT is found in
the closing chapters of Ezekiel. Three earlier chapters set the context: in Ezek.
1, the prophet sees the glory of the Lord on his throne by the Chebar River;
chapter 8 describes the impurity of the Jerusalem temple; and in chapter 10,
the divine glory leaves the temple.[42] In Ezek. 40:1–3, the prophet is taken up
in visions and set on "a very high mountain,"[43] where he encounters a man
"whose appearance shone like bronze." Chapters 40–42 constitute a visionary
tour of a temple with this guide, measuring the wall, the outer court with its
chambers, the inner court, porch (אולם, αἰλάμ), and sanctuary (היכל, ναός).
Notably, Ezekiel does not enter the most holy place, a point of connection

42. Note that Ezek. 1:1–3; 8:1–3; and 40:1–2 are the only places in the book to share a date
formula, the expression that the "hand of the Lord" is on the prophet, and an account of a
vision.
43. On this mountain's connections with Zion, Sinai, and Eden, see Levenson, *Program of
Restoration*, 5–53.

with some later heavenly ascents, including 1 En. 14–15 and T. Levi 2–5. This section is marked off by the word "wall," which forms an inclusio around Ezek. 40:5–42:20. Ezekiel 43:1–12 is a transitional section in which the divine glory enters and fills the temple, and the prophet is instructed to exhort the people to purity and to tell them about the plan of the temple.[44] Regulations relating to purity and service follow, combined with descriptions of the altar. The literary arrangement of these chapters is not self-evident.[45] They contain instructions and visions relating to temple, city, and land, with depictions of the holy district with the temple at its center (45:1–8), a river flowing from below the temple (47:1–12), and the boundaries of the land and the tribal portions (47:13–48:35).[46]

The transition within Ezek. 40–48 raises the important question of time. While we have already considered the temple's relation to protology in the ancient Near East and the OT, I have left eschatology to one side until now. Ezekiel 43–48 depicts a future sanctuary at the center of a renewed land. In this it is similar to Zech. 14, which envisages all Jerusalem becoming holy as a center for festival worship for all the nations, with waters flowing from it to the east and west (14:8, 16–21). There is debate over whether this is a concrete hope for restoration of the temple after returning to the land or an idealized eschatological vision not intended to be realized by the return-ing exiles.[47] In this light, Paul Joyce asks whether the temple of Ezek. 40–42 represents a reflection of Solomon's temple, a plan for the temple's restora-tion, or an eschatological temple.[48] He argues that, like the visions of Ezek. 1 and 8, it relates to a present reality. Yet in contrast to Ezek. 1 (where the divine throne comes to the Chebar River) and Ezek. 8 (which describes the defilement of the earthly temple), Ezekiel's ascent suggests that he enters a heavenly temple.

This interpretation is supported by strong echoes of Exod. 25 in the tran-sitional passage in Ezek. 43. Ezekiel is to "describe the temple to the house of Israel" so that they might "measure the pattern" (תכנית, Ezek. 43:10), a

---

44. John Kutsko (*Between Heaven and Earth*) traces the contours of Ezekiel's theology of divine presence, which combines God's absence from the temple in response to idolatry with his transcendent mobility and thus his presence in exile; this accounts for his return after Israel's purification in Ezek. 43.

45. Cook (*Ezekiel 38–48*, 3–8) regards Ezek. 40–48 as utopian literature, from the same au-thorial circles as the "proto-apocalyptic" chapters (Ezek. 38–39) despite the difference in genre.

46. Steven Tuell (*Law of the Temple*) identifies two sources within Ezek. 40–48, one associated with the prophet himself—for whom a perfect heavenly temple is guarded from defilement, un-like its earthly counterpart—and the other focusing on legislation for actual temple practice.

47. On the debate as to whether Ezekiel's temple vision is intended as an implementable program, see Strong, "Grounding Ezekiel's Heavenly Ascent."

48. Joyce, "Earliest 'Heavenly Ascent' Narrative?," 22.

word that differs by one consonant of similar shape (כ not ב) from the word for Moses's "pattern" (תבנית, Exod. 25:40). Some would emend Ezek. 43:10 to match Exodus, but even without this supposition, the vocabulary and sense evoke the Sinai revelation of the tabernacle in numerous ways. Ezekiel 43:11 adds further to this picture: "Make known to them the plan of the temple, its arrangement, its exits and its entrances, and its whole form—all its ordinances and its entire plan and all its laws; and write it down in their sight so that they may observe and follow the entire plan and all its ordinances." The "arrangement" is a rare architectural term (תכונה, cf. Job 23:3; Nah. 2:10; the LXX has no equivalent). The "plan of the temple [lit., house]" (צורת הבית) uses an unusual term (צורה, form, design), which is repeated four times in this verse and occurs nowhere else in the Hebrew Bible. The Septuagint employs a combination of a verb (διαγράφω), an omission, and two different nouns in the same verse (ὑπόστασις and δικαίωμα).[49] As in Exod. 25, the heavenly vision is the basis for human action in constructing a sanctuary.[50]

Although the vision is explicit and expansive compared to the revelation to Moses, the terminology of Ezek. 43:10–11 could still suggest that Ezekiel sees only a blueprint. The only measurements given for the building itself are on a two-dimensional, horizontal plane. Yet this terminology could equally refer to the heavenly temple he has been shown as an extant, three-dimensional reality, and this seems more likely, given the indications of material texture such as doors, carvings, and canopies.[51] The heavenly temple nevertheless does not (yet) appear to be in use: there are no furnishings, with the exception of the wooden incense altar (41:22).[52] This is either because heaven does not require items like bread of the presence and a lampstand[53] or, perhaps, because it is awaiting inauguration to serve in parallel to its earthly counterpart, or both, in that inauguration by the very presence of God could render certain cultic vessels unnecessary. The vision of the divine glory filling the temple (43:1–5) reflects its inauguration for service, but there is a studied ambiguity here. The

---

49. On the high level of textual uncertainty in Ezek. 43:11, see Lilly, "Scribal Composition in Ezekiel 43," 220–27. She argues that the MT here prioritizes learning Torah, whereas the LXX emphasizes the perlocutionary effect of the diagram.

50. Whether or not this is practically realizable is beside the point, contra Cook (*Ezekiel 38–48*, 182, 186, 191–92), who renders ועשו אותם in 43:11 "they must come to terms with them" rather than "do" or "follow."

51. Cook (*Ezekiel 38–48*, 8) suggests that the measurement "aims at structuring terrestrial, 'horizontal' spaces that soon become zones of contact with transcendent, 'vertical' reality. The architectural zones . . . await a *filling in* as God takes up bodily residence" (emphasis original).

52. Instructions for one other item of furniture for the eschatological sanctuary, the altar of burnt offering, are given more fully in 43:13–27.

53. So Joyce, "Earliest 'Heavenly Ascent' Narrative?," 30.

"gate facing east" through which the divine glory enters (43:1–2) is naturally read as the gate of the heavenly sanctuary (42:15), but this is also where God "will reside among the people of Israel forever" (43:7). Ezekiel regards the heavenly temple as both the *plan for* a new earthly temple and the *very place of* God's eschatological dwelling after Israel's purification.[54] These chapters reflect the notions that we have seen elsewhere—namely, of heaven as (or, here, containing) a temple and of correspondence and connection between the heavenly and the earthly temple. They also represent the fullest elaboration of this notion within the OT.

The Greco-Roman World

Greek and Roman Temples

The ritual and religious process in Greek and Roman religion had three core elements: prayers (εὐχαί), sacrifices (θυσίαι, whether of animals, cereals, or libations of wine or water), and votive offerings (ἀναθέματα, often statues of gods dedicated and given irrevocably).[55] The altar was the crucial item of cultic furniture, situated within a sacred precinct or temenos (τέμενος) delimited by marker stones or a wall. Here sacrifices and libations were offered. Water was often available at the entrance to the temenos for ritual purification.[56] The sacred precinct might be adjacent to a field where sacrificial animals could be kept and reared, though given limitations of space this was not a frequent feature within cities. Since the fundamental prerequisite for sacrifices to be offered was the altar, it follows that "a temple was not strictly necessary."[57]

Cult statues were manufactured, and major gods such as Zeus and Poseidon did not need temples, though they were appropriately honored by them. When a building was erected within the temenos, it was referred to as a "sanctuary" (Koine ναός, Ionic νηός, Attic νεώς; related to the verb "to dwell," ναίειν, used of gods, not of people; Latin *aedes* or occasionally *fanum*). The wider holy place, either equivalent to the temenos or a space within it, was referred to

54. Cook (*Ezekiel 38–48*, 187–89) uses language of "hypostatic union" to account for the divine presence's terrestrial manifestation without reducing itself only to this reality. Joyce ("Temple and Worship in Ezekiel," 154) observes that God's localization sits in the context of an "overarching theology of the freedom of God."

55. For a useful introduction to Greco-Roman temples, see Orlin, *Temples, Religion and Politics*; Stevenson, *Power and Place*, 37–114.

56. Burkert, "Temple in Classical Greece," 34–35.

57. Orlin, *Temples, Religion and Politics*, 11. Of course, cultic open areas were also known in Israel and the ancient Near East; see Haran, *Temples and Temple-Service*, 48–57.

as a "temple" (ἱερόν; in later Latin usage *templum*). This wider enclosure is distinct from the building itself, and the distinction is reflected in the terminology. But sometimes the terms are used without precision, and "temple" can be interchangeable with "sanctuary." As we shall see, Jewish authors writing in Greek transferred the terms easily to the Jerusalem temple, observing a uniform distinction between the temple complex (ἱερόν) and the actual temple building within it (ναός/νεώς). Greek and Roman temples typically had a single entrance, through columns that formed a kind of permeable boundary, inviting the worshiper in. Some temples were single-chambered, while others had an interior room (ἄδυτον, *cella*). This central chamber might be the location for the cult statue of the deity (in which case it likely stood open so that the statue could be seen), but on occasion it had little importance and served as a back storeroom, whether for cultic vessels or for votive offerings of statues of the deity.

The architecture of the Greco-Roman temple—well known in popular imagination, with its Ionic columns, triangular roof facade, and square or rectangular footprint—emerged in the eighth and seventh centuries BC under Egyptian influence. The development of such architecture reflected not a change in cultic practice *"but rather a decision to monumentalize,"* a demonstration of the wealth and power of the sponsors of temple building.[58] Despite the enduring popular image and the consistency in architectural presentation right through to the Hellenistic era, there was significant diversity as well.[59] The sheer glory and expense of these temples in light of their technical superfluity within the practice of religion made them the ultimate votive offering to the deity.[60] With the expansion of Greek and then Roman military and political power and cultural patronage, erecting a temple to a deity became a way of demonstrating a city's prestige and its commitment to the prevailing political power.[61] There were three prominent locations in which temples tended to cluster: high places (ἄκρα), public squares (ἀγορά), and marginal locations outside the city.[62] A multiplicity of coexisting temene and temples reflects the pantheon of gods, in contrast to the primary sponsoring deity of the ancient Near East city-state, and it was the particular constellation of temples that constituted a city's religious-political identity in the Greek and Roman worlds.

58. Marinatos, "What Were Greek Sanctuaries?," 229 (emphasis original).
59. Stambaugh, "Functions of Roman Temples."
60. Burkert, "Temple in Classical Greece," 43.
61. This becomes more prominent in the wake of the Roman Empire and development of the imperial cult; see Price, *Rituals and Power*, esp. 133–69.
62. Burkert, "Temple in Classical Greece," 42.

Temple Architecture and the Universe

Given temples' peripheral status for the actual practice of religion in the Greek and Roman worlds, it is unsurprising that they do not bear the weight of cosmic significance that ancient Near Eastern temples held. One exception to this is the temple at Delphi on the slope of Mount Parnassus in Greece, which was considered the center and omphalos, or navel (ὀμφαλός), of the world, reflecting the ancient concept of the axis mundi.[63] The sixth-century BC philosopher Anaximander of Miletus posited that the earth is a free-floating disk or cylinder, a development from the standard ancient cosmological understanding of a flat earth-disk floating on the seas or supported by pillars. Anaximander thus represents a break from the conventional three-tier universe with its solid firmament and a step on the way toward modern cosmologies. Robert Hahn has argued that Anaximander's cosmology reflects an alternative cultic symbology. The earth-cylinder is to be understood along the analogy of the cylindrical drums from which architectural columns were built, including those used in temples, with the earth forming one drum in a series of drums making up a celestial axis. Thus, "Anaximander imagined the cosmos to be a kind of temple, the cosmic house, along the analogy of the cosmic meaning of the column."[64] Intriguing as this suggestion is, it has been critiqued by Dirk Couprie. Column drums came in a wide range of diameter-to-height ratios, not just the 3:1 ratio that Anaximander postulated for the earth, which Hahn makes much of. More significantly, even if it is granted that Anaximander had in mind a celestial column, this is a very different thing from the full temple building of Greek antiquity.[65] Couprie presses a point of difference in meaning as well: whereas the celestial dome or firmament offers protection and refuge, Anaximander "blew up the celestial dome when he imagined the earth hanging free in space and the celestial bodies behind each other." His universe is thus not a refuge but "the opposite of a cosmic temple with a solid ceiling."[66]

Universe, Reverence, and Ethics

Although there is no evidence for a detailed connection between temple and cosmos in architectural terms, the two enjoy relatively widespread association in Greek and Latin writings for two purposes: (1) the universe, like a temple, is a muse that inspires awe, and (2) as such it impresses on humans the necessity

---

63. Burkert, "Temple in Classical Greece," 33.
64. Hahn, *Anaximander and the Architects*, 188. See also his "Architectural Technologies."
65. Couprie, *Heaven and Earth*, 153–60.
66. Couprie, *Heaven and Earth*, 160.

of right demeanor.[67] In his *Astronomica*, Marcus Manilius (early first century AD) connects his song to his theme as two shrines (*duo templa*), one fixed and the other "the vast celestial sphere" (1.20–24). In his *Olympic Discourse*, Dio Chrysostom (first to early second century AD) praises the temple of Zeus and celebrates him as the one "who dwelleth in mansions of cloud" (ὃς ὑπέρτατα δώματα ναίει, *Discourses* 12.24, using a verb that is cognate to ναός). He goes on to liken humanity's encounter with the wonders of the natural world to initiation into the Eleusinian Mysteries: the individual is placed "in some mystic shrine [εἰς μυστικόν τινα μυχόν] of extraordinary beauty and size," awed by the scale and sights therein (*Discourses* 12.33).[68] The Platonist philosopher Plutarch (second half of the first century AD), who also served as a priest at the Delphi oracle, approvingly cites Diogenes to the effect that every day is a festival. He affirms the sentiment: "For the universe is a most holy temple and most worthy of a god [ἱερὸν γὰρ ἁγιώτατον ὁ κόσμος ἐστὶ καὶ θεοπρεπέστατον]; into it man is introduced through birth as a spectator, not of hand-made or immovable images, but of those sensible representations of knowable things that the divine mind, says Plato, has revealed" (*Moralia* 477C [*On Tranquility of Mind* 20]).[69]

The created world draws human minds to the ideal realm, much as a temple raises our thoughts to a deity. Such awe-inspiring effects cannot but make an ethical impact. The Roman statesman and Stoic philosopher Seneca (first century AD), in his treatise *On Comets*, cites Aristotle, who draws exactly this implication, using a lesser-to-greater argument (*a minore ad maius*): "If we enter temples with composure [*si intramus templa compositi*], if when we are going to a sacrifice we have a humble demeanor, we straighten our toga, and we assume every mark of modesty, how much more ought we to do this when we are arguing about the stars, about the planets, about the nature of the gods, in order to avoid making incautious or ignorant assertions, or knowingly making false statements!" (*Natural Questions* 7.30.1).[70] The universe is like a temple and consequently demands appropriate humility of those who enter it.

A century before Seneca, the politician and writer Cicero in *The Republic* records a dream of Scipio in which he encounters his deceased grandfather and father. When he asks why he cannot come and join them, his father replies,

67. For this connection in classical writers, see Festugière, *Dieu cosmique*, 233–38.
68. Text and translation from Dio Chrysostom, *Discourses 12–30*.
69. Text and translation from Plutarch, *Moralia*, vol. 6.
70. The notes identify the Aristotle citation as frag. 14 Rose = 943 Gigon. Festugière (*Dieu cosmique*, 238) concludes that the idea of a world-temple goes back to Aristotle's *Peri Philosophias*.

"There is no possible way for you to come here, unless the god whose temple is this whole visible universe [*cuius hoc templum est omne, quod conspicis*] releases you from the bonds of the body. Human beings were born on condition that they should look after that sphere called earth which you see in the middle of this celestial space [*in hoc templo medium vides, quae terra dicitur*]" (*Republic* 6.15).[71] As noted above, the word *templum* came to denote the sacred precinct, but originally it described a part of the sky used for divination. One can see how both senses of the word are in play here, reflected in its translation by "temple" and then "space." Scipio's father continues by instructing him to "respect justice and do your duty," which is "the way of life which leads to heaven" (6.16).

Elsewhere, in *The Laws*, Cicero affirms a similar connection between ethical conduct and the world as a sacred space: "[Thales] said that people should believe that everything they saw was full of gods; then everyone would be more pure in heart, just as people are when they are in the most sacred temples [*quom in fanis essent*]." In this same passage, he rejects the Persian emperor Xerxes's inference that earthly temples should be destroyed because the gods' "temple and home consisted of the entire world [*quorumque hic mundus omnis templum esset et domus*]" (*Laws* 2.26).[72] That is to say, he accepts the premise but not the conclusion, much as Philo accepts the priority of the Jewish cult's symbolic significance yet resists the extreme allegorizers who infer that physical observances should therefore cease.[73]

A similar coexistence of universal and local temple is found in Josephus's account of Titus's siege of Jerusalem. When the general urges the city's leaders to surrender, they respond that they care little for their own lives and even for the city, given that the world is a better sanctuary for God than this one (ναοῦ ἀμείνω τούτου τῷ θεῷ τὸν κόσμον εἶναι, *J.W.* 5.458), yet they immediately add their confidence that God, who dwells in the Jerusalem temple, will preserve it (5.459).

The idea that the whole cosmos is a temple is a commonplace assumption within Greek and Roman writers from a range of times, places, and philosophical and religious backgrounds. Yet it is also one that is passingly or fleetingly made. It is not elaborated, and there is certainly no attempt to

71. Translation from Cicero, *The Republic and the Laws*. Latin text from www.perseus.tufts.edu.

72. Herodotus (*Persian Wars* 1.131) is also aware that Persian religion identifies the great god with the dome of heaven and involves sacrifice on mountains and to the elements. Winston (*Wisdom of Solomon*, 321) cites Pseudo-Heraclitus, *Ep.* 4, who levels a similar critique against earthly cults: "God is not wrought by hands and has not from the beginning had a pedestal, and does not have a single enclosure! Rather the whole world is his temple."

73. Philo, *Migration* 89–93; cf. *Heir* 123–24; *Drunkenness* 86–87.

develop any architectural correspondence as there is in the case of ancient Near Eastern and Israelite temples. Rather, the analogy draws attention to the awesomeness of creation, which is to be approached with religious reverence, and to the piety and moral behavior that people should display in their everyday lives, as they would in a temple or sacred precinct.

Conclusion

The shared cosmogony and cosmology of the ancient Near East attests to a conceptualization of creation, or a part of it, as the dwelling place of the gods. These creation myths also become the foundation myths for peoples, city-states, and their temples, which are erected in imitation of the universe by gods or their regents. Certain core motifs can be discerned, including the cosmic mountain, primordial waters, the world-center, and the tree of life.

Creation myths in the OT do not reflect the notion of a cosmic temple in the ways that comparable ancient Near Eastern texts do. Israel's sanctuaries nevertheless incorporate multiple aspects of similar cosmic temple ideology, including the mountain, representation of vegetation, and water sources. Moreover, the accounts of creation and tabernacle have been mutually shaped to mirror one another in certain respects. More widely, a number of OT texts witness to a variety of ways of connecting cosmos and cultus. Heaven is the location for revelation to Moses of blueprints for the tabernacle and is itself identified as God's sanctuary. In an extension of this, the whole of the created order is sometimes equated with God's dwelling place. A related but distinct notion of the connection of the earthly and heavenly sanctuaries finds anthropomorphic expression in the throne-footstool link and is also articulated in the Jerusalem temple's function as a focal place for prayer, which God will hear and answer from heaven. Ezekiel likewise has a strong sense of correspondence between a heavenly and earthly sanctuary, a relationship that is hard to disentangle fully given its eschatological framing. In his initial temple vision (Ezek. 40–42), we have, uniquely in the OT, a tour of a temple complex within heaven. These various conceptualizations are not highly developed, but they do sow the seeds for the more elaborate depictions of cosmic temples in the Second Temple period as we shall see in the following chapter.

Greco-Roman religious practice represents a point of contrast with ancient Near Eastern and Israelite ideology: temples are less fundamental to their rites and, with the exception of Delphi, are not imbued with cosmic significance.

While Greek and Roman writers often describe the universe as a temple, it is usually a brief and passing analogy that articulates the awe-inspiring and morally educative function of the natural world. We will see a similar analogy in Greek Jewish writers in the following chapter, but it is elaborated in a more detailed and thoroughly Jewish manner in which the specific structure of Israel's sanctuaries elucidates the cosmos.

2

Second Temple Literature

Blueprints and Buildings

The idea of a heavenly temple is widespread across the ancient world, though with different shades of emphasis and elaboration as we saw in the previous chapter. We now turn to Second Temple Jewish literature, which forms the most pertinent context within which to read the NT on this question. The material becomes expansive at this point, with a wide range of detailed accounts of the heavenly sanctuary, often but not only in visionary or ascent narratives. I begin with a review of existing scholarly proposals. While some have argued that the temple-as-microcosm is the only model for relating temple and cosmos in the period, others have seen an important distinction between microcosm and the discrete notion of a temple in heaven. Neither of these positions does full justice to the variety reflected in the texts, however. In their place, I introduce a new fourfold taxonomy of the relationship between heaven and temple in the period. This taxonomy describes a spectrum ranging from blueprints in heaven, through a temple building in heaven, temple and heaven as coextensive entities, to temple as cosmos. These four categories structure my discussion of a range of Second Temple texts in the rest of the chapter. Although the taxonomy emerges primarily from and accounts for Second Temple literature, its utility extends to texts discussed in the previous chapter, and brief reference to some of those texts will be made. The points on the spectrum are not rigid or reified "boxes" into which all texts must fit but instead represent a continuum. What emerges is both a sense of the widespread and foundational nature of the heaven-temple connection across these texts and also a picture of the great fluidity with which this basic tenet was elaborated and articulated in the Second Temple period.

Categorizing Heaven and Temple

Scholars are well aware of the heaven-temple connection but often do not push further than this. For example, Martha Himmelfarb's important study traces the impact of the "heavenly temple" concept on the development of ascent apocalypses, a phrase she uses interchangeably with "heaven as temple," without probing differing portrayals.[1] Christopher Rowland includes "the heavenly temple" as a single category among a diverse list summarizing temple ideologies in the period.[2] Another scholar, C. T. R. Hayward, focuses on the *significance* of the Jerusalem temple and identifies a number of key areas: cosmic order; cosmic symbolism; angelic worship; invocation of the Lord on Israel's behalf; and light.[3] These helpfully identify a range of different meanings that authors in the period associate with the temple, and many have some kind of cosmic connection. Yet this approach says little about the various cosmologies associated with the temple or about the specifics of their structure and architecture. Certain scholars, however, have addressed this question, and two main proposals can be identified.

Temple Only and Always as Microcosm

Crispin Fletcher-Louis argues that Jews in the Second Temple period operated with a single conception of temple as microcosm. In his major study of the Qumran document Songs of the Sabbath Sacrifice, he acknowledges that such a cosmology is not explicit in that text, but he argues that it "appears to be assumed" in the synchronization of cult and cosmos we find in some liturgical texts at Qumran.[4] He points to Sirach, Philo, and Josephus as explicit articulations of the temple-as-microcosm view, which he holds to be

1. Himmelfarb, *Ascent to Heaven*.
2. Rowland, "Second Temple." His other categories are Solomon's temple; second temple; sacrifice questioned; the indestructibility of the temple; the temple's destruction; building of new temple and city; and rejection of temple.
3. Hayward, *Jewish Temple*, 6–16. It is also worth mentioning Margaret Barker's many books on temple, which contain a rich wealth of detail, even if her method and conclusions in reconstructing a lost "temple theology" are problematic. See, e.g., Barker, *Gate of Heaven*; and Barker, *Temple Mysticism*.
4. Fletcher-Louis, *All the Glory of Adam*, 273–77, at 275; cf. 478–79.

uniform within the period. He regards the notion that a temple "up there" corresponds to the one "down here" as a later, rabbinic development.[5] In a subsequent essay that revisits his cosmological proposal, Fletcher-Louis states, *"In Israel's temple, the roofed sanctuary, especially its inner most portion, is heaven and the outer, open air, courtyard corresponds to the earth, or a particular point on the earth. . . .* The temple . . . is a complex whole comprising both roofed and unroofed portions that symbolise, or actualise, all parts of a several-tiered cosmos."[6] In support of this contention, Fletcher-Louis cites Josephus's identification of the tabernacle with the universe (*Ant.* 3.180–81). Josephus explicitly describes the 30 cubits of the tabernacle itself—the roofed sanctuary—as representing heaven, earth, and sea (10 cubits each), the components of the standard three-tiered ancient cosmos. Heaven (the most holy place) is "inaccessible to men," whereas the earth and sea (the 20 cubits of the holy place) are "accessible to all" (which here means the ordinary priests in their representative capacity).[7] However, Josephus does not say what Fletcher-Louis claims he says. The tabernacle's unroofed courtyard is nowhere in view, as Josephus is speaking only of the tabernacle's two chambers, both of which are enclosed. The outer chamber, equivalent to earth and sea, is "open" only in the sense that the priests are able to enter regularly, unlike the most holy place, which is essentially inaccessible to all but the high priest. We do find a presentation of roofed and unroofed portions of the temple as microcosm in Philo, and I will explore both that passage and the Josephus passage below, but these portrayals are not identical. What Fletcher-Louis rightly and helpfully highlights is that temple-as-cosmos is not simply a Hellenistic idea standing in opposition to a Jewish conceptualization of an actual structure in heaven. Indeed, as we saw in the previous chapter, Greco-Roman writers were not so much interested in temples as microcosms that elucidated the structure of the universe as in the passing analogy of the cosmos as a temple for its ethical implications. By contrast, the temple-as-microcosm finds a thoroughly Jewish expression in the Second Temple period.

5. "The notion that Jews in the Second Temple period believed in a heavenly temple up there as a model for the one down here is, I submit, a modern scholarly myth" (Fletcher-Louis, "Angels, Men and Priests," 154).

6. Fletcher-Louis, "Angels, Men and Priests," 153 (emphasis original). This piece notes his disappointment that his proposal has not received much traction. "It is as if temple-as-microcosm is an idea too strange or offensive to be taken seriously in some scholarly circles. What fearful ghosts does it conjure for a modern consciousness?" (153n28). I find the idea neither strange nor offensive; it is simply one among a range of positions held in the period, all alike potentially strange from a modern perspective. On this, see the concluding chapter of this book.

7. Translation from Mason, *Flavius Josephus, Translation and Commentary* (vol. 3 by Louis H. Feldman).

Temple as Cosmos versus Temple in Heaven

Bipartite categorizations of the heavenly temple have long standing in scholarship, as can be seen in G. B. Gray's treatment of "The Sacrificial Service in Heaven" a century ago.[8] He identifies two categories: First, the temple may be regarded as "the earthly equivalent of heaven itself, or more widely, the whole temple area may be regarded as a symbol or reproduction in miniature of the entire cosmos" (151). Second, others regarded "the earthly temple, including in the Jewish account an altar," as "built according to instructions given from heaven" (153). These two categories are distinct but not mutually exclusive. In his conclusion, he recapitulates two "broad lines." In the first, the earthly temple is a material representation of immaterial heavenly originals; the second "transfers to heaven more or less exact counterparts of the material things of earth and so makes heaven reproduce earth" (177). Despite insightful discussion of the variety of portrayals in a range of texts, it is not clear how Gray's closing two categories map onto his first two. The opening pair distinguishes temple-heaven equivalence from plans given in heaven, whereas the closing pair contrasts incorporeality with materiality. Heavenly immateriality could quite conceivably coincide with either temple-heaven equivalence or with heavenly instructions or plans for the tabernacle, as indeed it does in Philo.[9] In discussing Revelation, Gray makes a distinction between "heaven itself as a temple" and "a temple within heaven" (160–64). This distinction will be important below, but again it is unclear how he envisages these two categories relating to the others he enumerates. In short, Gray offers some acute analysis, but as they stand his categories are not sufficiently clear to be of use.

A key contribution to the scholarly discussion is offered by Jonathan Klawans, who draws a similar distinction between "temple as cosmos" and "a temple in heaven."[10] The former makes symbolic associations between the temple and the universe and regards the earthly cult as participating in a wider cosmic worship. The latter is more analogous in its conceptualization, with earthly worship imitating or reproducing heavenly worship. Given this mirroring, "an important prerequisite to the idea of the earthly temple *corresponding* to a heavenly one is a developed theology of divine emanation"—that is, of the divine Name, Presence, or Logos dwelling in the

---

8. This chapter appears in two parts in Gray's book. See G. Gray, *Sacrifice in the Old Testament*, 148–63, 164–78.
9. On which, see below. Gray's book was published posthumously from incomplete revisions of lecture notes, which may explain the lack of clarity.
10. Klawans, *Purity, Sacrifice, and the Temple*, 111–44.

earthly sanctuary. Also, a developed angelology "is an absolute prerequisite for the notion of a heavenly temple" (112). Klawans rightly critiques scholars for conflating these two notions and also for assuming too easily that the idea of a heavenly pattern (as found in Exod. 25:9, 40 and later reflection on it) must automatically entail a full-scale, operational heavenly temple. He readily acknowledges that the two ideas are "not contradictory" and "not completely incompatible." Yet he also states that "there are many tensions between them, and . . . it is a general rule that ancient Jewish sources will articulate only one or another of these approaches, and not both" (111–13).

Klawans's treatment is detailed and sophisticated, and the categories he identifies are a helpful development of the work of Gray and others. In particular, he eschews a simplistic apocalyptic-Hellenistic dichotomy, allowing Philo's and Josephus's portrayals of a cosmic temple to be treated as distinctively Jewish alongside other Jewish texts. Yet his own analysis undercuts itself: Philo's corpus is one of the key instantiations of the idea of the temple-as-cosmos (along with Josephus and later rabbinic and medieval Jewish texts), but at the same time it bears witness to a theory of divine emanation and a developed angelology,[11] items that Klawans associates with "a temple in heaven." As I show below, the key passage in *On the Special Laws* represents a borderline case, and this helps explain how Philo can hold together cosmic symbolism with angelology and emanation. Furthermore, Klawans's second category does not sufficiently distinguish between the two ideas that Gray identifies clearly: temple *within* heaven and temple as *coextensive with* heaven. By focusing attention on "a temple in heaven" and downplaying heaven itself as a temple, Klawans excludes what is in fact a middle term between his two, and thus his evaluation of the evidence remains too dichotomous.

A New Taxonomy

The approach here is thematic rather than chronological, as my intention is to identify differing conceptualizations, not dependence or development (though we will note the development of ideas found in some of the OT texts discussed in chap. 1). Rabbinic texts and later apocalypses are included on the basis that they may well preserve earlier traditions and that they further illustrate categories that can be well established on the basis of texts firmly within the period. While the texts studied here are demonstrably Jewish, it is important to acknowledge the likelihood of Christian redaction in some

---

11. Klawans (*Purity, Sacrifice, and the Temple*, 113) acknowledges this but shrugs it off, commenting that "there are many overlapping aspects of these notions as developed by ancient Jews."

places, especially in view of the reality that many apocalypses were more popular within (and therefore more often preserved by) Christian circles. Scholarly debate continues over the relative Jewish and Christian aspects of many of these texts, even as the very posing of the question is recognized to be fraught with complexities of definition as much as of historical record. A text such as the Ascension of Isaiah, treated in chapter 8, could arguably be included here, but the assignment of such texts between these two chapters does not substantially affect the conclusions drawn.

In reading the texts, two principles are borne in mind. First, we will presume consistency within a particular text or author. This is a presumption, not an absolute law, and allows that variation may be present, particularly in an oeuvre written over many years or in multiple parts. Second, we must recognize that in describing the heavenly sphere—particularly in the context of dreams or visions—writers quite understandably push at the boundaries of human thought and language and may therefore deliberately offer apparently contradictory portrayals and descriptions. An example related to our theme is Enoch's description of heavenly structures as both "hot like fire and cold like ice" (1 En. 14.13), though not all instances are so directly juxtaposed as this. We need to treat this as a paradox rather than dismissing it as incoherent. These two principles stand in a slight but not insurmountable tension with one another. Together, they suggest that alongside the challenge of defining how a particular text construes the heaven-temple relationship, allowance needs to be made for cases where a text or author might in fact display fluid or multiple conceptualizations.

My proposal is that we should conceive portrayals of the heavenly sanctuary in the period on the model of a spectrum, described via its four most salient points. The first point is a *temple-plan in heaven*, whereby there is a blueprint of some kind in the heavenly realm that is shown to a human being (usually Moses) who then proceeds to construct the earthly sanctuary. Next comes the notion of a *temple in heaven*, where there is an actual structure within the heavenly domain. The third category (which is a kind of excluded middle from Klawans's two categories) is *temple as heaven*, where heaven lacks any distinct structure as such but rather is itself a sanctuary—that is, heaven and the temple are coextensive. Finally comes *temple as cosmos*, where the whole universe is a temple, usually with (the highest) heaven as its most sacred precinct and earth and sea as outer chambers or courtyards. It is worth reiterating that these four headings do not represent silos but rather form the key points along a spectrum of views ranging from minimalist to maximalist in their understanding of the scale of the cosmic temple, and they shade into one another at the edges. This will become clearer as we turn to examine actual texts.

Temple-Plan in Heaven

The idea that there is a plan or blueprint for the tabernacle or temple in heaven is most directly associated with Exodus, as we saw in chapter 1.[12] When Pseudo-Philo describes Moses's forty days with God on Mount Sinai, he takes up language from this episode: "He commanded him about the tabernacle [and its furnishings]. . . . And he showed him their likeness [*ostendit ei similitudinem eorum*] in order that he might make them according to the pattern that he had seen [*secundum exemplar quod viderat*]" (LAB 11.15; cf. 19.10).[13] The Greek terminology of "form" (εἶδος), "model" (παράδειγμα), and "pattern" (τύπος)—translating Hebrew or Aramaic terms drawn from Exod. 25—and the conceptuality of plans or blueprints in heaven can be discerned here.

Philo also comments on the Exod. 25 tradition. In keeping with his Platonist-Jewish synthesis, he describes Moses as seeing incorporeal ideas, an archetype and models (ἀρχέτυπος, παραδείγματα), which he then reproduced accurately in matter in constructing the tabernacle (*Moses* 2.74–76; cf. QE 2.90). Given the superiority of the incorporeal realm and the importance of the term "model" (παράδειγμα) within Platonist thought, these are not simply building plans but rather eternal forms on which created things are based. Whether Philo imagines a perfect form of the sanctuary or the sanctuary imitating the eternal realm more widely remains unclear,[14] but the shared language of "model" (παράδειγμα) and the notion of correspondence make it easy for him to draw Plato (cf. *Timaeus* 29a6–b1) and the Septuagint together here. Hebrews employs similar language in relation to Exod. 25, though with different ends, as I shall argue in chapter 4.

The rabbis noticed the terminological variation between "pattern" (תבנית) in Exod. 25:9, 40 and "ordinance" (משפט) in 26:30, which emphasizes the oral nature of God's instructions to Moses. The Septuagint, by contrast, continues the visual emphasis in its use of the word "form" (εἶδος) in 26:30. The Babylonian Talmud makes a distinction between "ordinance" (משפט) in 26:30, which is related to the tabernacle as a whole and interpreted as (verbal) instructions, in contrast to "pattern" (תבנית) in 25:40, which is related to the furnishings and which is taken to imply that Moses saw actual fiery models

---

12. On the reception of Exod. 25, see Wilcox, "'According to the Pattern.'"
13. Latin text from Jacobson, *Pseudo-Philo's Liber Antiquitatum Biblicarum*; English translation of this and other pseudepigraphal texts is from *OTP*.
14. In *Alleg. Interp.* 3.96–103, Philo identifies God as the ultimate παράδειγμα, with the tabernacle, like humanity, made via a series of images (εἰκών), which in turn become παραδείγματα for lesser images.

of an ark, menorah, and table, which he was then to copy (b. Menahot 29a).[15] These translation decisions and interpretations mirror the textual complexities of Ezek. 43, discussed in chapter 1, and the different emphases of the Hebrew and Greek versions. Philo and the rabbis here demonstrate that the notion of a heavenly pattern remained important, but they also illustrate how such a pattern grew in size, scope, and ontological significance. That is, alongside Ezek. 40–42 they indicate the development toward more maximal depictions of a heavenly sanctuary. Like many of the texts of the period, these authors draw on Exod. 25 for the fundamental principle of correspondence between heaven and an earthly sanctuary and do not limit it to its likely original meaning of "blueprints."

Temple in Heaven

A number of texts indicate that the earthly sanctuary imitates an actual structure in heaven. The Wisdom of Solomon offers a tantalizingly brief reference to what might at first appear to be an idea similar to Exod. 25: "You have given command to build a temple on your holy mountain / and an altar in the city of your holy habitation, / a copy of the holy tent [μίμημα σκηνῆς ἁγίας] that you prepared from the beginning" (Wis. 9:8). What is significant here is not just the different terminology—"copy" or "imitation" (μίμημα) as opposed to "pattern" (παράδειγμα, τύπος, or εἶδος)—but its application to the earthly sanctuary alongside explicit mention of a heavenly sanctuary, in this case a "holy tabernacle." That is, the direction of travel (heaven to earth) remains the same, but the scales have been reversed: this is not a movement from blueprints, plans, or a small model to a building, but from an extant structure to another derivative, lesser one. This preexistent heavenly sanctuary dates "from the beginning," presumably indicating creation (cf. 9:1–2). Another wisdom text, Sirach, depicts Wisdom coming to dwell in Zion as a parallel to her original dwelling in heaven: "I encamped in the heights. . . . In the holy tent [ἐν σκηνῇ ἁγίᾳ] I ministered before him, / and so I was established in Zion" (Sir. 24:4, 10 NRSVue). As in the Wisdom of Solomon, the "holy tent" appears to denote a celestial tabernacle that precedes the earthly sanctuary in Jerusalem.

The Syriac Apocalypse of Baruch witnesses to a similar idea but with a couple of significant differences:

> Do you think that this is the city of which I said: On the palms of my hands
> I have carved you? It is not this building that is in your midst now; it is that

---

15. Note that Exod. 25:40 speaks of תבניתם (*"their* pattern"), whence the inference of multiple exemplars. Numbers Rabbah 15.10 also describes Moses being shown a menorah of fire.

which will be revealed, with me, that was already prepared from the moment that I decided to create Paradise. And I showed it to Adam before he sinned. But when he transgressed the commandment, it was taken away from him—as also Paradise. After these things I showed it to my servant Abraham in the night between the portions of the victims. And again I showed it also to Moses on Mount Sinai when I showed him the likeness of the tabernacle and all its vessels. Behold, now it is preserved with me—as also Paradise. (2 Bar. 4.2–6)

The first notable difference here is that the revelation to Moses becomes the third in a series, with Adam and Abraham seeing what he later saw. It would appear that even Adam had access to these heavenly realities, which he lost upon expulsion from paradise. Abraham's connection with the cult is elaborated in other texts that expand on the covenant sacrifice of Gen. 15 and the Akedah in connection with both temple and heaven.[16] Second, the heavenly reality is not only an actual structure but is the entire city of Jerusalem. This city was built at creation, is preserved with God in the present age (even as earthly Jerusalem is destroyed), and waits to be revealed in the future. It contains a tabernacle, and there is a clear "likeness" or correspondence between the heavenly and earthly city and sanctuary (see also 2 Bar. 59.4); again we see the influence of Exod. 25. Second Baruch represents a borderline case from the previous category, because the heavenly sanctuary does not appear to be currently functioning.[17] Instead, it is a model for the earthly one and is preserved through Israel's tribulations, ready to be revealed as the lasting city in the next age. A similar notion, with Jerusalem appearing as a woman before her transformation into a city, is encountered in Ezra's visions (2 Esd. [4 Ezra] 10:25–28, 51–55).[18]

Thus 2 Baruch highlights the importance of eschatology: many of the texts to be surveyed below envisage a currently functioning cultus in the heavenly realm to which earthly worship corresponds. Yet there is an intermediate position between a blueprint and a functioning sanctuary—namely, a sanctuary

---

16. For Gen. 15, see Apoc. Ab. 12–15 (Abraham rebuilds Adam's altar); for Gen. 22, see Tg. Ps.-J. of Gen. 22:2–4, 9–10 (Isaac sees angels in heaven) and Sifre Deut. 352 (Abraham and Isaac both see the temple built, ruined, and rebuilt).

17. Although the Jerusalem temple's furnishings are removed by angels, this is for safekeeping (2 Bar. 6.7–9; 80.2; cf. Num. Rab. 15.10), not to be used in heaven.

18. On the connection between heavenly temple and heavenly Jerusalem, see Safrai, "Heavenly Jerusalem." An eschatological transformation of the temple is envisaged in the Enochic Book of Dreams, with a "greater and loftier" house replacing the "ancient house" whose pillars and columns are removed (1 En. 90.28–36), though this would seem to be primarily earthly as it is set up "in the first location." Contrast the Apocalypse of Weeks, where following the destruction of the "house of the kingdom" there is no indication of a rebuilding (1 En. 93.7–8).

that awaits construction or inauguration.[19] This is what we find in Ezek. 40–48, as I suggested in chapter 1. The Temple Scroll from Qumran offers a different take on a similar principle, envisaging an idealized, utopic sanctuary with great detail on its structure, equipment, and rites. It is destined to be created at the eschaton and to last forever (11QT[a] XXIX, 10).[20]

As we move to texts where the temple in heaven is operational, I briefly note a somewhat unusual scene in the Apocalypse of Abraham: on his heavenly tour, the eponymous hero sees an altar opposite an idol, with "boys being slaughtered on it" (25.1–2). This is not simply a scene of idolatrous sacrifice, however, for a "handsome temple" is also present (25.3). This appears to be a scene of judgment more than a rightly ordered cult (cf. 25.4, 6), but it indicates that a temple is the kind of thing one might expect to find in a heavenly journey.

One of the clearest examples of a temple in heaven occurs in the Enochic Book of the Watchers.[21] Enoch is rushed up to heaven on the winds and comes to a wall of white marble and tongues of fire (1 En. 14.8). He passes through this and approaches a "great house" (14.10–14). Within this house, he has a further vision of "a second house which is greater than the former" made entirely of tongues of fire (14.15–17). Within this second house, Enoch sees a throne with wheels, cherubim, and "the Great Glory" sitting on it, attended by angels who cannot come near to him (14.18–23). Enoch is summoned to approach and is addressed directly with a message to take back to the Watchers (14.24–16.3). The terminology is not explicitly cultic, but the indication of a temple is clear:[22] the wall demarcates the outer court, while the first and second houses represent the outer and inner chambers of the temple, respectively.[23] The inner chamber is the dwelling place of God, where his

19. Four possibilities as to *when* the heavenly temple is built can be identified: before creation (b. Pesahim 54a; b. Nedarim 39b), at creation (Gen. Rab. 1.4), simultaneous with the earthly sanctuary (Num. Rab. 12; Pesiq. Rab. 5), or at the eschaton (1 En. 90).

20. Much of the structural material on the sanctuary proper and its furnishings (cols. 3–12) is highly fragmentary. Lawrence Schiffman ("Jerusalem Temple") characterizes the Temple Scroll as picturing utopia.

21. Suter ("Temples and the Temple," 207) rightly notes that "microcosm in fact might not be the right word to use in this case to describe the relation between celestial temple and cosmos" in 1 Enoch.

22. Contra the extended argument of Esler, *God's Court*. Esler rightly and masterfully draws attention to the royal-palace imagery but overreaches in his argument that this is to the exclusion of cultic-temple imagery. Rather, these two notions in relation to a god in heaven coexist and are mutually reinforcing throughout ancient Near Eastern and Second Temple Jewish texts. For the temple interpretation, the scholarly consensus is well represented: e.g., Himmelfarb, *Ascent to Heaven*, 9–28, esp. 14–16; Suter, "Temples and the Temple."

23. Note that Josephus (*J.W.* 5.209) describes the outer chamber as "the first house" (ὁ πρῶτος οἶκος).

throne is located. It might be suggested that 1 En. 14 implies a tripartite depiction of heaven, with the outer wall as its boundary and heaven subdivided
into three sections, but in fact Enoch approaches the outer wall some way
into his heavenly ascent, and the sanctuary proper is described as a house,
which shows that the conceptualization is very definitely of a structure within
heaven.[24]

The Enochic Book of Parables (1 En. 37–71) can also be mentioned here.
It contains general indications of heavenly worship (angels interceding and
standing to bless God with the Trisagion, 39.5; 39.12–40:2; the prayers and
blood of the righteous ascending into heaven, 47.1) and of a heavenly throne
(45.3), which might suggest a temple-as-heaven perspective. But as the book
reaches its climax, Enoch is taken to "the heaven of heavens" and sees "a
structure built of crystals" (71.5) and "countless angels . . . encircling that
house" (71.8). In this case, greater specificity emerges over the course of the
text, showing that what is envisaged is a temple in heaven.

A more explicit cult is found in the Songs of the Sabbath Sacrifice. The extant material is replete with indications of heavenly temple architecture, with
pillars and "all the corners of its structure" (4Q403 1, I, 41), "sanctuaries,"
"seven elevated holy places" (4Q403 1, II, 10–11),[25] and "vestibules" by which
enter "the spirits of the most holy inner Temple" (4Q405 14–15, I, 4).[26] The
greatest attention is given to the heavenly holy of holies, the dwelling place
of God, described variously as the "glorious innermost Temple chamber,"
"the inner Temple" (4Q400 1, I, 1–4, 19), the "glorious innermost Temple
chambers" (4Q405 14–15, I, 6–7). This rich variety of structural terminology
is "drawn from the technical language of the cult," with strong influence from
Ezek. 40–48.[27] The temple is furnished with "ornaments of the innermost
sanctuary" (4Q403 1, II, 13–14) and "the image of the throne-chariot above
the firmament" (4Q405 20–22, II, 8–9). Particularly striking is the animate
nature of the structure and the ornaments, which offer praise and prayers. In
this they join the angels who serve constantly as priests and ministers of the
divine Presence.[28] The Sabbath Songs contain more extensive indications of
celestial cultic architecture than 1 Enoch, while at the same time maintaining

---

24. Contra Fletcher-Louis ("Angels, Men and Priests," 154), who argues that Enoch does
not enter a temple but moves from earth-as-courtyard to heaven-as-roofed-building. Enoch's
passage through the wall before reaching the first house tells against this interpretation.

25. In connection with the seven sanctuaries, note the variation between singular and plural
forms. Carol Newsom (*Songs of the Sabbath Sacrifice*, 49) sees this as an attempt "to com-
municate something of the elusive transcendence of heavenly reality."

26. English translations are from Vermès, *Dead Sea Scrolls*.

27. Newsom, *Songs of the Sabbath Sacrifice*, 47, 51–58.

28. Newsom, *Songs of the Sabbath Sacrifice*, 23–38.

a focus on heavenly worship in which the community joins.[29] It is therefore harder to tease out the actual structural arrangement, but it appears to have multiple chambers and a most holy place, much as the earthly temple did.[30] The mirroring principle is still in operation but remains largely implicit. Where a temple in heaven is operational, as in these texts, it entails angelology, as the angels serve in the role of priests.

One later text merits brief mention here. In the Babylonian Talmud, an exegetical discussion of the seven heavens and their names locates Jerusalem, the temple, and the altar on which Michael makes offerings within Zebul,[31] the fourth heaven (b. Hagigah 12b).[32] This is less usual, in that a temple in heaven is normally located centrally (so far as indications permit us to discern), with its inner chamber as the throne room of God, whereas God's throne and dwelling here are in Arabot, the seventh heaven. We will see below that the highest heaven is often identified as the sanctuary or its most holy part. A step toward this is identifying heaven and sanctuary as coextensive. We turn next to portrayals of heaven as *constituting* rather than *containing* a temple.

Temple as Heaven

The Testament of Levi displays significant dependence on the Enochic literature.[33] In response to his prayer for deliverance and vengeance after his sister Dinah's rape, Levi sees heaven opened in a vision and is invited by an angel to enter. He sees a first and second heaven and is given an explanation of the three heavens (T. Levi 2–3). The "uppermost heaven of all" is where God dwells "in the Holy of Holies superior to all holiness" (3.4). God is served by archangels, offering "a rational and bloodless oblation," and receives eternal praises (3.5–8). After Levi is assured that his prayer has been heard, the gates of heaven are opened to him, and he sees "the Holy Most High sitting

29. For Fletcher-Louis (*All the Glory of Adam*, 277), temple as microcosm is the hidden assumption that explains why humans and angels can mix as they do in the Sabbath Songs: "That the human community should encounter the heavenly world and its population in the Temple is a logical corollary of the fact that the Temple is a microcosm of the universe which makes available in an accessible space and time realities otherwise out of human reach."

30. Christopher Morray-Jones ("Temple Within," 149–70) sees this temple as heaven, with the seven heavens representing seven sanctuaries.

31. Compare Michael's role in 3 Bar. 12–14, where he takes bowls of righteous deeds into the fifth (and apparently highest) heaven into which Baruch cannot enter.

32. In 1 Kings 8:13//2 Chron. 6:2, Solomon describes his temple as a בית זבל. Note that some texts locate the heavenly temple in the third (e.g., Testament of Levi) or fifth heaven (e.g., Re'uyot Yehezkel; Safrai, "Heavenly Jerusalem," 15.

33. For similarities in the ascent to the heavenly temple, see Nickelsburg, "Enoch, Levi, and Peter," 588–89.

on the throne," who gives him the priesthood and commissions him to take vengeance on Shechem (5.1–3). There is evidence in the textual tradition of development, and some text-forms expand 3.1–8 to include seven heavens.

The earlier Aramaic Levi Document survives only in fragmentary form, pieced together from manuscripts from the Qumran caves, the Cairo Genizah, and other sources, and it is particularly fragmentary in chapter 4, which has a brief account of Levi's visionary ascent to heaven.[34] In his vision, Levi is above the heavens and approaches the gates of heaven (תרעי שמיא), but no further details have been preserved. Robert Kugler suggests that both the three- and the seven-heaven cosmologies were "clumsily inserted into Original *Testament of Levi* sometime after the document's initial composition."[35] He concludes that the original text went directly from 2.6 to 4.2, with a single heavenly opening at 5.1. While the traditions with a multi-tiered heaven make its cultic aspect more explicit, all alike regard the highest heaven as the dwelling place of God on his throne. Unlike 1 En. 14, there are no architectural specifications, and it is clear that heaven is coextensive with the sanctuary: opening "the gates of heaven" yields a direct vision of the throne (5.1).[36] This represents an important distinction from the texts under the previous heading, while there is continuity in the clear indications of a heavenly cult and access via ascent.

Numerous texts feature multiple heavens, usually three or seven.[37] These are auspicious numbers in Jewish thought, and they are also cosmically salient given the ancient three-tier cosmology of sea, earth, and heaven and the Aristotelian cosmology with its seven planetary spheres. Third Baruch proceeds through a series of five heavens, and the fifth is the most holy—indeed, so holy that Baruch is not permitted to enter. The gates remain closed until Michael comes (3 Bar. 11.2–5; 15.1), and after his departure, they close again (14.1; 17.1). Indications of cultic activity are attenuated, but Michael holds a vast bowl to receive "the virtues of the righteous and the good works

34. Greenfield, Stone, and Eshel, *Aramaic Levi Document*.
35. Kugler, *From Patriarch to Priest*, 180–83; cf. A. Y. Collins, *Cosmology and Eschatology*, 25–30.
36. Himmelfarb (*Ascent to Heaven*, 33) notes this distinction between 1 En. 14 and Testament of Levi but makes little of it.
37. In addition to the texts treated here, see, e.g., Mart. Ascen. Isa. 7–9; Ep. Ap. 13; 51; and 2 Cor. 12:2, which I discuss in chap. 8. The fragment of Apoc. Zeph. in Clement (*Strom.* 5.11.77) mentions the "fifth heaven." The ten heavens of 2 Enoch are probably an emendation of an original seven: the longer recension differs from the shorter in containing a brief reference to the eighth and ninth heavens (21.6) and naming the tenth heaven Arabot, like the seventh heaven in b. Hagigah 12b. See Rowland, *Open Heaven*, 82. The seven heavens acquire great importance in the Hekhalot literature of Merkavah mysticism (see Gruenwald, *Apocalyptic and Merkavah Mysticism*, 48–51 and passim).

which they do" (11.9),[38] which is filled by angels and which he then takes to offer in heaven (12.1–8). On his return, he brings oil as a reward (15.1–4).[39] Details of the contents of the fifth heaven and its worship are sparse, as it is a closed and inaccessible space. While I think this is most likely identified with the sanctuary, it is not inconceivable that a building might lie *within* the fifth heaven, locating 3 Baruch with the texts under the previous, "Temple in Heaven" heading.

Alongside 3 Baruch, and even less detailed, we should note the Testament of Abraham, which together with descriptions of heaven's gates and a golden throne (10.15; 11.1–9) has clear indications of angelic worship as Abraham is taken into heaven (20.12–14[A]; 4.4[B]). Another brief indication of heaven's equivalence with a temple is found in the Prayer of Azariah, which proclaims, "Blessed are you in the temple of your holy glory. . . . Blessed are you in the firmament of heaven" (31, 34). A similar notion in a rather different setting is found in Jubilees, which retells the Genesis and Exodus accounts with an emphasis on extending the sacrificial cult back into the days of the patriarchs. For example, Noah's sacrifice takes on particular importance (Jub. 6), and Abraham is first to celebrate the Festival of Booths/Tabernacles (16.20–31). An additional emphasis is on the precise regularity and eternity of the cult offered in accordance with a solar calendar (e.g., 49.7–8). One aspect that undergirds this regular cult is its mirroring of the heavenly cult, although again indications are fairly sparse: Levi and his descendants are to minister before God just as the angels do, "to serve in his sanctuary as the angels of the presence and the holy ones" (30.18; 31.14; cf. the angels' keeping of the sabbath in heaven, 2.18–19).[40] As with 3 Baruch, it is hard to specify with certainty whether the Testament of Abraham and Jubilees evince a temple in heaven or temple as heaven.

Although Philo of Alexandria is often taken to equate temple with cosmos, he in fact displays a variety of approaches to temple symbolism. A key passage is in *On the Special Laws*: "The highest, and in the truest sense the holy, temple of God [τὸ μὲν ἀνωτάτω καὶ πρὸς ἀλήθειαν ἱερὸν θεοῦ] is, as we must believe, the whole universe [τὸν σύμπαντα . . . κόσμον], having for its sanctuary [νεώ] the most sacred part of all existence, even heaven [οὐρανόν], for its votive ornaments the stars, for its priests the angels who are servitors to His powers, unbodied souls" (*Spec. Laws* 1.66 LCL). He does not simply equate the entire cosmos with the temple. Rather, Philo makes a careful distinction between the

---

38. Greek; the Slavonic has "the prayers of men."

39. H. E. Gaylord (*OTP* 1:657) describes Michael as a high priest, taking these good works "to the temple in an upper heaven to offer upon the altar."

40. On the earth-heaven parallelism, see esp. J. Scott, *On Earth as in Heaven*.

temple complex (denoted consistently with ἱερόν) and the sanctuary proper, the temple building itself with porch and outer and inner chambers (which is consistently indicated with νεώς).[41]

We were alerted to this distinction in chapter 1 in relation to Greco-Roman temples. While authors writing in Greek and Latin were not always consistent in applying the terminology outlined there, when we come to Jewish authors writing in Greek, we find that the distinction is carefully observed. To equate the whole universe with the temple complex entails identifying heaven itself with the actual temple building. And thus we find ourselves with a picture that is only marginally different from the portrayal of heaven as coextensive with the sanctuary.[42] The temple-as-microcosm model that Fletcher-Louis advocates, with earth as courtyard and heaven as roofed sanctuary, is explicitly articulated only here in extant texts from the period. Moreover, Philo does not here dwell on the outer courts or elaborate their significance or symbolism in relation to aspects of the visible or physical universe but instead moves on to describe the Jerusalem temple (1.67–78) before then discussing the cosmic symbolism of priestly garments (1.79–97). His primary interest in 1.66 is the heaven-as-temple-proper correspondence, and in line with this he has here, as Klawans notes but underplays, a clear angelology and also (throughout his corpus) a developed theory of emanation of the divine presence. This is an impeccably borderline case: both temple(-sanctuary) as heaven and temple(-complex) as cosmos. As such, it well demonstrates the gradation of understandings of heavenly temple in the period and pivots us directly into the final heading.

Temple as Cosmos

As we turn to the last point on the spectrum, we will look initially at Josephus before correlating his perspective with another key passage in Philo. Josephus's interest is largely descriptive, with historically important descriptions of the tabernacle (*Ant.* 3.102–257) and the temples of Solomon (*Ant.* 8.63–98) and Herod (*Ant.* 15.230–425; *J.W.* 5.184–247).[43] In describing the

---

41. Cf. *Spec. Laws* 1.72; Josephus makes the same distinction (e.g., *Ant.* 15.219; *J.W.* 5.184, 207, 209). Philo (e.g., *Moses* 2.178) also distinguishes between the sanctuary as a whole (νεώς) and the most holy place (ἄδυτον). The words νεώς/ναός can also be used to refer to pagan temples (e.g., Philo, *Spec. Laws* 1.21; *Embassy* 139).

42. Jutta Leonhardt (*Jewish Worship in Philo*, 218) rightly notes traditional Jewish connections here but is wrong to suggest that the idea that "the universe is the first Temple of God" must derive from Hellenistic philosophy, given that it is a commonplace across the ancient world.

43. On the varying historical accounts, see Levine, "Josephus' Description of the Jerusalem Temple."

tabernacle, however, he compares it to the universe (a passage we considered briefly above). The tabernacle was fashioned as an "imitation and representation of the universe" (εἰς ἀπομίμησιν καὶ διατύπωσιν τῶν ὅλων, *Ant.* 3.180). Moses divided the tabernacle's thirty-cubit length into three equal parts, and by appointing two of them for the priests as a space "accessible and in common, he signifies the earth and the sea [ὥσπερ βέβηλόν τινα καὶ κοινὸν τόπον τὴν γῆν καὶ τὴν θάλασσαν ἀποσημαίνει], for these also are accessible to all [πᾶσίν ἐστιν ἐπιβατά]." But the third portion (that is, the most holy place, a cube of ten cubits) is restricted to God, because "the heaven also is inaccessible to men" (διὰ τὸ καὶ τὸν οὐρανὸν ἀνεπίβατον εἶναι ἀνθρώποις, 3.181; cf. 3.123). Within the physical creation represented by the tabernacle's outer chamber, the twelve loaves of showbread represent the twelve months, and the sevenfold lampstands the seven planets (3.182). Juxtaposed with the passage from Philo's *Special Laws*, the differences become clear: Josephus equates the tabernacle sanctuary alone with heaven, earth, and sea, whereas Philo identifies the temple complex with the universe, and heaven with the sanctuary. It is only with this description from Josephus that we actually land fully in a temple(-sanctuary)-as-cosmos model.

However, a similar tradition was known to Philo. In *Questions and Answers on Exodus*, he describes the inner chamber as "holy and truly divine," whereas the outer chamber "indicates the changeable parts of the world which are sublunary" (2.91; cf. 2.94; note the Aristotelian cosmological terminology). And in *On the Life of Moses*, he describes the tabernacle at some length (2.71–160). When he comes to the incense altar, he notes that it was placed "in the middle of earth and water, as a symbol of thanksgiving" (μέσον μὲν τὸ θυμιατήριον γῆς καὶ ὕδατος σύμβολον εὐχαριστίας, 2.101).[44] In this context, he identifies the cherubim of the ark as God's creative and royal powers (2.98–99)[45] and the seven-branched lampstand as the seven planets, and he relates the table to the winds, which provide nourishment (2.102–4). This passage is consonant with Josephus's description (though direct dependence is unlikely), but it represents a perspective that is different from Philo's *Special Laws*.

Worthy of brief mention is Bar. 3:24–25, which exclaims, "O Israel, how great is the house of God, / how vast the territory that he possesses! / It is great and has no bounds; / it is high and immeasurable." This is underdetermined, but the text goes on to speak of the birthplace of the giants and

---

44. Cf. Josephus's connection of the incense altar with the habitable and uninhabitable parts of the earth (*J.W.* 5.218).

45. He first considers and dismisses their equation with the hemispheres (ἡμισφαίριον) above and below the earth, that is, the firmament and the underworld, with the earth as a disc between the two.

then of the heavens and seas (3:26–30), which suggests that the whole world as God's temple might be in view. Whatever one's judgment on Baruch, it is clear that Josephus and Philo stand in a category apart in terms of the detail of correspondence between sanctuary and universe they envisage.

In another passage, Philo speaks of two temples: one is the rational soul, and the other is the universe (κόσμος, *Dreams* 1.215). Here he does not dwell on cosmological details but compares the high priest in the universe with the "true person" (ὁ πρὸς ἀλήθειαν ἄνθρωπος) within the soul. Later he elaborates on the status of the high priest as the Logos, the divine rational principle operative within creation, who both represents and also surpasses humanity in his intermediary function (supremely on the Day of Atonement, 2.185–89).[46]

A notion related to the temple-as-rational-soul is cosmic-cultic symbolism, whereby items associated with the cult are invested with cosmic significance. We find this extensively in Josephus and Philo, particularly with regard to the high priest's garments, which are in themselves a microcosm. Their threads symbolize earth, air, heaven, and water (the four classical elements); the two shoulder pieces represent the hemispheres or the sun and moon; the bells and pomegranates signify harmony and water or thunder and lightning, and so forth.[47] Cosmic symbolism is also found in the depiction of the high priest Simon son of Onias in Sir. 50:5–7, who is like the celestial bodies—the morning star, sun, and moon—in the splendor of his temple service.[48] So also the four colored threads of the temple veil represent the four elements (Josephus, *Ant.* 3.183; *J.W.* 5.210–14), and sacrificial animals and incense are susceptible to similar interpretations (Philo, *QG* 3.3; *Heir* 196–97). These elucidations underline the sense of the Jerusalem cult's cosmic significance, but they operate at the level of symbolism rather than correspondence. That is, rather than holding that the universe or heaven is or contains a temple and that the earthly sanctuary represents this greater reality, these explanations of cultic garments and accoutrements connect specific aspects to particular cosmic phenomena, usually without regard for a broader coherent picture or correspondence.[49] They are not unrelated to the material above, but spatial and systematic aspects of the sanctuary-cosmos correspondence are missing.

46. Cf. Let. Aris. 99, which describes the high priest as someone coming from outside this world.

47. Philo, *Moses* 2.109–35; *Spec. Laws* 1.82–97; Josephus, *Ant.* 3.184–85; *J.W.* 5.231; cf. Wis. 18:24. On the universal significance of the high priest in Philo, see Leonhardt, *Jewish Worship in Philo*, 128–29. On Josephus, see Pena, "Wearing the Cosmos."

48. On Simeon's portrayal, see Fletcher-Louis, "High Priest in Ben Sira 50," 94–98, 110; Hayward, *Jewish Temple*, 49–55, 78.

49. Indeed, as Hayward (*Jewish Temple*, 126) notes, Philo is capable of substantial variations in his explanations of cultic furnishings.

One other point bears mentioning here. The core motifs of ancient Near Eastern temple ideology noted in the previous chapter—mountains, waters, and paradise—are often found in one form or another in Jewish writings. Thus the portrayal of Eden as sanctuary, which is at best implicit in Gen. 1–3, becomes explicit in a text like Jubilees, where Eden is described as "the holy of holies and the dwelling of the Lord" (8.19).[50] In T. Levi 18.10–11, the opening of the gates of paradise apparently mirrors the opening of the heavenly temple (cf. 18.6). In 1 En. 25, the patriarch encounters a tree that will be planted "upon the holy place—in the direction of the house of the Lord" and a tall mountain "whose summit resembles the throne of God" (25.1–5). In 2 Esd. (4 Ezra) 8:52, the opening of paradise, planting of the tree of life, and building of the city are juxtaposed as symbols of the eschaton. These identifications are not quite the same thing as equating the whole of creation with a temple, but they represent a closely related set of ideas and a perpetuation of the cosmic symbolism of the ancient world.

Conclusion

The notion of a heavenly temple held great importance for Second Temple texts and authors and was a rich source of varied reflection. Previous proposals for temple-as-microcosm as the only model in the period and for a twofold categorization of temple-in-heaven over against temple-as-universe are inadequate, especially where the latter distinction is correlated with an apocalyptic versus Hellenistic fault line. The issue with this binary distinction is primarily its missing middle term. Treating the idea of temple-as-heaven separately reveals that there is only a small step from this to temple-as-cosmos, because some temple-as-heaven texts equate heaven or the highest heaven with a single-chambered sanctuary, leaving open the possibility that outer chambers or courts might reflect lower parts of the cosmos. It is precisely this possibility that Philo exploits, and a close reading of *On the Special Laws* reveals *both* temple-sanctuary as heaven *and* temple-complex as cosmos in the same passage, thus distinguishing him from Josephus's equation of the cosmos with the tabernacle alone. In contrast to Greco-Roman depictions of the universe as a temple, which are often fleetingly made and show little

50. Eden is designated one of three "holy places" alongside Mount Sinai and Mount Zion; cf. Jub. 4.26, which counts four holy places, adding Mount Qater, where Enoch offered incense. See also Tg. Ps.-J. of Gen. 2:7, 15, where Adam is formed from dust from the place of the sanctuary and offers sacrifice on the first altar.

interest in associating temple structure with tiered cosmologies, Philo and Josephus present elaborate and distinctively Jewish construals of the universe's equivalence to Israel's sanctuaries. Indeed, the gradations of holy space that were present in the tabernacle and were extended in Solomon's and Herod's temples naturally lent themselves to a variety of graded approaches to the universe.[51] The texts explored in this chapter alert us to the existence, the extent, and the range of heavenly temple reflections in the period and thus prepare and inform our encounter with similar ideas in the NT.

---

51. Rowland (*Open Heaven*, 84) plausibly suggests that temple design influenced developing cosmology.

3

Revelation

Judgment and Salvation

The book of Revelation is the epicenter of heavenly temple imagery within the NT, and it is therefore fitting that we start our investigation of NT texts here. The heavenly sanctuary recurs extensively as the setting for the major sequence of visions in the center of the work. The book as a whole is replete with cultic symbolism, encompassing spaces, furniture, vessels, servants, and offerings. The imagery is fluid, with language of both tabernacle and temple and a range of perspectives on the heavenly sanctuary in different visions. In particular, Revelation's opening and closing visions (Rev. 1; 21–22) treat temple themes in ways quite different from the book's central section. The heavenly sanctuary is nevertheless a place of worship and refuge and hence a source of assurance and a focus for earthly believers' praise, much as in Hebrews and in some of the other texts we will encounter later in our study. Yet Revelation is distinctive not only among NT texts but also among apocalypses in its insistent identification of the heavenly temple as the originating locus of God's judgment. My thesis in this chapter is that the emphasis on judgment emanating from the heavenly temple is in keeping with its function as a place of worship and refuge and is also consistent with the transformation of heaven in Revelation's closing vision of the age to come. The heavenly temple's holiness and openness together account for these portrayals that at first sight seem rather divergent.

This chapter proceeds in four parts. First, we look at the temple's significance. Revelation's opening vision along with a few other passages suggest the temple might in part signify the church. The temple is also a place of worship of the Lamb and of refuge for the righteous. Second, we explore the temple's architecture, focusing on a key item of furniture that it contains (the golden incense altar) and on its structure as a single chamber that is both throne room and most holy place. Third, we examine the striking association, recurrent and emphatic, of temple with judgment. In light of other literature, Revelation's way of connecting these two themes is shown to be all the more distinctive. In the fourth and final part, we explore the book's closing vision. Here I argue that the heavenly sanctuary is not absent but is instead transformed to become coterminous with the New Jerusalem.

Temple Significance

Temple as People and Place

Revelation's opening address mentions the divine throne and names believers as priests (1:4, 6). The throne is foremost a royal image, but as we have seen the distinction between religious and political motifs in the ancient world was minimal. Indeed, in relation to a deity, the throne is the location of his temple, and vice versa. As Revelation continues, the throne will be described in terms that are increasingly cultic.[1] John is "in the spirit" (1:10), indicating a visionary experience, and the first thing he sees in his vision is "seven golden lampstands" (1:12). The imagery is drawn from Israel's sanctuary: the tabernacle had a single, seven-branched menorah (Exod. 25:31–32), while Solomon's temple had ten golden lampstands (2 Chron. 4:7).[2] Herod's temple, like the tabernacle, had a seven-branched menorah, which can be seen on the Arch of Titus in Rome, which commemorates the sacking of Jerusalem in AD 70.[3] The lampstands stood in the holy place, the first or outer compartment of the sanctuary. The "one like the Son of Man" (Rev. 1:13) is dressed in glorious apparel, which combines features of levitical and pagan priestly dress.[4]

1. Gallusz, *Throne Motif*, 100–101.
2. Rabbinic tradition infers that the seven-branched menorah stood between the ten lampstands, five on the north and five on the south (b. Menahot 98b).
3. It is unclear what Zerubbabel's temple contained. The lampstand in Zechariah's vision (Zech. 4:2) has seven branches, apparently with seven wicks on each.
4. The words ποδήρης and ζώνη describe the priestly robe and sash in Exod. 28:4 LXX (cf. Josephus, *Ant.* 3.159; Exod. 39:29 [36:36 LXX]). On pagan goddesses wearing a sash around their breasts, see Paul, *Revelation*, 73. Blount (*Revelation*, 44), citing 1 Macc. 10:89, connects the robe with Aaron's garment and the sash with kings.

While other indications of sanctuary architecture are lacking, the lamp-stands and high priest figure might suggest that the holy place of the temple/tabernacle is the setting. If the vision is thought to be on earth, then this could indicate a temple-as-cosmos concept, with heaven as the most holy place. Yet the vision is at this stage too indeterminate. "In the spirit" (1:10) is identical to the description of how John comes to have his vision of heaven (4:2), though the open door and the invitation to come up are missing in Rev. 1. Moreover, the lampstands are identified as the seven churches (1:20), which suggests a symbolic perspective whereby churches form part of the temple furniture.

A similar notion is encountered in the letter to the church in Philadelphia. Here "the one who overcomes" (NASB) is promised, "I will make you a pillar in the temple of my God" (στῦλον ἐν τῷ ναῷ τοῦ θεοῦ μου, 3:12). This sixth letter has a strong cultic framing, reinforced by the mention of the New Jerusalem in the same verse. The terminology is consistent with sanctuary terminology elsewhere, where "sanctuary (of God)" (ναός [τοῦ θεοῦ]) denotes the heavenly sanctuary. The "pillar" may well draw on the Greco-Roman practice of incorporating pillars carved as human figures in their sacred architecture. Here the image represents both permanence and service of the deity.[5] There are also similarities with the animate temple architecture in Songs of the Sabbath Sacrifice, which sings God's praise.[6] The promise is that the believer will become a pillar in the heavenly sanctuary, and reference to the New Jerusalem coming down from heaven harks forward to Rev. 21, as does repeated mention of "the one who overcomes" (ὁ νικῶν) in the letters and in 21:7. It therefore seems that this is a future and not a present depiction of the believer, consonant with but not identical to the identification of churches as lampstands.

The identification of believers with the sanctuary is in keeping with Revelation's use of tabernacle/dwelling terminology. At Michael's defeat of the dragon, the heavens "and those who dwell in them" (οἱ ἐν αὐτοῖς σκηνοῦντες, Rev. 12:12) are exhorted to rejoice. In the paired vision of the following chapter, the first beast blasphemes God's dwelling or tabernacle (σκηνή), "that is, those who dwell in heaven" (τοὺς ἐν τῷ οὐρανῷ σκηνοῦντας, 13:6). Such language connects with the promise of the eschaton, when God will "spread His tabernacle" (7:15 NASB) over his people and "dwell" with them (21:3, σκηνώσει in both cases). These visions again relate to heavenly or eschatological reality, as does the letter to the Philadelphians,

5. Stevenson, *Power and Place*, 246–51.
6. Regev, *Temple in Early Christianity*, 238.

and not to the churches' present existence as in Rev. 1; we will return to them below.[7]

Heaven as a Setting for Worship

Revelation 4:1 marks a significant transition in the book's structure,[8] from the seven letters to the heavenly setting, which will dominate the central section up to Rev. 20. Leaving aside the proleptic tilt toward Rev. 21 in 3:12 examined above, this is the first direct mention of heaven in the book. A door stands open (θύρα ἠνεῳγμένη) already and permanently, presumably opened by God.[9] This is apparently the same door as in the greeting of the letter to Philadelphia, which describes Christ as "the holy one, the true one, / who has the key of David, / who opens and no one will shut, / who shuts and no one opens" (3:7). He then states, "I have set before you an open door [θύρα ἠνεῳγμένη] that no one is able to shut" (3:8). The description of Jesus is drawn from Isa. 22:22, which establishes Eliakim's power and legitimacy over that of Shebna. The targum interprets this as the key of the "house of the sanctuary,"[10] and both the Jerusalem temple and pagan temples had doors.[11] In combination with other temple architecture references in the same letter and the use of the same phrase to denote the opening to the heavenly sanctuary in Rev. 4:1, it seems right to identify Philadelphia's open door not as generic opportunity but more concretely as the way to the heavenly temple.[12] What is new is that John is enabled to see it and through invitation and being "in the spirit" to pass through it, much as Enoch and Levi are invited to approach.[13] Structurally, the door might open into heaven itself or stand

7. Gundry ("People as Place") argues that in Rev. 21–22 the New Jerusalem is a cipher for God's people. See my discussion in the final section, "Temple Transformed," below.

8. Harrington, *Revelation*, 78.

9. "Gott selbst hat dem Seher das Tor geöffnet" (Schimanowski, *Die himmlische Liturgie*, 68). On the opening motif, see van Unnik, "Die 'geöffneten Himmel'"; Lentzen-Deis, "Das Motiv der 'Himmelsöffnung.'" For this motif in relation to the heavenly temple in Revelation, see Moore, "God's Sanctuary in Heaven Was Opened."

10. Tg. Ps.-J. of Isa. 22:22. For an account of the meaning of Isa. 22:22 and its reception, see Rucker, *Temple Keys*, 1–25, 59–96.

11. The temple of Artemis in Ephesus had a door symbolizing the epiphany of the goddess (Aune, *Revelation 1–5*, 280–82). Greek and Roman authors also report temple doors springing open spontaneously (Stambaugh, "Functions of Roman Temples," 569). For the doors to the inner and outer compartments of Solomon's temple, see 1 Kings 6:31–35. Note also the doors in Ezekiel's visionary temple (Ezek. 41:23–25).

12. Contra Rucker (*Temple Keys*, 97–133), who regards the open door as the opportunity for Jews to become part of the church construed as new temple.

13. In contrast to Revelation's permanently open door, in Ezek. 1:1 it is the opening of heaven that initiates Ezekiel's vision.

within heaven, opening onto the throne room. The invitation to "come up" seems to imply the former.[14]

What John sees is both a royal throne room and a sanctuary. Regal and cultic imagery coexist and are not in competition.[15] The divine throne (4:2) is represented by the ark of the covenant and its atonement cover.[16] Jasper, carnelian, and emerald are three of the precious stones on the high priests' breastplate (Rev. 4:3; Exod. 28:15–21). The twenty-four elders may represent the Levite divisions of service (Rev. 4:4, 10; 1 Chron. 24:4–19). The seven burning torches recall the seven branches of the lampstand (Rev. 4:5; Exod. 25:31–39), and the crystal sea is like the tabernacle laver or Solomon's bronze sea.[17] The four living creatures evoke those in Ezekiel's visions (Rev. 4:6–9; Ezek. 1:5–14 and implicitly in 43:2–3), and they and the elders hold harps and bowls of incense, ready for priestly service (Rev. 5:8).

This place is a setting for worship first of all: the Trisagion of the creatures alludes to Isaiah's temple vision ("holy, holy, holy," Isa. 6:3) and is accompanied by a song from the elders (Rev. 4:8–11). Revelation 5 continues in the same setting. The possibility that the sealed scroll cannot be opened is averted by the "Lamb standing as if it had been slaughtered" (ὡς ἐσφαγμένον, 5:6), who is worthy to open the scroll. The Lamb is described as having been slaughtered and as redeeming (ἐσφάγης καὶ ἠγόρασας, 5:9) people from every tribe, tongue, people, and nation. The significance of the Lamb's slaughter is debated. The verb "slaughter" (σφάζω) is found only in Revelation and 1 John in the NT, clearly denoting in several places nonritual killing (see 1 John 3:12; Rev. 6:4). In the Septuagint, it can likewise refer to the act of killing in general (e.g., Jer. 52:10). Yet it is also used frequently in relation to a variety of sacrifices, whether the burnt offering (Lev. 1:5; Ezek. 44:11), peace offering (Lev. 17:5), sin offering (4:4), guilt offering (7:2), or Day of Atonement offerings (16:11, 15). The *tamid* offerings of a lamb every morning and evening took the form of a burnt offering, and might also be in view here (Exod. 29:38–42). We will explore sacrificial process in greater detail in chapter 4 in relation to Hebrews and the Day of Atonement. For now, we note that while ritual slaughter is only an early step within the process of animal sacrifice and not its sum total, it remains an integral part of it.

14. In 1 En. 14.8–25, Enoch sees through an open door into the next part of the heavenly temple (R. Davis, *Heavenly Court Judgment*, 149).

15. *Pace* Schimanowski (*Die himmlische Liturgie*, 67n25; 103), who unnecessarily downplays the significance of temple motifs here. For studies of the temple in Revelation, see also Spatafora, *From the Temple*; Snyder, "Combat Myth"; Briggs, *Temple Imagery*; Tóth, *Der himmlische Kult*.

16. Hall, "Living Creatures"; Hannah, "Cherubim."

17. Rev. 4:6; Exod. 30:18–21; 1 Kings 7:23–26; 1 Chron. 18:8. See R. Davis, *Heavenly Court Judgment*, 123.

In Revelation, the animal slain is a lamb, or possibly a ram given that it has seven horns (Rev. 5:6). A ram would suggest the guilt offering (Lev. 5:15; 6:6), whereas a lamb would suggest the Passover (Exod. 12:3–6) or the *tamid* or peace offering (Exod. 29:38, 42; Lev. 3:6–11).[18] The Lamb's location on the throne might imply the Day of Atonement, if the throne is to be identified with the ark (as I will argue below). Only the blood of the Yom Kippur sacrifices was applied to the throne, with the carcass disposed of outside the camp (Lev. 16:27–28), although we should not expect exact correspondence in this christological permutation. It is conceivable that the blood is brought into the most holy place in the very person of the risen, exalted Christ (this is what we shall see in Hebrews in the following chapter). Nevertheless, the Lamb's presence on the throne is likely due more to the royal motif than to a particular construal of sacrificial process. One other salient portrayal of a slain lamb is in Isaiah's fourth Servant Song, where the servant is silent "like a lamb that is led to the slaughter, / and like a sheep . . . before its shearers" (Isa. 53:7). The Septuagint's terms for the animal are at variance—"sheep" and "lamb" (πρόβατον, ἀμνός), whereas Revelation uses "little lamb" (ἀρνίον)— but the idea in combination with "slaughter" (σφαγή) is very close. Many interpreters see regal aspects as the only contributing factor in this portrayal of the Lamb, who has emerged from battle or martyrdom.[19] The identification of martyrdom with sacrifice is not secure in this period, though it is likely emerging as demonstrated by 4 Maccabees, written in a similar time frame to Revelation (see further my discussion in chap. 8).

As stated above, royal-militaristic and cultic-sacrificial images are not mutually exclusive in Revelation's understanding of heaven, and both are in play. The sacrificial aspect of the Lamb's portrayal is inescapable in a context where other indications of temple worship are clearly present: "bowls full of incense, which are the prayers of the saints," are offered, as is singing accompanied by harps, and the ransomed people are named both a kingdom and priests (5:8–10). Exactly what kind of sacrifice the Lamb constitutes is left underdetermined, and there may well be an allusion to the guilt and

18. While the origins of the Passover may not have been sacrificial, by the Second Temple period it was well integrated as an important annual sacrifice and festival, with the slaughter of the paschal lambs performed by Levites. Haran (*Temples and Temple-Service*, 327–48) argues that both the festival and its association with the temple are early.

19. E.g., Massyngberde Ford (*Revelation*, 90–91) writes, "The slaughter of the lamb and the function of his blood must be seen against the background of battle and/or martyrdom." He goes on to connect martyrdom with sacrifice and with the Akedah. Blount (*Revelation*, 109–12) sees the Lamb as executed for his faithful witness, with little or no sacrificial connection. For a recent study of the power dynamics of martyrdom in Revelation, see Middleton, *Violence of the Lamb*.

peace offerings. Given the prominence of Passover as an image for Jesus's death in the Gospels, however, it seems likely that paschal resonances are foremost.[20] As Rev. 5 continues, a vast gathering of angels is introduced before every creature in the whole cosmos joins the song (5:11). As I will argue below, Revelation exhibits little interest in structural gradations of holiness beyond the earth-heaven distinction, but it offers a gradation of concentric circles of worship moving outward to encompass the whole created order.[21] A crescendo of worship in Rev. 4–5 builds through five songs and culminates in a song to both God and the Lamb together.[22] At the center of this worship, in the middle of the heavenly temple, stands a Lamb who was slain—both a victorious suffering servant-martyr and a living sacrifice.

Temple as a Place of Refuge

Heaven is primarily portrayed as a location for heavenly beings, but humans are present there too. At the opening of the fifth seal, the heavenly sanctuary is revealed to be a place of refuge for the souls of the faithful who have been slaughtered (αἱ ψυχαὶ τῶν ἐσφαγμένων, 6:9). The use of the same verb that was used for the Lamb identifies them closely.[23] They take shelter "under the altar" (θυσιαστήριον). This could be the altar of burnt offering, which stood outside the sanctuary proper, or the incense altar (mentioned in 8:3, 5; 9:13); we will return to this question shortly.[24] It is not unknown for temples to function as places of asylum. In the OT, both Adonijah and Joab flee to the sanctuary and cling to the horns of the altar of burnt offering in their attempt to avoid execution at Solomon's orders, though both are ultimately executed (1 Kings 1:50–51; 2:28). Greco-Roman sanctuaries, particularly those located near the sea, were an ideal place for political refuge due to their location, their sanctity, and, more practically, the presence of cult meadows outside the temenos where livestock providing sacrificial animals could be kept.[25]

This brief glimpse in Rev. 6 is consonant with the more expansive vision of Rev. 7. Chapter 7 (esp. vv. 16–17) has extensive connections with Rev. 21–22 and forms a bridge between the worship scene of Rev. 4–5 and the book's closing vision. The 144,000 servants of God are sealed for their protection (7:3–8). The great multitude from every nation joins in the praise of the angels,

---

20. Osborne, *Revelation*, 255–56; Shauf, *Jesus the Sacrifice*, 137–41.
21. Blount, *Revelation*, 89–90.
22. See R. Davis, *Heavenly Court Judgment*, 143–44.
23. Bauckham, *Revelation*, 77–78.
24. Osborne (*Revelation*, 284–85) suggests that Revelation's one heavenly altar combines functions of both earthly ones.
25. Sinn, "Greek Sanctuaries"; Schumacher, "Sanctuaries of Poseidon."

elders, and creatures. Like the martyrs of 6:9, they have emerged from a great ordeal, with white robes washed in the blood of the Lamb. Their location is significant: "They are before the throne of God, / and worship him day and night within his temple, and the one who is seated on the throne will shelter them" (7:15). The multitude is near the throne (7:9), just like the altar of 8:3 (the same phrase, ἐνώπιον τοῦ θρόνου, is used for both), which reinforces the connection with the martyrs of 6:9. This location is further specified as "within his temple," and language of tabernacling (σκηνώσει, 7:15) is used to describe their protection by God himself. The vision of Rev. 7 fulfills the expectation in 6:9–11 that others will join the faithful martyrs. Heaven is open to receive those who have remained faithful to Jesus through tribulation and even death. The temple building and its altar are again a place of refuge in 11:1–2, contrasted with the court, which is to be trampled by the nations. Part of the function of the heavenly temple, then, is to offer asylum, refuge, or indeed "sanctuary" (in another nuance of the English word) to God's people.

Temple Architecture

The Altar

We turn now to explore the architecture of the heavenly temple as Revelation presents it. The altar, like the throne, is an important item of heavenly furniture in John's visions. The same word (θυσιαστήριον) is used eight times in the book, and the question of which altar(s) and the implications of its or their location is complex.

In Rev. 8:3–5, an angel stands at the altar with a censer and is given incense to offer with the prayers of the saints. The altar is "before the throne" (ἐνώπιον τοῦ θρόνου), and the angel fills the censer with fire from the altar and throws it onto the earth, indicating a clear distinction between the altar in heaven and the earth. The incense altar was situated in the holy place of the earthly sanctuary, not the most holy place, but its location is often specified with respect to the curtain, ark, and atonement cover within the inner chamber, much as Revelation relates the altar here to the throne.[26]

At the blowing of the sixth trumpet, a voice comes from the "four horns of the golden altar before God" (9:13).[27] Both the incense altar and the altar of burnt offering had horns at each of their corners, to which blood was ritually

26. An exception is Heb. 9:4, discussed in the following chapter, which represents a possible interpretation of Exod. 30:6.
27. Some manuscripts omit "four," which could readily have been supplied from knowledge of the OT but does not substantially affect the meaning here.

applied (for the altar of burnt offering, see Exod. 27:2; 38:2; Lev. 4:25, 30). In the case of the incense altar, blood was applied on the Day of Atonement (Exod. 30:10). The atonement cover over the ark had blood sprinkled on and toward it (Lev. 16:14–15) but did not have horns to which blood was directly applied. That the altar in Rev. 9:13 is "golden" (τοῦ χρυσοῦ, cf. Exod. 30:3) and "before God" (ἐνώπιον τοῦ θεοῦ) strongly suggests it too is the incense altar, as in 8:3–5, which as noted previously is closely proximate to and correlated with the ark and God's presence above it in the most holy place.

In Rev. 11:1–2, John is told to measure the altar (τὸ θυσιαστήριον) along with the temple (ναός),[28] but not the court outside. It is unusual for an altar to be mentioned here alongside the temple building and its court. Given that the altar of burnt offering was located in the courtyard, which is not to be measured, we are probably again dealing with the altar of incense, as in the previous occurrences.[29] This reading is reinforced by the consideration that the court is handed over to the nations to be trampled, whereas the temple building and the altar (which presumably must be within the sanctuary) are a place of refuge, as in Rev. 6–7. In 14:18 an angel emerges from the altar (ἐκ τοῦ θυσιαστηρίου). The angel has "authority over fire," which was used on both altars (for the perpetual fire on the altar of burnt offering, see Lev. 6:9–13). However, given that this is the third in a series of angels, the first of whom came "out of the temple" and the second "out of the temple in heaven" (14:15, 17),[30] the altar again appears to be located inside the temple like the incense altar.

The final reference to an altar in Revelation fits this emerging pattern. The altar itself responds to an angel who declares God's justice, saying: "Yes, O Lord God, the Almighty, / your judgments are true and just!" (16:7). Prior to this, the emptying of the seven bowls of wrath is initiated by "a loud voice from the temple" (μεγάλης φωνῆς ἐκ τοῦ ναοῦ, 16:1) instructing the angels. Once the seventh bowl has been poured out, again "a loud voice came out of the temple, from the throne [φωνὴ μεγάλη ἐκ τοῦ ναοῦ ἀπὸ τοῦ θρόνου], saying, 'It is done!'" (16:17). The two loud voices seem to be identical, as both come from the temple and respectively initiate and close the judgment of the seven bowls. Therefore, the altar is most naturally understood as the incense

28. Revelation uses ναός 16× and ἱερόν never. Nevertheless, 11:1–2 demonstrates a clear distinction between the sanctuary building proper (ναός) and its outer courts (here αὐλή).

29. Contra Aune, *Revelation 6–16*, 596–98, 603–7. He takes θυσιαστήριον here to refer to the "altar area," used together with the sanctuary as a symbol for the people of God. He thinks 6:9, 14:18, and 16:7 all refer to the altar of burnt offering (see also Aune, *Revelation 6–16*, 405–6).

30. A few manuscripts, including 051, have "out of heaven" in 14:15; while "temple" is likely the original reading, this indicates the close connection and even interchangeability of these terms to early readers.

altar within the temple. It is not identical with the throne, but the two are closely associated, as we have seen.

It appears, then, that when Revelation mentions an altar, it refers consistently to the golden altar of incense, located within the temple.[31] It is closely related to the throne, which was represented in earthly sanctuaries by the ark of the covenant with its atonement cover. The close association of the two and their location within heaven and within the temple suggests that the distinction between the holy place and the most holy place is of little or no importance for Revelation. Whether this signals the unification of the two chambers, a single chamber from the outset, or simple lack of interest is difficult to say without looking at further evidence.

Structure of the Heavenly Temple

As noted above, the opening vision of Jesus as a priest among the seven lampstands could suggest the equation of the temple with the cosmos, where earth is the holy place and heaven the most holy place. This would be consistent with John entering the most holy place when he ascends to heaven in Rev. 4–5. Yet the incense altar's location within heaven, close to the throne and the divine presence, problematizes this apparently straightforward initial impression. Other structural indications are also somewhat ambivalent.

In Rev. 11:1–2, John is told to "measure the temple of God [τὸν ναὸν τοῦ θεοῦ] and the altar and those who worship there" but not to measure "the court outside the temple" (τὴν αὐλὴν τὴν ἔξωθεν τοῦ ναοῦ). This is because the nations "will trample over the holy city [τὴν πόλιν τὴν ἁγίαν]." The temple is again a place of security and refuge for God's people. If the temple here is equivalent to heaven, as would seem most natural given the previous references to God's people worshiping him there (5:13; 6:10; 7:15), the court is presumably on earth, because it is vulnerable to "the nations."[32] It is not explicitly

---

31. Contra Blount (*Revelation*, 165n9), who claims that "John jumps between the sacrificial and incense altars" but that both "can be clearly identified in John's text." Kistemaker ("Temple in the Apocalypse," 436) suggests that the altar of burnt offering is absent because it is rendered obsolete by Jesus's death. However, if the slain lamb alludes to peace and guilt offerings, then Jesus's death is associated with the altar of burnt offering in Revelation, at least obliquely. Whether or not Revelation connects Jesus's death with the altar of burnt offering, it is not clear that the latter is necessarily made obsolete. With the possible exception of Heb. 9:14, the two are not connected elsewhere in the NT. On the potential connection of "eternal spirit" with "perpetual fire," see Vanhoye, "Esprit éternel." The altar of burnt offering did have a role on Yom Kippur: it was the source of the coals for Aaron's censer (Lev. 16:12) and was smeared and sprinkled with blood (16:18–19; Milgrom, *Leviticus 1–16*, 1036–40).

32. Bachmann ("Himmlisch," esp. 475–78) notes that temple, altar, and worship are all heavenly phenomena and suggests that identifying the sanctuary as the Jerusalem temple is a

stated that anyone is present in the court, but its equation with the "holy city" suggests that it is inhabited, as do the frequent references to tribulations elsewhere in the book (note also the use of πατέω for the trampling by the nations here, and for treading the winepress of wrath in 14:20; 19:15—both of which imply the suffering of a group of people). The similarity to Ezekiel measuring the heavenly eschatological sanctuary could suggest that this passage is future-facing, much like Rev. 7, but the specific and limited duration of the trampling (forty-two months, the same period as the 1,260 days, 11:2–3) indicates that it occurs during the period of tribulation before the end.[33] If the earth is the temple's courtyard, this would imply that heaven itself is the sanctuary proper. The cosmology would then be different from Josephus's parallel between the tabernacle and creation, and would instead be closer to Philo's identification of the sanctuary (νεώς) with heaven and of the temple complex as a whole (ἱερόν) with the universe (*Spec. Laws* 1.66; see the discussion in chap. 2 above).

At the end of Rev. 11, following the seventh trumpet, "God's temple in heaven was opened, and the ark of his covenant was seen within his temple" (11:19). Three features are noteworthy here. First, the sanctuary is explicitly described as "in heaven" (ὁ ναὸς ... ὁ ἐν τῷ οὐρανῷ) rather than simply equated with it as in Rev. 4–5. Similar descriptions are found in 14:17 and 15:5, and I discuss the significance of the phrase "in heaven" below. Second, at the temple's opening the ark of the covenant is seen, though we are not told by whom. This is the only mention of the ark in Revelation, and it should be equated with the divine throne.[34] The two are linked via the ark-as-footstool traditions (1 Chron. 28:2; Pss. 99:5; 132:7; cf. Isa. 66:1), by the depiction of God as enthroned between the cherubim over the ark (1 Sam. 4:4; 2 Sam. 6:2; 1 Chron. 13:6), and by the fact that in Revelation both throne and ark are the source of lightning, rumblings, and thunder (Rev. 4:5; 11:19).[35] Unlike the altar, the ark's location is not specified with reference to God or the throne because it is the very site of his presence.

---

more complex thesis because it requires spiritualization alongside a literal reference to the temple and because the temple had been destroyed by Revelation's date of composition. For 11:1 as the earthly temple, see Blount, *Revelation*, 203–4; Kistemaker, "Temple in the Apocalypse," 435–38; and Harrington, *Revelation*, 119. Beale (*Temple and the Church's Mission*, 315–20) has an unusual dualistic reading in which the temple is the church spiritually, and the outer court represents the bodies of the faithful on earth.

33. On the temporal sequence here, see Giblin, "Revelation 11.1–13," 438–40.
34. So Gallusz, *Throne Motif*, 234–43.
35. By contrast with the ark's absence from the second temple (for various treatments of the reason for this absence, see Jer. 3:16; 2 Esd. [4 Ezra] 10:22; 2 Macc. 2:4–8), the presence of the ark in heaven offers assurance and guarantees the enacting of covenant blessings and curses. See Gallusz, "Ark of the Covenant," 116–21.

And third, the opening of the sanctuary as a singular event implies one veil or door into a single chamber, although it is possible to envisage the simultaneous opening of two veils or doors (all heavenly openings in Revelation occur automatically, without express indication of agency). This opening must be toward the earth, given the emanation of meteorological portents of judgment that elsewhere affect the earth (e.g., 8:5; 11:13; 16:18–19). The use of the aorist tense for the action of opening (ἠνοίγη) differs from the perfect tense forms in 3:8 and 4:1, which suggest a more lasting access. This makes sense as here we have an opening for judgment, which turns out to be temporary (see below), whereas in the other passages the opening is for assurance and revelation. Initially one might wonder whether "sanctuary" refers only to the innermost chamber where the ark was located, but this usage is unlikely as it is nowhere found in the Septuagint (although ναός can denote the inner part of Greco-Roman temples).[36]

Another important passage to consider in this connection is Rev. 15:5, which states that "the temple of the tent of witness in heaven was opened" (ἠνοίγη ὁ ναὸς τῆς σκηνῆς τοῦ μαρτυρίου ἐν τῷ οὐρανῷ). "Tent of testimony" (ἡ σκηνή τοῦ μαρτυρίου) is the commonplace Septuagint term for the "tent of meeting" (usually translating the Hebrew אֹהֶל מוֹעֵד), denoting the tabernacle.[37] Whether the Greek translators were seeking distance from potential anthropomorphic connotations of God meeting with Aaron, or wanted to increase terminological consistency, or both, their translation connects more closely with the (again, relatively common) phrase "ark of the testimony" (κιβωτὸς τοῦ μαρτυρίου). The term "testimony" (μαρτύριον, עֵדָת) refers to the tablets inscribed with the Ten Commandments that were deposited within the ark (see Exod. 25:16, 21; 40:20). This particular phrase, then, draws attention both to the ark of the covenant, and to the tablets of the covenant within it, and it is therefore of a piece with Rev. 11:19. The connection is reinforced by the motif of opening common to both texts.

The full phrase "the temple of the tent of testimony" (AT, ὁ ναὸς τῆς σκηνῆς τοῦ μαρτυρίου) is unusual. This phrase might refer to the "(inner) sanctuary of the tent of testimony," in which case it would be the only explicit indication of an outer chamber to this heavenly structure. Yet, as noted above, ναός does not refer to the most holy place in Greek Jewish writing. There is no exact OT parallel to this phrase, although perhaps the closest is Num. 9:15, which

---

36. Aune, *Revelation 6–16*, 877. In the Septuagint it normally translates הֵיכָל (temple, palace), referring either to the whole of the temple, or to the holy place, or to the porch (אוּלָם). For the pagan usage, see, e.g., Herodotus, *Persian Wars* 1.183; 6.16.

37. The phrase אֹהֶל הָעֵדָת, of which ἡ σκηνή τοῦ μαρτυρίου is a more direct rendering, occurs just 4× in Numbers and once in 2 Chron. 24:6.

refers to "the tabernacle, the tent of testimony" (AT, הַמִּשְׁכָּן לְאֹהֶל הָעֵדֻת, which the LXX renders τὴν σκηνήν, τὸν οἶκον τοῦ μαρτυρίου).[38] Given the lack of any further indications or exploitation of this potential distinction in the text, it is probably best to take the phrase in Rev. 15:5 as epexegetical: "the temple, that is, the tent of testimony."[39] The meaning is then very close to 11:19. Interestingly, this shows that Revelation is quite happy to switch between temple and tabernacle language, even as the former tends to describe the place and the latter the action of dwelling or those who dwell.[40]

The remaining structural question regarding Rev. 11:19, 14:17, and 15:5 is whether "in heaven" (ἐν τῷ οὐρανῷ) indicates a temple structure within heaven. This exact phrase is used recurrently in Revelation (eighteen of the fifty-two occurrences of οὐρανός in Revelation appear in this phrase) and denotes a heavenly location for furniture, characters, and events. It identifies a sphere or realm in general, often in opposition or contrast to the earth (e.g., 12:1–4). We are thus dealing with something very different from the visions of 1 En. 14–15, where Enoch enters a heavenly realm and progressively encounters a structure within it, including seeing the outside of the wall and house. Instead, the evidence taken together suggests that Revelation envisages a single-chambered heavenly temple-cum-throne room, with the throne-ark at its center and the incense altar nearby and a door open toward the earth.

Temple and Judgment

Heavenly Temple as Originating Locus of Judgment

The presence of the scroll in the heavenly worship scene of Rev. 5 prepares the way for the scenes of judgment that will follow. The opening of the scroll's seven seals unleashes a series of judgment events and gives way to the seven trumpets and seven bowls of wrath. The opening of the sixth seal results in a variety of portents (6:12–14). Alongside an earthquake and the removal of mountains and islands, several of these portents relate to heaven: the sun is darkened, the moon becomes as blood, and the stars fall to earth. Revelation 6:14 adds an interesting detail: "The sky vanished like a scroll rolling itself

---

38. The function of the *lamed* preposition is difficult here, but it disrupts what would otherwise (without the article on מִשְׁכָּן) be a construct phrase, explaining the LXX use of the accusative (rather than the genitive as in Rev. 15:5). Most translators read the Hebrew as apposition or gloss, so NRSV; Milgrom, *Numbers*, 71. Ashley (*Numbers*, 184) suggests, "The thought is probably that the tent of the testimony enclosed the tabernacle."

39. So Osborne, *Revelation*, 569; Aune, *Revelation 6–16*, 877–78; Blount, *Revelation*, 290–91.

40. Σκηνόω: Rev. 7:15; 12:12; 13:6; 21:3; σκηνή: 13:6; 15:5; 21:3.

up." The NRSV translation "vanished" obscures the nuance of separation in the verb (ἀποχωρίζω). The simile "like a scroll being rolled up" suggests either that the sky recedes from one end of the heavens to the other or that it splits in the middle and the two parts both roll up. In combination with the verb "separate," the second interpretation should be favored.[41] This resonates with the use of "tear" (σχίζω) in Mark 1:10 to describe the rending of the heavens at Jesus's baptism, but it is somewhat different from what we find elsewhere in Revelation.

There are, nevertheless, strong heavenly and cultic associations: natural phenomena in Revelation symbolize the supernatural realm, and it can be hard to say whether "heaven" (οὐρανός) denotes the visible sky or "the unseen place of God's throne."[42] Once the sky is split and rolled back, "the one seated on the throne" and "the Lamb" are seen by the rulers of the earth, who attempt to flee (6:15–17, echoing Hosea 10:8; cf. Luke 23:30). That is to say, as the heavens are parted, the rulers see into the same heavenly throne room-sanctuary as John did in Rev. 4–5, but with the difference that the vision is a revelation of wrath instead of worship.

This picture intensifies as Revelation continues, with specific reference to heaven's cultic nature. Already in 4:5, introducing the initial scene of worship in heaven, "lightning and rumblings and peals of thunder" come from the throne. In 8:5, the same portents result directly from the angel taking fire from the altar and throwing it to earth,[43] with "an earthquake" added to the list. In 9:13–19, the sixth trumpet prompts a voice from the horns of the incense altar, releasing four angels who direct a plague of cavalry. This judgment against unrepentant human idolatry fittingly emanates from the place of true worship (9:20–21). The seventh trumpet blast initiates a worship scene (11:15–18), which is reminiscent of Rev. 4–5 and cedes immediately to the opening of the temple and a vision of the ark of the covenant (11:19). The juxtaposition indicates that Revelation sees worship (including the worship of people taking refuge in the heavenly temple) as going hand-in-hand with the judgment of those who do not honor God. If it is right to identify the ark with the throne, this scene is very close to the earthly rulers' vision of the throne as a sign of wrath in 6:16. The same list is found in 4:5 and 8:5, with the addition of "heavy hail."[44]

41. BDAG (s.v. ἀποχωρίζω) offers "the sky was split" for this verse. LSJ (s.v. ἀποχωρίζω) has "separate, detach." Osborne (*Revelation*, 293n31) allows that "either picture is possible." Yet ἀποχωρίζω makes the sense of splitting more likely. Contrast the use of ἑλίσσω alone in LXX Isa. 34:4; Heb. 1:12, citing Ps. 101:26 (102:27 LXX), which has ἀλλάσσω.

42. McDonough, "Revelation: The Climax of Cosmology," 180.

43. As Blount (*Revelation*, 165) comments, "There can be no clearer image of divine wrath."

44. On the progressive intensification here, see Bauckham, *Revelation*, 202–4; R. Davis, *Heavenly Court Judgment*, 124.

The high point of the correlation between temple and judgment comes in Rev. 14:14–16:21. Two angels emerge from the temple and one from the altar with sickles to reap the harvest of wrath (14:15–20). The angels carrying the plagues of God's wrath are dressed in bright linen like priests and are given bowls, cultic vessels, by the four creatures who are around the throne (15:6–7). As in Rev. 11, a scene of worship is interspersed (15:2–4). The sanctuary is opened in order for the angels to exit and receive the bowls of wrath, and then it is "filled with smoke from the glory of God and from his power, and no one could enter the temple until the seven plagues of the seven angels were ended" (15:8). The smoke may partly reflect the clouds of incense on Yom Kippur (Lev. 16:13) but more directly recalls the cloud of God's glory that fills both the tabernacle and Solomon's temple at their inauguration (Exod. 40:34–38; 1 Kings 8:10–11; cf. Num. 9:15 and the fire preventing entry in 1 En. 14.19, 21–22).[45]

Just as Moses could not enter (οὐκ ἠδυνάσθη . . . εἰσελθεῖν, Exod. 40:35) and the priests could not perform their cultic service (οὐκ ἠδύναντο οἱ ἱερεῖς στῆναι λειτουργεῖν, 1 Kings 8:11) because of the cloud, so also in Revelation no one is able to enter the sanctuary while the smoke is present (οὐδεὶς ἐδύνατο εἰσελθεῖν, Rev 15:8). In Revelation, the sanctuary is opened for judgment, not inauguration, and for no other purpose until that judgment is complete.[46] Yet the judgment and the opening that facilitates it are temporary and do reach a conclusion. The seven bowls are poured out like libation offerings,[47] but once emptied they are finished. In confirmation of the judgment's completion, after the seventh bowl is poured out, a voice comes "out of the temple, from the throne," to declare, "It is done!" (16:17).

One further passage calls for attention. The first part of Rev. 19 is another worship scene, located in heaven, with a familiar cast: a great multitude, the elders, and the four creatures worshiping the one on the throne, with the saints clothed in bright linen (19:1–10). The mood is celebratory following the judgment of Babylon, looking back to the just enactment of God's judgments and forward to the wedding feast of the Lamb with his bride (19:7–9; cf. 21:2). The scene that follows is martial and regal, with the Word of God riding out on a horse at the head of the armies of heaven (19:11–16). Yet it is wrong to suggest that "the heavenly sanctuary/throne room has faded from view."[48] The

45. The similarities include the cloud of smoke, which is of divine origin and thus represents God's glory and presence; its filling of the whole sanctuary; and the inability of anyone to enter.
46. "In 11:19 the ark may have been a sign of mercy, but here it is a sign of judgment" (Osborne, *Revelation*, 569).
47. Rev. 16; cf., e.g., 1 Sam. 7:6; Isa. 57:6. The third bowl in Revelation (16:4–7) elicits affirmation of the justice of God's judgment from an angel and the altar.
48. Paulien, "Cultus, Sanctuary, and Temple," 254.

conception of heaven as sanctuary is well established by this point in the text, and the strong sanctuary connections of heavenly worship and the throne up to this point make it hard to deny cultic overtones.[49] What is more, the vision of Jesus riding the horse begins with the statement "I saw heaven opened" (εἶδον τὸν οὐρανὸν ἠνεῳγμένον, 19:11). Unlike the openings of 6:14, 11:19, and 15:5, which occur in the course of the vision, the perfect passive participle "opened" is identical to 3:8 and 4:1 and suggests that heaven stands open already. This is a climactic and definitive opening, one that implies a total identification of heaven with sanctuary. The final judgment that emerges from it is a response to the saints' prayers for vindication and results in their praise (6:10; 19:2).[50] There is no closing of heaven, simply a series of closures: a final battle (19:17–21), the binding and defeat of Satan (20:1–10), and the court judgment with books (20:11–15). With these complete, the scene is set for the final vision.

Temple and Judgment in Other Literature

Before turning to Revelation's climax, we need to pause to ask where else this striking association of judgment with the temple is found. It is not unusual for divine wrath to be visited on people who violate the sanctity of the tabernacle or Jerusalem temple. Examples include Nadab and Abihu, who offer unauthorized fire and are consumed by fire that comes out from the Lord's presence (Lev. 10); Miriam, who becomes leprous for challenging Moses's authority in the tent of meeting (Num. 12); and Korah's rebellious insistence on offering incense and Levitical service, which ends when he and his followers are swallowed up by an earthquake (Num. 16). In the Second Temple period, similar accounts continue, often with foreign emperors. Ptolemy IV Philopator's attempt to enter the most holy place in 3 Macc. 1–2 results in temporary paralysis (2:21–24), and 2 Macc. 9 presents Antiochus IV Epiphanes's affliction and death as divine punishment for his desecration of the temple (9:4–5). Pompey's entrance to the temple earns Josephus's scorn (*Ant.* 14.71–73), just as Caligula's attempts to place pagan statuary in the temple prompt the Jewish protests represented in Philo's *Embassy to Gaius* (306–8). Greco-Roman writers also record meteorological phenomena preventing an enemy from attacking a temple, and a voice threatening vengeance if a temple is damaged.[51]

49. Stevenson, *Power and Place*, 235n42.
50. Aune (*Revelation 17–22*, 1046–47) expresses the consensus that this scene relates to the parousia.
51. E.g., thunder, rockfall, and a shout of triumph from Athene's temple at Delphi (Herodotus, *Persian Wars* 8.37); a voice threatening vengeance (Livy, *Hist.* 6.33.4–6); see Stevenson, *Power and Place*, 100–101.

In Revelation, however, judgment moves outward from the sanctuary to the whole earth, rather than touching only those who transgress its own holiness directly. In connection with martial portrayals of judgment, as in Rev. 19:11–21, it is worth noting the importance of the ark of the covenant in Israel's early military campaigns (esp. 1 Sam. 4:1–7:2), although Revelation gives no indication of the ark leaving the heavenly sanctuary. While the notion of judgment emanating from heaven is not uncommon (e.g., Ezek. 1–3; 3 Macc. 6:18–19), heavenly *sanctuary* and judgment do not really coalesce in the OT, except perhaps in Isa. 63–64, where there are intimations of heaven's cultic status and an appeal to God to rend the heavens and come down, to intervene in judgment and salvation in a decisive manner (cf. esp. Isa. 63:15, 18; 64:1). In this case, the expressed hope is that God himself will intervene directly. This differs from his operation via heavenly agents such as angels as we find in much apocalyptic literature, including Revelation, though it is closer to the Word of God riding out to judge in Rev. 19:11.

The closest comparison to Revelation's opening of the sanctuary in order for heavenly figures to be equipped and commissioned for judgment is found in the Testament of Levi, which we first encountered in chapter 2. In the context of his sister Dinah's violation, Levi receives a vision of a heavenly sanctuary (T. Levi 2–4), including its open gates (5.1), and in 5.2–4 he is equipped with a shield and sword and told to execute vengeance, which he then does (chap. 6). This episode is a gloss on the narrative of Gen. 34:25–31 and in particular counters Jacob's apparently negative assessment of Simeon and Levi's bellicose behavior (34:30) with an explanation and supreme legitimation of their conduct. Given its particular narrative setting, the episode in the Testament of Levi is relatively narrow in scope, unlike the global eschatological judgments of Revelation.

The unusual nature of this connection between the sanctuary and judgment can be seen by comparison with the earlier Enochic Book of the Watchers (1 En. 1–36). Here the heavenly temple is less directly linked with judgment, perhaps surprising in a text that is largely concerned with the latter theme. Yet although God himself comes down to Sinai to execute judgment at the outset of the book (1 En. 1.3–4), and judgment recurs throughout (e.g., 1 En. 10; 19; 21; 27), Enoch's vision in the heavenly sanctuary (1 En. 14–15) unfolds rather differently from Levi's. Enoch is not commissioned to execute vengeance on the Watchers or to extend clemency. Rather, his attempt to mediate for them is reversed, and he becomes a go-between to take a message back to them. This message explains the consequences of their actions but does not prescribe direct or immediate judgment. Instead, "the flesh . . . will corrupt without incurring judgment" (16.1). Their transgression carries its own recompense, which flows naturally from it, and thus they will have no peace "until the great age is consummated" (16.1, 3). This is not the active execution of judgment emanating from the sanctuary that we find in the Testament of Levi and Revelation.

Ultimately, Revelation's correlation of judgment and sanctuary is the product of several factors. One is the utter holiness of God and of his dwelling place.[52] It is a commonplace in the OT and the Second Temple period that contact between the holy and anything morally or ritually impure is dangerous. Another factor is the specific temporal location of Revelation's visions during the time of final tribulations and plagues, climaxing just before the eschaton. In this period, more than at any time before, God's judgment is active but temporally limited, and Revelation clearly frames certain judgment sequences that are both initiated *and* concluded by action from the temple. The third factor is the motif of opening: in this period before the end, the sin and wickedness of the world cannot but elicit the emanation of divine wrath when the heavenly temple is opened. The barrier of the temple door or veil does not so much protect God's dwelling from defilement as protect what is outside it from destruction, and when the barrier is removed, God's dynamic holiness emerges in the form of judgment.

Temple Transformed

New Jerusalem as New Temple

In the final two chapters of Revelation, we reach the book's climax and close, indicated by multiple motifs at the outset of chapter 21: the new heaven and earth, the New Jerusalem, its descent from heaven, and God's renewal of all things (21:1–5). Toward the end of this chapter, we read a striking statement about the sanctuary: "And I did not see a sanctuary in it [the city], for the Lord God Almighty is its sanctuary, and the Lamb" (Rev. 21:22 AT).[53] Does this mean that "Revelation introduces a brand-new concept according to which the eschaton will lack a Temple,"[54] or that "any and all sorts of temples are

52. In Revelation, the term ἅγιος describes God and Christ (3:7; 4:8; 6:10), Jerusalem (e.g., 11:2; 21:2), and angels (14:10). It is most frequently used as a substantive to denote the saints (e.g., 14:12 and passim).

53. Citing 4Q511 (Songs of the Sage) and T. Dan 5.9, 13–14 among the few parallels, Aune (*Revelation 17–22*, 1168) describes the absence of a temple from the New Jerusalem as "unique" and notes that the affirmation of God as temple is "striking."

54. Regev, *Temple in Early Christianity*, 243.

but tokens of the old order"?[55] The apparently straightforward statement in this verse, which at first sight resembles the Fourth Gospel's portrayal of Jesus as temple, is complicated by two features of the text: tabernacle language and temple architecture.

At the outset of the chapter, a voice declares, "Behold, the tabernacle [σκηνή] of God is with people, and he will tabernacle [σκηνώσει] with them" (21:3 AT). Craig Koester points out that this comes at the center of a chiasm spanning 21:1–5a. It also accompanies a key eschatological refrain from the OT, "They shall be his people, and God himself will be with them [as their God]" (21:3 RSV; cf. Exod. 6:7).[56] That is, the tabernacle's purpose, God dwelling in the midst of his people, has been fulfilled in the New Jerusalem. Numerous interpreters argue that God's people have become his sanctuary.[57] Although this view is a minority report within Revelation, what evidence there is relates especially to the eschaton, as we saw at the outset of this chapter. The identification of the seven churches with lampstands is the one earthly and eschatologically realized employment of temple imagery in relation to God's people. The other architectural identification is of the believer who overcomes becoming a temple pillar (3:12), relating to the age to come.

All other intimations of community-as-temple notions within Revelation play on the dwelling imagery associated with the tabernacle and cognate terms. One of the two references to "those who dwell [οἱ σκηνοῦντες] in heaven" is appositional to God's "tabernacle" (σκηνή) and appears to be a gloss on it (13:6; cf. 12:12). Apart from these few references, however, Revelation's emphasis is on *God*, who spreads a tent or shelter over his people (σκηνώσει ἐπ' αὐτούς, 7:15) and dwells with them (σκηνώσει μετ' αὐτῶν, 21:3). In Rev. 21 and those parts of the book that presage it, there is firmer ground for identifying the temple with God than with his people.[58] Heaven is a place where God's people tabernacle with him, but supremely it is a place where God tabernacles with them. As God's presence defines his dwelling place as its sine qua non, it is an easy step for John to describe God and the Lamb as the temple to the exclusion of a separable or identifiable temple building.

Architecturally, there are numerous indications that the New Jerusalem incorporates features of Israel's sanctuary, going beyond the basic and

55. Briggs, *Temple Imagery*, 104.
56. Koester, *Dwelling of God*, 120–21.
57. See esp. Gundry, "People as Place"; Beale, *Temple and the Church's Mission*, 328–31.
58. So Regev, *Temple in Early Christianity*, 245; Stevenson, *Power and Place*, 239. Briggs (*Temple Imagery*, 103–8) identifies the temple with God's people until the eschaton, and with God himself thereafter.

commonplace association of the holy city and Mount Zion with the temple. In his second vision of the New Jerusalem, John is accompanied by an angel, whom he had earlier encountered carrying a bowl with one of the seven plagues from the temple, dressed in priestly linen (15:5–8). This angel-priest takes him up "a great, high mountain" (ὄρος μέγα καὶ ὑψηλόν, 21:10), which may evoke Mount Zion, where the Lamb stood receiving worship from the 144,000 earlier in Revelation (14:1). The city is a perfect cube, like the most holy place (21:16; cf. 1 Kings 6:20); it is the place of God's throne (Rev. 21:3) and glory (21:11, 23), a place from which all impurity is excluded (21:8, 27). The city's twelve foundation stones set against gold echo the twelve precious stones on the high priest's breastplate, also set in gold (cf. Rev. 21:19–20 with Exod. 28:17–20).

There are also extensive connections with Ezekiel's and Zechariah's visions of an eschatological temple.[59] In Zechariah's final vision, the holiness of the temple expands to encompass the whole city, including its common vessels; living waters flow from Jerusalem to eastern and western seas; and all nations go up to worship and observe the Festival of Booths/Tabernacles (Zech. 14:7–8, 16–21). Revelation's "river of the water of life" flowing from the throne is also indebted to Ezekiel's river, which flows east from underneath the temple (Rev. 22:1–3; Ezek. 47:1–12). Revelation shares with these texts an emphasis on holiness and purity, with intimations of the exclusion of those who are impure (Rev. 21:8, 27; cf. Ezek. 43:7–9; 44:5–14).[60]

These shared features suggest that the sanctuary has not disappeared from view in Rev. 21–22. There is no sanctuary *in* the city because the whole of the New Jerusalem *is* a garden-city-sanctuary. It is the place where God not only meets but permanently dwells with his people. The importance of the spatial dimension should not be overridden: heaven and earth have not disappeared in the New Jerusalem but have come together.[61] The cultic aspects of heaven do not vanish but are changed. "Revelation does *not* claim that there is no temple in the New Jerusalem. Rather, Rev. 21:22 redefines the temple. Involved here is not the removal of the temple from the city, but the *transformation* of the idea of the temple."[62]

59. Moyise, "Ezekiel," 52–56.
60. In contrast to Zech. 14:20–21, where the whole city becomes sanctified, Ezekiel (44:15–27) retains the distinctions between courts and grades of purity and makes this a key function of the priests.
61. Note by contrast Jordaan's ("Cosmology in the Book of Revelation") reading of Revelation's cosmology as essentially eschatological/temporal.
62. Stevenson, *Power and Place*, 268 (emphasis original); cf. Deutsch, "Transformation of Symbols," 113–16; Snyder, "Combat Myth," 187–89.

Accessibility of the Eschatological Temple

While many have recognized the affinities between the New Jerusalem and the temple, the continuities and differences between the New Jerusalem and the sanctuary as portrayed elsewhere in Revelation are less fully explored. I focus here on two aspects: structure and access. The city is a perfect cube, just like the most holy place. While in Rev. 4–20 we infer that the heavenly sanctuary and throne room are the most holy place, here it is spelled out. We thus expect no partitions within it. The scale of this city-sanctuary is so utterly massive—12,000 stadia (roughly 1,500 miles) in each dimension—that it fills all of creation. There is "a new heaven and a new earth" (21:1), but this is not so much the setting within which the New Jerusalem descends (21:2, 10) as it is a way of saying the same thing twice. There is mention of people entering the city: the kings of the earth bringing "their glory" into it and people bringing in "the glory and the honor of the nations" (21:24, 26). Yet there is no indication of where they are coming *from* or of a place that is *outside* the New Jerusalem. Instead, it seems that they bring these things with them as they come into the city from the old earth and the former age. What is outside the city is a place for the unrighteous (22:15), but as their place is the lake of fire and sulfur (21:8; cf. 20:14–15), it is in fact a place of nonbeing, like the old creation, intimated by the absence of any sea, which represents chaos (21:1). Moreover, because in the New Jerusalem judgment is complete, and absolute purity has been established (21:8, 27), there is no longer need for a distinction between holy and common, clean and unclean, or for spatial or ritual transitions between these states. In short, the need for mediation through spatial division, ritual action, or priestly intervention has now passed.[63]

There is limited indication of what is within the city. We are told that "the throne of God and of the Lamb" is at its center as the focus of worship (22:1, 3), just as it was in the heavenly temple. The river of the water of life flows from the throne down the middle of the city's street, much as the primordial Gihon spring flowed from the temple mount in Jerusalem and the river flows from Ezekiel's temple (Ezek. 47:1–12). The tree of life is present—apparently on both sides of the river—and produces twelve kinds of fruit, bearing each month (Rev. 22:2). The lack of mention of the altar does not necessarily indicate its absence, but this would be fitting. The altar, like the throne and the temple, was both a source of judgment and a place of refuge, associated also with the angels offering the saints' prayers. As both judgment and threat to God's people have ceased, and as they "see his face" and can therefore

63. Stevenson, *Power and Place*, 269; Deutsch, "Transformation of Symbols," 115.

commune with him directly, none of these functions of the altar is required any longer. Revelation 21–22 thus offers a picture of the most holy place becoming all in all—filling the whole of creation and knowing of no division or distinction within it. In this it is continuous with the heavenly temple in being a single chamber containing the ark-throne, but it also surpasses it in its unification with earth rather than separation from it.[64] In recognition of this, earthy imagery of the garden of Eden enters the frame as well.

With respect to access, the depiction of the city gates is significant: there are twelve of them (three in each side), and "on them" (or "in them," ἐπί with genitive) are twelve angels (21:12). "Its gates will not be shut by day, for there will be no night there . . . and nothing profane will enter into it" (21:25, 27 AT). The twelve gates (οἱ πυλῶνες) of the city give access to a space shaped like the holy of holies. The presence of an angel in each gate evokes the entrance to the most holy place, which had a veil emblazoned with cherubim, just as cherubim guarded the entrance to Eden (Exod. 26:31; Gen. 3:24). The symbolism of the number twelve is linked to the tribes of Israel (Rev. 21:12) and increases the sense of access. The most holy place is no longer a space reserved for one member of one family of one tribe of Israel to access via its one entrance on one day of the year. Instead, the gates have been thrown open to all Israel, offering permanent access every day because the gates are never shut since there is no night (21:23, 25; 22:5, 14; cf. Zech. 14:7).

This is a superlative degree of access and at the same time is fully consistent with its sacred status, as no one unrighteous and nothing profane (κοινός) can enter it. Such free access for the righteous fulfills the idea in 6:9–11 of heaven's sanctuary as refuge and the proleptic picture of protection for the saints in Rev. 7. The transformation lies in the permanence of this openness, in its availability to all God's people, and in its association with salvation and security rather than with judgment.

Conclusion

The heavenly temple is fundamental to Revelation's vision of reality. Worship scenes serve a key purpose within the book's literary structure. Heaven as temple is the setting for its cosmic vision of God and the Lamb in their sovereignty—following the Lamb's sacrifice and martyrdom—as the focus of

64. Thus, I find Beale's (*Temple and the Church's Mission*) emphasis on the expanding nature of the temple accurate but not its connection to people alone.

universal worship. The heavenly temple is furnished with the throne-ark at its center and the golden incense altar as a place of refuge and prayer. Revelation does not envisage any internal divisions within this heavenly sanctuary, though whether this was an original feature is unclear, as are any connections between Jesus's sacrifice and the absence of an internal veil, doors, or partitions. Whatever the case, as a permanent feature of this cosmic temple, holy-place furniture (the incense altar) is located close to holy-of-holies furniture (the throne-ark) with no barrier between the two. Heaven is populated with living creatures, elders, angel-priests, and white-robed martyrs who conduct the ongoing service. Revelation plays with the polyvalence of dwelling/tabernacle language to portray the people of God in heaven as God's tabernacle, but its overwhelming interest is in God's dwelling with his people rather than vice versa. This interest in community-as-temple does not override the emphasis on heaven (and later the new heavens and new earth) as the spatial context in which people meet with God and know his protection.

As the location of the full measure of God's holiness, heaven is not only a place of purity but also the originating locus for God's judgment, which emanates from within the temple, from its altar and throne-ark, toward the earth, often implemented by angelic-priestly mediators. Such judgment in connection with the temple is not unprecedented in earlier and contemporaneous literature but is unparalleled in its extent. It is dependent on the openness of the temple, whereby any barrier (Revelation speaks explicitly of doors on a couple of occasions) to the emanation of divine wrath is removed. Yet this judgment is also defined and time limited, with the temple and its angelic servants marking its end as well as its beginning. Once judgment is complete, the way is clear for the eschaton, in which the heavenly temple is merged with earth. Here it is transformed to become a city-garden-sanctuary, coextensive with the New Jerusalem. The single-chambered heavenly temple is now an immense holy of holies, perfectly cubic in shape, and with twelve open gates rather than a single, screened entryway. The permanence and extent of this openness is greater than that seen elsewhere in the NT but nevertheless represents a point of connection with Hebrews, to which our attention turns in the following chapter.

4

Hebrews

Atonement and Access

Like Melchizedek, king of Salem, who makes a brief cameo in Genesis, Hebrews can pass fleetingly across the consciousness of readers of the NT, leaving little trace. Yet the letter's reflection on the notion of heaven as sanctuary represents a high point within the Christian canon alongside Revelation. Where Revelation speaks about the present worship and future trajectory of the heavenly throne room and temple, the focus of the author of Hebrews is on the past and present cultic work of Jesus and on the present position of believers. Hebrews thus complements what we have already seen in Revelation by revealing something of the backstory of heaven, cast as a tabernacle, and its status in the immediate wake of the earthly ministry and heavenly ascent and offering of Jesus.

The chapter proceeds in three parts. First, I establish the ontological and temporal *priority* of Hebrews' heavenly tabernacle, which forms the model for the earthly tabernacle constructed by Moses. Despite some shared vocabulary, Hebrews' dualism is to be understood primarily in line with the Second Temple apocalyptic literature explored above in chapter 2 rather than in Platonic terms. The heavenly sanctuary is not a metaphor for the believing community but refers concretely to a preexisting cosmic place that was likely built at creation. In this it is similar to, though not identical with, related images of promised rest and the heavenly Jerusalem. Second, I explore the *structure* of the heavenly tabernacle. Given that the earthly tabernacle was modeled on the heavenly, it in turn shows what heaven is like. Yet Hebrews' typology does not operate at a level of simple correspondence alone. Instead, I argue that a decisive structural shift occurs in the ministry of Jesus in fulfilling and combining the two spaces of the Mosaic tabernacle and leaving only a single chamber now decisively opened and inhabited by Jesus. This leads, third, to consideration of the *service* of the heavenly tabernacle. The celestial tabernacle is the locus for Jesus's singular Day of Atonement offering, his sitting on the throne, and his ongoing high priestly intercession. Through Jesus, heaven becomes the focus for believers' priestly sacrifices of praise and good deeds. The principal contribution of this chapter is that Jesus's ascension is a pivotal moment for the availability of heavenly space, achieved not only through cultic process (the Day of Atonement sacrifice) and his person (as high priest) but also through a structural change to the heavenly place itself. Hebrews' focus on the most holy place suggests that this is not only the center but conceivably the whole of heaven, and it is, moreover, emphatically open in the drawing aside of the curtain to form a permanent entryway.

The Priority of the Heavenly Tabernacle

On Earth as in Heaven

Hebrews' "chief point" (κεφάλαιον, 8:1) is that Christians have a high priest and a heavenly holy place. This epicenter of the letter affirms a correspondence between heaven and Israel's sanctuary, citing Exod. 25:40 like several of the texts discussed above in chapter 2: "[The levitical priests] offer worship in a sanctuary that is a sketch and shadow of the heavenly one; for Moses, when he was about to erect the tent, was warned, 'See that you make everything according to the pattern that was shown you on the mountain'" (Heb. 8:5). This is a maximal interpretation of the tabernacle instructions in Exodus: the "pattern" (τύπος) Moses saw was not simply a blueprint, but was itself a heavenly sanctuary, "the true tent" (ἡ σκηνὴ ἡ ἀληθινή, 8:2). Hebrews adds "everything" to the citation, an addition that derives from Exod. 25:9 and cements this expansive understanding of Moses's heavenly vision.[1]

The same notion is found a little later: "Thus it was necessary for the sketches of the heavenly things to be purified with these rites, but the heavenly things themselves need better sacrifices than these. For Christ did not enter a sanctuary made by human hands, a mere copy of the true one, but

---

1. On maximal and minimal interpretations of Moses's vision in Philo and the rabbis, see D'Angelo, *Moses*, 208–22.

he entered into heaven itself, now to appear in the presence of God on our behalf" (Heb. 9:23–24). The phrase "heavenly things" (τὰ ἐπουράνια) is a neuter plural adjective functioning as a noun. While "things" is a possible translation, it is better to take it as an abbreviation of "the heavenly holy places" given the use throughout Hebrews of the neuter plural of "holy" (ἅγια) to refer to the sanctuary, including in 9:24 and 25. In the following section, I argue that the reference is more specific still, denoting the most holy place, but for now what matters is the reference to cultic place rather than cultic vessels.[2] The same is true of the earlier passage, 8:5, which does not contain the word "sanctuary" in Greek. Here the NRSV translators have correctly taken "a sketch and shadow of the heavenly one [ὑποδείγματι καὶ σκιᾷ . . . τῶν ἐπουρανίων]" as referring to the sanctuary. What is envisaged in 9:23, then, is purification of the heavenly sanctuary, which, just like the earthly sanctuary, was defiled by the fact of human sin.[3]

These passages attest a tight correspondence between the heavenly and earthly sanctuaries: what Moses saw on Mount Sinai, the heavenly tabernacle, was the pattern or *type* (τύπος, 8:5), and the tabernacle he subsequently built on earth was the copy or *antitype* (ἀντίτυπος, 9:24). These terms are not used in the technical way that later Christian interpretation would use them, but they are internally consistent. Typology will use "type" to denote a historically prior person, event, or institution, and "antitype" to denote the later thing that corresponds to it.[4] For Hebrews, the "type" is likewise historically prior and the "antitype" later, but there is also a spatial distinction that reflects an ontological difference: the "type" is above, and the "antitype" below. Accordingly, the tabernacle was "made by human hands" (χειροποίητα, 9:24), whereas the heavenly tent was pitched (ἔπηξεν [from πήγνυμι], 8:2) by God himself. In this light, the apparently esoteric description of the tabernacle's structure and furniture in 9:1–5 makes sense. If the earthly reflects the heavenly, then it is of interest not in itself alone but for what it teaches about heaven. We will return to this point below.

Platonist Shadows

Hebrews uses two other terms to describe this correspondence: the tabernacle is both a "shadow" (σκιά, 8:5) and a "sketch" (ὑπόδειγμα, 8:5; 9:23) of

---

2. Though the cultic vessels are quite probably included with the sanctuary; cf. Heb. 9:21.
3. On heaven's need for purification, see Jamieson, "Cleansing of the Heavenly Tabernacle"; Bloor, *Purifying the Consciousness in Hebrews*, 93–98.
4. The classic study is Goppelt, *Typos*. On typology in Hebrews, see C. Richardson, *Pioneer*, 7–8; Caird, "Exegetical Method"; Ounsworth, *Joshua Typology*, 32–40, 51–54.

its heavenly counterpart.[5] These words have been the subject of some debate. "Shadow" is a term used in Platonist discourse to refer to created reality, most famously and foundationally in the allegory of the cave.[6] In addition, the term in Hebrews usually translated "sketch" or "(mere) copy" (ὑπόδειγμα) is cognate with a favorite Platonist term for a model (παράδειγμα), and the two can be synonymous.[7] This language thus has an undeniable Platonist ring to it, and numerous commentators have seen Hebrews as drawing on Platonist dualism in its cosmology.[8]

Yet there are important differences in the way the terminology is employed.[9] Within Platonist thought, the realm of ideas is frequently denoted by the term "model" (παράδειγμα), and what is fashioned after these ideas is described both allegorically as a "shadow" and technically as a "copy" (μίμημα, e.g., Plato, *Timaeus* 48e–49a; cf. Wis. 9:8) or "image" (εἰκών, e.g., *Timaeus* 29b). This is quite different from Hebrews. In Heb. 10:1 the law has "a shadow of the good things to come and not the true form of these realities," a statement that contrasts "shadow" (σκιά) with "true form" or "image" (εἰκών). The "image" for Platonists is always derivative, whereas Hebrews uses the term to denote what is ultimate.

This difference becomes clear when we compare Hebrews with Philo of Alexandria, for whom the vocabulary of the Septuagint offered multiple avenues for integration with a Platonist thought world. The Septuagint's use of "image" (εἰκών) to describe God's creation of humanity in Gen. 1:27 and of "model" (παράδειγμα) to describe the heavenly pattern (translating תבנית, Exod. 25:9, the same term rendered τύπος in 25:40) are conducive to a harmonizing interpretation. For example, in a discussion of the tabernacle's construction in Exodus, Philo comments on the name of the craftsman Bezalel, which means "God in his shadow":

> But God's shadow [σκιά] is His Word, which he made use of like an instrument, and so made the world. But this shadow [σκιά], and what we may describe as the representation [ἀπεικόνισμα], is the archetype [ἀρχέτυπος] for further creations.

5. I take "sketch" to be a serviceable translation of ὑπόδειγμα, as it can denote both a copy and a model for something later, and indeed both at the same time. See further below.

6. Plato, *Republic* 514a–20a: the prisoners in the cave see nothing "but the shadows cast by the fire" (πλὴν τὰς σκιὰς τὰς ὑπὸ τοῦ πυρός, 515a).

7. Schlier, "δείκνυμι," *TDNT* 2:25; LSJ, s.v. ὑπόδειγμα. Runia ("'Exemplar' as Example," 358) points to Diogenes Laertius (*Lives* 3.71) and Aëtius (*De placitis philosophorum* 1.7.4) as evidence of synonymity.

8. Eisele, *Ein unerschütterliches Reich*; Thompson, *Beginnings of Christian Philosophy*; Thompson, "EPHAPAX"; Thompson, "What Has Middle Platonism to Do with Hebrews?"

9. See further Ribbens, *Levitical Sacrifice*, 89–94; Gäbel, *Kulttheologie*, 112–27.

For just as God is the Pattern [παράδειγμα] of the Image [εἰκών], to which the title of Shadow [σκιά] has just been given, even so the Image [εἰκών] becomes the pattern [παράδειγμα] of other beings, as the prophet made clear at the very outset of the Law-giving by saying "And God made the man after the Image [εἰκών] of God." (*Alleg. Interp.* 3.96 LCL)

Philo envisages a chain of being in which God, the ultimate model, forms images and shadows of himself. Because of their likeness to God, these things (his word, his image) in turn can take on that same power and become models for things below them (the world, humanity). This is a Jewish and Philonic iteration of the Middle Platonist notion of the intermediary realm between the ideal and the material. Hebrews, by contrast, is interested in two levels rather than many. In a reversal of Platonist usage, it employs a word close to "model" (ὑπόδειγμα) for the earthly domain and "image" (εἰκών) for the heavenly.[10] And while the term "shadow" (σκιά) is employed in a way that is similar to Platonist usage, in Heb. 10:1 it has a connotation that is more temporal than spatial, referring to the law as it *fore*shadows eschatological goods.

Eschatological Sanctuary

Lincoln Hurst is one scholar who has done much to demonstrate that Hebrews' language here does not reveal a Platonist worldview. However, he argues that the term "sketch" (ὑπόδειγμα) in Greek literature only ever means the basis for something that comes later.[11] This would disprove my contention above that Hebrews regards the heavenly tabernacle as something that precedes Moses's vision and his construction of the earthly tabernacle. Instead, Moses was shown blueprints, and the heavenly tabernacle is an eschatological reality patterned *after* the earthly one. For Hurst, the construction of the heavenly tabernacle is an eschatological event, timed to coincide with what Jesus achieved in his ascension "in these last days" (Heb. 1:2).[12]

Hurst's argument has been taken up and developed by Philip Church, but with a significant difference. Church argues that the eschatological sanctuary remains future from the perspective of Hebrews and "is not a structure, either

---

10. Runia ("'Exemplar' as Example," 354–60) makes an important case that the philosophical and particularly the Philonic usage of such terms remains essential background.

11. "There is no instance in known Greek literature where ὑπόδειγμα can be demonstrated to mean 'copy'" (Hurst, "How 'Platonic,'" 157). His argument was found sufficiently convincing to lead the NRSV committee to use "sketch" in Heb. 8:5 and 9:23 rather than "copy" as in the RSV. See also his wider discussion of Platonism in Hurst, *Background*, 7–42.

12. We noted in chapter 2 that construction of a heavenly sanctuary at the eschaton is attested in Ezek. 40–48 and 1 En. 90.

in heaven or on earth. Rather, it is a metaphor for the eschatological dwelling of God with his people."[13] Believers in the present time constitute an interim temple.[14] The identification of the eschatological sanctuary with the community of the people of God is a well-known trope in the period, most notably in Paul and at Qumran,[15] though it is harder to see it represented in Hebrews.[16] It is notable that interpreters tend to gravitate toward community-as-temple readings of a range of NT texts, and perhaps especially when studying the NT as a whole, even where a cosmological or spatial reading is more natural.[17] We will encounter such readings at several points in the following chapters, and I shall return to this observation in the book's conclusion with some reflections on why this might be the case. Church reads a number of terms relating to the heavens in nonspatial ways, all of which are possible readings. Essentially, however, his argument is dependent on Hurst's reading of correspondence language, and I therefore focus on that here.[18]

It is true that the term "model" (παράδειγμα) is used much more widely than "sketch" (ὑπόδειγμα) in the period, including (but not only) by Platonists for whom it is a technical term, as we have seen.[19] Yet the two words have a significant semantic overlap, referring to showing or indicating what something else is like, irrespective of whether that thing exists, and the same is true of their related verb forms. Hebrews could not use the term "model" (παράδειγμα) to describe the earthly sanctuary because the exact same word is used as a synonym for the heavenly "pattern" (τύπος, both translating תבנית) in the same part of LXX Exodus (25:9, 40). We should therefore not overread the significance of the choice of "sketch" (ὑπόδειγμα).[20]

Hurst's contention that these words never mean a copy of something else is overstated. Herodotus describes the wooden models of corpses (παρα-δείγματα νεκρῶν ξύλινα) used by Egyptian embalmers to indicate the three

13. Church, *Hebrews and the Temple*, 435.

14. Church, *Hebrews and the Temple*, 88, though this notion is "at best, muted."

15. 1 Cor. 3:10–17; 6:19; 2 Cor. 6:14–7:1; 1 Pet. 2:4–8; 1QS VIII, 6–10; IX, 3–6; 4Q174 I, 6–7.

16. One verse that might suggest this idea is Heb. 3:6, "we are his house" (cf. Num. 12:7), though the primary wordplay here is with house as both building and household. Grässer (*Hebräer*, 1:168–69) sees this as describing the church in a contemporary cultic sense as well as in its eschatological orientation.

17. Prominent examples include Congar, *Mystère du Temple*; McKelvey, *New Temple*; Beale, *Temple and the Church's Mission*.

18. For a detailed account of Hurst's and Church's case and a fuller version of my argument in this section, see Moore, "True Tabernacle."

19. Hurst, "How 'Platonic,'" 157. Josephus's extant corpus uses ὑπόδειγμα 6× and παρά-δειγμα 22×, against ὑπόδειγμα 4× and παράδειγμα 88× in Philo, nicely illustrating the Middle Platonist bias toward the latter term.

20. So also Runia, "'Exemplar' as Example," 358.

mummification options (with their three price points, no less!).[21] These are imitations (μεμιμημένα) based on previously mummified corpses. Similarly, Aëtius in *De placitis philosophorum* (first century AD) can describe Plato as teaching "that the visible world was made as a representation [παράδειγμα] of the ideal world" (2.6 AT).[22] The term "sketch" occurs in the Septuagint of Ezek. 42:15, where the angel measures "the ὑπόδειγμα of the house [i.e., the heavenly temple] from all around in order." This is relatively hard to interpret: it corresponds to nothing in the Hebrew Masoretic Text, which has "and he measured it all around" (ומדדו סביב סביב), but it must mean something along the lines of "outline" or "dimensions." It is striking that it is used in regard to the heavenly temple, just as "model" (παράδειγμα) is used of Moses's vision in Exod. 25:9. More significant still is Aquila's revision of the Septuagint (early second century AD), which uses the term to denote idolatrous carvings, which are representations of animals in Deut. 4:17 and Ezek. 8:10 (in both cases translating תבנית). Within a couple of generations of Hebrews, then, we have usage of the same term to mean a copy, image, or representation.

Thus "representation," a pattern of something that comes before and not only after, is a possible sense for this term, as indeed for the English term "sketch," which Hurst proposes as a suitable translation. After all, an artist might produce an in situ sketch of a landscape that she will later use as the basis for a painting in studio. At this point, we return to Heb. 8:5, where the earthly sanctuary is described as a "sketch and shadow" of the heavenly one, just as (or "because"—both are possible meanings for καθώς) Moses was told to build according to a heavenly pattern. The second half of the verse illuminates the first, either by comparison or by providing causal grounds.[23] The reading I offered above stands: the heavenly tabernacle precedes the earthly one, ontologically and temporally. This means that the earthly tabernacle in turn can reflect and foreshadow heaven and Jesus's ministry within it, as we will explore below.

Other Heavenly Motifs

Before we turn to the heavenly tabernacle's inauguration, it is worth noting several other motifs within Hebrews that also describe heaven. The first is

21. Herodotus, *Persian Wars* 2.86.
22. LSJ, s.v. παράδειγμα.
23. Hurst argues that Heb. 8:5a and 5b should be distinguished, and he discerns Ezek. 40:2–4 and 42:15 behind the citation of Exod. 25:40, which would supply an eschatological context. Thompson (*Hebrews*, 169) also reckons that ὑπόδειγμα in Heb. 8:5 is probably due to the influence of Ezek. 42:15. Yet the spatial reference in the explicit quotation of Exodus cannot be overridden by a temporal reference in a possible allusion to Ezekiel.

"rest," which denotes Canaan (though neither "Canaan" nor the "promised land" are mentioned explicitly).[24] Hebrews 3–4 explores this motif by quoting and expounding Ps. 95, with the narrative account of the Israelites' failure to enter the land at Kadesh Barnea in Num. 13–14 in the background. The author argues that if Joshua had truly given the Israelites rest by entering the land, God would not *later* have promised rest as he does through David in Ps. 95. This rest, described in the psalm as *"my* rest," prompts a search for other scriptural passages describing God's rest (a technique known as *gezerah shawah*), which yields Gen. 2:2, the seventh day following creation when God rested from his works.[25] God's rest therefore remains open to the people of God now, though as for the wilderness generation this is a time-limited offer, and care must be taken to ensure that the rest is entered by faith (Heb. 4:1, 11).

Rest is clearly spatial in its framing in Heb. 3–4. It is a resting *place*, equivalent to the land of Canaan and supremely the city of Jerusalem, Mount Zion, where the ark and temple will come to rest (Josh. 1:15; 23:1; 2 Chron. 6:41; Ps. 132:14). It is also a state, as indicated by Gen. 2:2 (where God is the subject) and by its characterization in Heb. 4:9 as *"sabbath* rest" (σαββατισμός, the first occurrence of this term in extant Greek literature), denoting the celebration of the sabbath.[26] The rest motif is geographically horizontal and temporally future for the people of God. Yet it is comparable to the notion of heaven as sanctuary in that it is entered following the completion of work (Heb. 4:10): God rests after his work of creation, and believers rest after their work in this life, just as Jesus himself sits down after his priestly work of atonement (Heb. 1:3; 10:12–13).[27] Rest is not identical with the tabernacle, but there are significant parallels between the two. This gives grounds to think Hebrews' author may have envisaged the heavenly tabernacle's construction as occurring with or just before the creation of the world, ready for God to rest in it on the seventh day. As we saw in chapters 1 and 2, the building of the heavenly sanctuary is located before or with creation in a number of rabbinic texts,[28] and tabernacle construction in the OT parallels the creation account.

---

24. Key studies are Hofius, *Katapausis*; Laansma, *"I Will Give You Rest,"* 252–358; Wray, *Rest*.

25. This relies on the Greek, not the Hebrew, for the connection between κατέπαυσεν and κατάπαυσις; Gen 2:2 MT has וישבת, and Ps. 95:11 MT has מנוחתי.

26. Laansma (*"I Will Give You Rest,"* 276–83) characterizes σαββατισμός as the activity that occurs within the resting place.

27. For an argument that "the one who entered rest" is Jesus, see Moore, "Christological Reading of Hebrews 4.10."

28. Gen. Rab. 1.4: the throne of glory is made before creation, as is the decision to make the temple. See also b. Pesahim 54a 8, 11 (in the context of a discussion about the creation of Gehenna's fire on sabbath eve); b. Nedarim 39b 4, 10.

Other motifs in Hebrews are like rest and tabernacle in that they draw from Israel's geography and history to denote heavenly realities. Abraham becomes a sojourner because by faith he anticipates "the city that has foundations" (Heb. 11:10). He and the patriarchs seek not the land they have left, but a better, heavenly homeland (πατρίς, 11:14–16). This homeland is "heavenly" (ἐπουράνιος) and is closely linked with the city God has prepared. The enduring nature of this city is expressed in terms of its "foundations," which chimes with the later sentiment that "here we have no lasting city, but we are looking for the city that is to come" (13:14, with a neat wordplay between "lasting," μένουσαν, and "coming," μέλλουσαν). The city also occurs in a comparison of the two mountains, Sinai and Zion, in 12:18–24. Here believers have drawn near "to the city of the living God," which is juxtaposed with Mount Zion and "the heavenly Jerusalem" ('Ιερουσαλὴμ ἐπουρανίῳ, 12:22, the only mention of Jerusalem in the letter) as equivalents.[29]

Two points are noteworthy: this is the location of a "festal gathering" (πανήγυρις, 12:22) of angels and the spirits of the righteous, much as rest is a location for sabbath celebration.[30] And there is a strong emphasis on creation: God is the "architect and builder" (τεχνίτης καὶ δημιουργός, 11:10) who has prepared the city (ἡτοίμασεν, 11:16), just as he is "the builder" of all things (ὁ κατασκευάσας, 3:4). In this regard, just like rest, the fact that the city is *future* from the perspective of believers (13:14) does not contradict its already having been created by God. This is consistent with the building of the heavenly tabernacle at or before creation, as suggested above.

Despite the parallels between these motifs, Hebrews at no point explicitly relates them. Why is this? In part, land, Jerusalem, Zion, and temple are readily associated within Jewish thought, as we have seen, and easily stand in for each other by metonymy. Yet also, Hebrews' thoroughgoing interest in the exodus and its appeal to wilderness figures, events, and institutions, including the tabernacle, stands in some tension with the post-conquest images of land and city. They lend themselves to different aspects of the author's exhortatory and pastoral program: land and city as believers' ultimate goal and tabernacle as Jesus's location and thus a source of present help. Yet if heavenly realities are also future realities, an association between them is inescapable for the

29. For a full account of Hebrews' treatment of the Sinai theophany, see Kibbe, *Godly Fear*, esp. 182–212.

30. The NT hapax legomenon πανήγυρις is well attested for cultic festivals in pagan literature. Syntactically it could describe the angels (most likely), the church of the firstborn, or be freestanding, but the difference is slight. On both points, see Grässer, *Hebräer*, 3:313–15.

attentive reader.[31] The author of Hebrews does not suggest that the heavenly Jerusalem contains a temple or that the promised rest contains a city. This leaves open the possibility that they are equivalent, possibly even coextensive. We turn next to the structure of the heavenly tabernacle, which is integrally related to the ascension of Jesus.

The Structure of the Heavenly Tabernacle

In Heaven as on Earth

If the heavenly tabernacle is the model for the earthly tabernacle, then the latter tells us what the former is like. David Moffitt describes this correspondence as "an important hermeneutical correlate," noting that "because the heavenly structure is ontologically prior, the earthly tabernacle and sacrifices are instructive for understanding what happens in heaven."[32] This brings us back to Heb. 9:1–5, which describes the earthly sanctuary. It had a first tent (σκηνὴ . . . ἡ πρώτη, 9:2), which contained the lampstand, table, and showbread. Another tent was separated from this by "the second curtain" (τὸ δεύτερον καταπέτασμα, 9:3), which implies a curtain at the entrance to the first chamber as described in Exod. 36:37. The second tent contained the incense altar,[33] the ark of the covenant with its contents, and the cherubim over the atonement cover (9:4–5).[34]

Hebrews thus divides the tabernacle into two cultic places. The multiple spaces of later temples and even the courtyard of the tabernacle are nowhere in view. These two cultic places relate to two classes of cultic personnel, priests and the high priest, who perform two different cultic processes (9:6–8). The priests go "continually" (διὰ παντός, 9:6) into the outer chamber to perform their services. The phrase διὰ παντός does not mean "constantly" or "at any time" but denotes "regular" service. In the Septuagint, it translates the Hebrew term *tamid*, which came to stand for the morning and evening sacrifices composed of grain, animal, and incense offerings. It clearly has this technical sense in Heb. 9:6.[35] The high priest, by contrast, goes only "once a year" (ἅπαξ

31. Rest is thus not merely a "theological metaphor" without christological connection, *pace* Wray, *Rest*, 89–94.

32. Moffitt, *Atonement*, 225n18.

33. This seems unusual or incorrect in that in both tabernacle and temple the incense altar was located in the holy place, in front of the veil of the most holy place. It is, however, a possible reading of Exod. 30:6 that the incense altar is before the atonement cover, with blood applied to it on Yom Kippur.

34. On the furnishings here, see Gäbel, "'You Don't Have Permission.'"

35. Esp. in the Pentateuch, where διὰ παντός qualifies cultic items or activities, in particular the regular offerings, 26×: Exod. 25:30; 27:20; 28:30, 38; 30:8; Lev. 6:6, 13; 24:2, 8;

τοῦ ἐνιαυτοῦ) into the second chamber on the Day of Atonement, taking blood to offer for sins of ignorance (9:7; cf. Lev. 16).

This account of the tabernacle forms part of an extended analogy or typology with heaven (indicated by the discourse markers μέν ... δέ in 9:1, 11). Christ is the high priest who has now come, and he entered "once for all" (ἐφάπαξ) into the sanctuary with his own blood (9:11–12). What is often missed is that *both chambers* of the tabernacle and *both kinds of priestly service* find their fulfillment in Christ's action. There is a widely recognized intensification of the high priest's work on the Day of Atonement, from a once-a-year to a once-for-all entrance, from the second tent to heaven, and from animal blood to his own blood. But there is also an intensification from the *twice-daily* service of the priests (which the high priest could also perform, see 7:27) to the *eternal* redemption that Christ obtains (just as he *always* intercedes, 7:25).[36] Below we will return to the matter of the service of the heavenly tabernacle. For now, the question that arises is this: If the heavenly tabernacle's cultic personnel and ritual processes represent a combination of those found in the earthly sanctuary, are there implications for its *space* as well?

The Most Holy Place

To answer this question, we need to look closely at the language Hebrews uses to describe the sanctuary. The favored phrase, as noted above, is a neuter plural adjective functioning substantively: "holy [things/places]" (τὰ ἅγια). This term with the article denotes the tabernacle's second chamber, the most holy place, in 9:8, 25, and 13:11. In each of these occurrences, the earthly high priest's Day of Atonement entrance is clearly in view. One therefore can presume that it indicates the most holy place in its other three occurrences as well, an assumption confirmed by the salience of Jesus's entrance or presence within the most holy place as high priest in every case (8:2; 9:12; 10:19).[37] The term occurs without the article in 9:24, but this can be explained by the accompanying adjective "made by hands," which emphasizes its earthly rather than heavenly nature. In other respects, 9:24 is parallel to the most holy place in the verse that follows (a form of the verb εἰσέρχομαι, "entered," occurs in both 9:24 and 25). The three exceptions to this consistent usage all come in

---

Num. 4:7; 28:10, 15, 23, 24, 31; 29:6, 11, 16, 19, 22, 25, 28, 31, 34, 38; Deut. 33:10. There are only 5 noncultic occurrences of the term: Lev. 11:42; 25:31, 32; Num. 9:16; Deut. 11:12. See Hamm, "Praying 'Regularly.'"

36. For a full account of this typology, see Moore, *Repetition in Hebrews*, 178–88.

37. So Schenck, *Cosmology and Eschatology*, 145–47; Koester, *Hebrews*, 397; Bénétreau, *Hébreux*, 2:72; Weiß, *Hebräer*, 457; contra Ounsworth, *Joshua Typology*, 160.

9:1–5, where the earthly tabernacle *as a whole* is described with the singular "the holy [place]" (τό ... ἅγιον, 9:1), and then the outer chamber is called "holies" (ἅγια, 9:2, without the article) and the inner chamber "holies of holies" (ἅγια ἁγίων, 9:3, the only occurrence). This is not inconsistency on Hebrews' part but is rather an appeal to what they are called in general (note the passive forms of the verb "to say": λέγεται, λεγομένη, 9:2–3).

That Hebrews should be interested in the most holy place is only natural, given its articulation of Jesus's ascension in terms of the Day of Atonement. This does not, however, demonstrate that Hebrews conceives of the heavenly tabernacle as unicameral, having only one chamber. The evidence elsewhere in Hebrews is complex. For example, Jesus as high priest "has passed through the heavens" (4:14). The term "heaven(s)" (οὐρανός) is somewhat fluid in Hebrews. Both the singular and the plural can denote the heavenly realm in which Jesus, angels, and the assembly of the firstborn are presently located (8:1; 9:23–24; 12:23, 25), but they can also indicate the physical heavens (1:10; 12:26). The notion that Jesus traversed the heavens and is presently higher than them (7:26) could refer either to the visible heavens or to multiple heavens before the highest heaven (including, possibly, heavens construed as prior chambers).[38]

One Chamber or Two?

At the letter's epicenter, the author describes Jesus's high priestly position as "seated at the right hand of the throne of the Majesty in the heavens" (Heb. 8:1) and immediately adds that he is "a minister in the sanctuary and the true tent" (τῶν ἁγίων λειτουργὸς καὶ τῆς σκηνῆς τῆς ἀληθινῆς, 8:2). The word "sanctuary" here is "holy [places]," which as I have just argued refers to the most holy place rather than to the sanctuary in general. This is confirmed by Jesus's seated position on or adjacent to the divine throne, which is equivalent to the ark of the covenant. But what is "the true tent" or "tabernacle"? It could refer to the whole sanctuary (in distinction from the most holy place as its inner part) or to the outer chamber (compare 9:2–3, where σκηνή refers to a single chamber rather than to the whole tabernacle). In either of these cases, the result is the same, a bicameral heavenly sanctuary.

This question can be decided only by examining Heb. 9 (here) and Hebrews' discussion of the tabernacle curtain (in the following section). In 9:11–12, Christ enters the most holy place "through the greater and more perfect tent

---

38. Church (*Hebrews and the Temple*, 372–77) takes διέρχομαι in 4:14 as "moving around [to minister]," citing 1 Sam. 2:30, 35, which would make "heavens" in Heb. 4:14 consistent with the majority of occurrences but still leaves 7:26 unexplained.

(not made with hands, that is, not of this creation)" (9:11 RSV). Here we
have the same two terms as in 8:2, "holy [places]" and "tent," coordinated in
an apparently straightforward manner: Christ goes *through* the tent (either
the whole tabernacle, or its outer chamber) to *enter* the holy places (inner
chamber).[39] On either reading of "tent," however, this solution has insurmountable problems. If the "tent" is the entire sanctuary *in contradistinction
to* one of its parts, it makes little sense to describe Jesus as passing *through*
it when he is in fact still within it, indeed in its most central part.[40] I do think
that "tent" refers to the whole sanctuary, but as will become clear, I do not
think this is distinct from its inner chamber. The spatial imagery works better
if, on the other hand, the "tent" is the outer chamber, but the way in which
the tent is qualified again poses problems. Why would the author describe the
outer chamber in such superlative terms when he does not here qualify the
inner chamber at all? This would be all the more surprising given that nowhere else in the letter is the outer chamber a focus of attention, with the
exception of the description of the earthly holy place in 9:2, and even there it
is overshadowed by the description of the inner chamber (twenty-one words
compared to forty-seven, 9:3–5).

It is better to take the preposition διά in a modal sense instead, indicating
that Christ serves as high priest *by means of* the greater and more perfect
tent.[41] This is in keeping with the use of διά twice in 9:12 to indicate that he
entered "by means of" his own blood and not "by means of" animal blood. It
suggests that the phrase in 9:11b relates to Christ's *institution* as high priest
(9:11a) more than to the *movement* of his entrance (9:12; against NASB, which
repeats "he entered" in 9:11). Thus "Christ came as high priest . . . by means
of the greater and more perfect tent" (AT). That is, the prepositional phrase
does not connect with what follows to describe how he entered. Rather, it
connects with what precedes, indicating the means by which he acts as high
priest. This is the flip side of the statement that Christ cannot serve as a priest
when he is on earth (8:4); he is high priest of eschatological goods because
of his relationship to the heavenly sanctuary.

The relationship between the tabernacle and its two chambers is addressed
between the descriptions of the heavenly (9:11–14) and earthly (9:1–5) tabernacles. The Holy Spirit was indicating by the priestly service of the old covenant that "the way into the most holy place" (AT, τὴν τῶν ἁγίων ὁδόν) had

39. For four options (mythological [= temple in heaven], cosmological [= heaven as temple],
christological, and ecclesiological), see Vanhoye, "Par la tente"; Vanhoye, "Sanctuaire terrestre,
sanctuaire céleste." Both essays appear in English translation in Vanhoye, *Perfect Priest.*
40. Contra, e.g., Jamieson, *Jesus' Death*, 59–60.
41. So Schenck, "Hebrews' Tabernacle Imagery," 250–51.

not been revealed—or, more straightforwardly, was not visible—while the first tent "had standing" (AT, ἐχούσης στάσιν, 9:8).[42] This is true as a description of the physical reality of the tabernacle as it has been set out in 9:1–5: no one could see the inner chamber from outside the tabernacle, and even the high priest obscured his view using incense on the Day of Atonement.[43] Yet the description is also a temporal one: the way to the most holy place was *not yet* visible *while* the first tent was in operation.[44] This first tent is "a symbol of the present time" (9:9; σκηνή is the natural antecedent for the feminine singular relative pronoun ἥτις), the time when gifts and offerings for external purity are offered—that is, the period of the old covenant. This suggests that "first tent" is polyvalent here, describing the sanctuary's outer chamber when viewed spatially and, when viewed temporally, the sacrificial system pertaining to the first covenant (compare use of "first," πρώτη, to relate to covenant in 8:13–9:1). Thus, in the "time of reformation" (9:10 NASB), these last days, there will be no "first tent," neither the earthly sacrificial system whose dispensation is passing away (8:13) nor any outer chamber. Some commentators protest that it makes no sense to conceive of the outer chamber of the tabernacle as absent.[45] Yet Hebrews' point is not that the outer chamber of the earthly tabernacle was taken away but that as long as it was there, it visually blocked the way to the most holy place. Given that believers can now approach the "throne of grace" (a term for the ark, 4:16) and, indeed, can "see Jesus" (2:9), it seems that the outer chamber to the heavenly tabernacle has in fact "lost its standing" by being combined with the most holy place.

The Final Curtain

The combining of the two chambers of the heavenly tabernacle is confirmed by Hebrews' argument concerning the curtain that separated them (9:3). By his entrance into heaven as a forerunner, Jesus has breached the curtain (6:18–20), and Christian hope is likened to an anchor "within the curtain" (εἰς τὸ ἐσώτερον τοῦ καταπετάσματος, 6:19 AT). This phrase in the Pentateuch relates closely to the ark[46] and thus locates Jesus within the most holy place.

---

42. This phrase generally relates to physical position, not existence; see e.g., Herodotus, *Persian Wars* 9.21; Plutarch, *Isis and Osiris* 368D.

43. See Philo, *Spec. Laws* 1.27; *Drunkenness* 136; Josephus, *J.W.* 5.208–12; *Ant.* 3.125; note the rabbinic tradition that the veil to the inner chamber was doubled, m. Yoma 5.1; m. Middot 4.7.

44. Young, "Hebrews 9," 200; Stanley, "'Parable' of the Tabernacle," 394. Note also that the *tamid* service ceased while the high priest was in the most holy place on Yom Kippur.

45. E.g., Koester, *Hebrews*, 405.

46. Exod. 26:33; Lev. 16:2, 12, 15. See Davidson, "Christ's Entry 'Within the Veil.'"

Recognizing this helps make sense of the (rather odd) nautical imagery, in that Jesus's presence over the ark's atonement cover moors believers' hope to a concrete location just as an anchor does. The curtain is presented as something that has been breached, establishing a connection between Jesus within the most holy place and believers outside of it.[47]

The curtain receives a third mention in 10:19–20. The grounds for the exhortations that follow is that believers have "confidence with respect to the entryway to the most holy place by the blood of Jesus, which he inaugurated for us as a new and living way through the curtain" (AT). Here I take εἴσοδος ("entryway," 10:19) in a substantive rather than verbal sense, as referring to an entryway rather than to the act of entering. This makes more sense of the phrase "a new and living way" in 10:20, which is appositional to "entryway."[48] This way is the entrance to the heavenly most holy place and has become—through the drawing aside of the curtain that normally screens it off—prominent as a place of access instead of a barrier.[49] The opening of the way is described in terms of "inauguration" (ἐγκαινίζω, cf. 9:18), suggesting that Christ's ascension to offer himself as a Day of Atonement sacrifice inaugurates the new covenant by the very act of atoning for sins.[50] That the way to the most holy place is now visible and the curtain no longer screens the ark-throne within means that believers can see Jesus (2:9) and have confidence to approach him (4:16; 10:22). The removal of the curtain unites the two chambers into one, a change that is straightforward given that the chambers of the tabernacle are equal in width and there is no other structural distinction between them. The widespread emphasis on vision and proximity is a corollary to the notion of a single-chambered sanctuary. We are now in a position to return to 8:1–2, where "the true tabernacle" should be taken as epexegetical to "the most holy place," glossing the same space in different terms because of the removal of the curtain, whereby the entire sanctuary has become "most holy." This unicameral sanctuary is not figurative or Hellenistic[51] but is presented along concretely spatial, apocalyptic lines in keeping with the spectrum of possibilities outlined in chapter 2.[52]

47. Moore, "'Once More unto the Breach.'"
48. Moore, "'In' or 'Near'?," 195–96.
49. Mackie, "Jewish Mystical Motifs," 93–95.
50. Inauguration of the new covenant cannot therefore be easily identified with Jesus's death alone or separated from his ascension and offering, *pace* Moffitt, "Wilderness Identity."
51. Asumang and Domeris, "Ministering in the Tabernacle"; Schenck, "Hebrews' Tabernacle Imagery," 246–51.
52. Scholars who see apocalyptic background as most salient here tend to envisage two chambers, e.g., Barnard, *Mysticism of Hebrews*, 110–13; Attridge, *Hebrews*, 222–24; Moffitt, *Atonement*, 220–28. Ribbens (*Levitical Sacrifice*, 94–99) is not explicit about the number of

The Service of the Heavenly Tabernacle

Christ as High Priest and Sacrifice

Christ's priesthood and priestly work is rightly identified as a central feature of Hebrews, appearing in its exordium (1:3) and periodically (2:17; 4:14–16) in the buildup to the major central section of the letter that explores his priesthood (5:1–10; 7:1–28), covenant mediation (8:1–13; 9:15–22), and sacrifice (9:1–14; 10:1–18). This sacrifice is described primarily in terms that evoke the annual Yom Kippur / Day of Atonement ceremony. Many commentators have regarded Hebrews as mapping Jesus's death and ascension onto this rite, with death equivalent to the slaughter of the animal and ascension equated with the high priest's entrance into the most holy place.[53] We have seen that the latter point is right in terms of the heavenly architecture and location of Jesus in his ascended state. However, the rest of the picture leaves something to be desired. On this model, it is entirely possible to conceive of Jesus's ascension as a purely spiritual event, perhaps coterminous with his death, and thus to read Hebrews in a more thoroughgoing Platonist direction or as part of a nascent gnostic tendency within early Christianity.[54] Yet as several scholars have pointed out, most recently and extensively Moffitt, this reading misconstrues the nature of Jewish sacrifice in general and of the Yom Kippur rite in particular.[55]

Sacrifice is a process that, in the case of *animal* sacrifice, begins with the selection and slaughter of the victim. The Israelite cult then has various requirements for different parts of the animal, depending on what kind of sacrifice is being offered; various parts may be burned, eaten, or otherwise disposed of. Its blood in particular is collected and can be applied to the altar, sprinkled in the outer chamber of the sanctuary, or, in the case of Yom Kippur, applied to the atonement cover of the ark by the high priest. It is thus incorrect to identify only the slaughter of the animal with sacrifice, and the terminology of "offering" (which etymologically relates to "bringing near," קרב/προσφέρω) indicates movement at a later stage of the process, whether

---

chambers but would seem to favor this view. Moffitt extends gradations of heavenly cultic space further in "Serving in the Tabernacle in Heaven." Cockerill (*Hebrews*, 352–57) offers an interpretation along lines similar to mine.

53. For a survey of scholarship, see Moffitt, *Atonement*, 3–41.

54. The classic study in positing a gnostic redeemer myth, still important though not widely followed on this point, is Käsemann, *Das wandernde Gottesvolk*; ET Käsemann, *Wandering People of God*. As an example of disregard for sacrificial process in Hebrews, Giambrone (*Bible and the Priesthood*, 226–29) can speak only in vague terms of a "hybrid cult" and of the "blending of the heavenly with the earthly realm" in Jesus's offering.

55. Brooks, "Perpetuity"; Nelson, "Sacrifice in Hebrews"; Moffitt, *Atonement*.

to burn the fat parts or the entire animal on the altar of burnt offering in the courtyard or to apply the blood.[56]

Rereading Hebrews with this in mind presents a rather different picture from the common view of sacrifice—a view that remains persistent in popular understanding—that it consists exclusively in the victim's death with no remainder. Several descriptions in the letter of Jesus's sacrificial or priestly work do not spell out the ancient understanding of the sacrificial process and therefore remain susceptible to the popular equation of sacrifice with death. In Heb. 1:3, Jesus sat down *after* he had made purification for sins (reading the aorist middle participle ποιησάμενος as indicating action prior to the main verb that follows it).[57] This tells us little about the process before his heavenly session. Similarly, in 2:17 Jesus became human in order to be "a merciful and faithful high priest in the service of God, to make a sacrifice of atonement for the sins of the people." The language of atonement here connects with sin offerings and supremely with Yom Kippur, but again indication of process is minimal, and we should not overread the present tense of the infinitive verb "to atone" (ἱλάσκεσθαι) as signaling ongoing action.[58] Hebrews 4:14–16 describes Jesus's ascension as "pass[ing] through the heavens" and alludes to his intercession there through mention of sympathy, mercy, grace, and timely help. This heavenly intercession becomes explicit in 7:25 and is ongoing, but its relation to his sacrifice is unclear.

Shortly afterward, Jesus's sacrifice is characterized as offering himself "once for all" in contrast to the daily sacrifices of the human high priests (7:27). "Once for all" ([ἐφ]άπαξ) is a key term that recurs several times in Hebrews (7:27; 9:7, 12, 26–28; 10:10), and as we saw above, it is Yom Kippur terminology. The Day of Atonement is the only one of the annual Israelite festivals to be explicitly characterized as "once a year" in the OT (ἅπαξ τοῦ ἐνιαυτοῦ/אחת בשנה, Exod. 30:10; Lev. 16:34). While Second Temple texts such as Jubilees extend this terminology to the other annual festivals for the sake of neatness,[59] the prominence of Yom Kippur in Hebrews indicates that

56. See esp. Jacob Milgrom's (*Leviticus 1–16*) detailed treatment of the sacrificial rites in Lev. 1–7 (133–439) and his synthetic comments on sacrifice (440–89); also Eberhart, *Bedeutung der Opfer im Alten Testament*; Shauf, *Jesus the Sacrifice*, 7–93. For Hebrews specifically, see Moffitt, "Jesus's Sacrifice in Hebrews."

57. Fanning, *Verbal Aspect*, 407; Porter, *Verbal Aspect*, 380–81; Barnard, *Mysticism of Hebrews*, 132–33.

58. Contra Gäbel, *Kulttheologie*, 226–27. Kleinig (*Hebrews*, 125–26, 140–41) seeks to distinguish between Christ's "vicarious atonement by his sacrificial death" and "his bestowal of its benefits on sinners" and relates ἱλάσκεσθαι here to the latter only.

59. Yom Kippur: Jub. 5.18; 34.18–19; Festival of Weeks: 6.17, 20; Passover: 49.7–8, 15 (the Latin text of Jubilees has *semel in anno*, "once a year," matching the Vulgate of Lev. 16:34 and Heb. 9:7).

this is what is in view when "once" is used. It does not necessarily indicate numerical singularity: the high priest entered the most holy place multiple times on Yom Kippur.[60] Rather, it conveys an emphatic focus on the theological sufficiency of the Day of Atonement taken as a whole, which is a most holy day, a "sabbath of sabbaths."[61]

Sacrificial Process in Hebrews

Only when we come to Heb. 9–10 does sacrificial process really come to the fore. Christ "entered once for all into the most holy place . . . by means of his own blood, thus achieving eternal redemption" (9:12 AT). Scholars debate whether the phrase "finding/having found eternal redemption" (εὑράμενος, an aorist middle participle) locates redemption before or after Christ's entrance. An aorist participle following a main verb more normally indicates coincident or subsequent action[62] and in combination with the emphasis on blood (*not* animal blood but his own) suggests that the NRSV ("thus obtaining eternal redemption") is right to take this as following his entrance rather than prior to it, during Christ's suffering on the cross. The mention of blood and the imagery of Yom Kippur implies that Christ enters heaven not in a purely spiritual state but in his resurrected, bodily form (he carries his blood within his living person). Thus, along with the crucifixion and ascension, the resurrection is one crucial plank in Hebrews' Christology and soteriology. The portrayal of heaven evokes Middle Platonist terminology, albeit used in distinctively Jewish ways, as argued above. But Jesus's physical entrance into heaven decisively subverts this understanding in a way that is consistent with many of the Second Temple apocalyptic texts examined in chapter 2.[63]

Hebrews 9:23–28 is also interested in process. Christ "entered into heaven itself, now to appear [ἐμφανισθῆναι] in the presence of God on our behalf" (9:24). He entered not to offer repeatedly like the earthly high priests (9:25), which would have required repeated suffering (9:26a), but "he has appeared once for all" (ἅπαξ . . . πεφανέρωται) at the end of the ages to put aside sin by his sacrifice (θυσία, 9:26b). The imagery again maps closely onto Yom Kippur but is distinguished from the earthly performance of this rite. Yom Kippur occurred once within the frame of a year, whereas Christ's offering occurred

---

60. Philo (*Embassy* 306–7) counts exactly two entrances; m. Yoma 7.3–4 notes at least two; Lev. 16:12–13 may imply three (first for incense).

61. Calaway, *Sabbath and the Sanctuary*, 139–77.

62. Porter, *Verbal Aspect*, 385–87.

63. Moffitt, *Atonement*, 220–56. Wedderburn ("Sawing Off the Branches") rightly notes the subversion but regards this as inconsistency on Hebrews' part.

once within the frame of the ages. From this perspective, emphasis falls on
the repetition of Yom Kippur year by year.

So it is clear that Christ entered heaven in order then and there to make an
offering, one not equivalent to his death alone.[64] What is less clear is whether
"once" means that the offering is finished at (or shortly after) Christ's entry
into heaven or whether it continues until his second coming. The end of this
passage speaks of Christ "having been offered once" for sins, then appearing
"a second time" with salvation (9:28).[65] Some have seen here a further parallel with the Day of Atonement—namely, the emergence of the high priest
from the sanctuary.[66] If this is so, "once" could refer to the entire period of
Christ's presence in heaven before his second coming. "Having been offered"
(προσενεχθείς) is an aorist passive participle, and like all participles, its time
reference is relative to the main verb. Here the main verb is future, "he will
appear" (ὀφθήσεται), so "having been offered" indicates completion not necessarily from the perspective of the writer but completion only by the point
when Christ appears again. Ultimately Heb. 9:23–28 in itself is inconclusive
and could be read either way. I will argue below that Hebrews regards Christ's
atoning offering as already decisively finished, but contrary to much opinion,
the term "once (for all)" does not on its own determine this. For now, I note that
"a second time" is nowhere used in connection with Yom Kippur, and therefore I suspect that this rite does not underlie the portrayal of Christ's return.

Ceasing and Sitting

Only when we give attention to the heavenly session of Christ, his act of sitting down at the right hand of God's throne, does the timing of the end of his
offering become clear.[67] Christ's session is referred to many times in Hebrews
(1:3, 13; 2:7–9; 8:1; 12:2) and indeed in many other NT texts, often accompanied by quotation of or allusion to Ps. 110:1, "The LORD says to my lord, 'Sit
at my right hand.'" In fact, this is the most frequently cited OT verse in the
NT. Hebrews emphasizes the action of sitting and the throne more than other
NT texts, which tend to highlight Christ's ongoing presence at God's right

64. Though, as Jamieson (*Jesus' Death*, 127–79) argues, Jesus's death under the figure of
"blood" is part of what he offers.

65. There is a parallel in 9:27–28 between human death "once" and Christ's being offered
"once." The context equates offering with Christ's entrance into heaven and presence before
God in heaven, and thus the parallel does not equate Christ's offering exclusively with his death
but rather includes his death as part of his offering and highlights the eschatological judgment/
salvation that follows.

66. E.g., Kleinig, *Hebrews*, 464.

67. The argument of this and the following section is given more fully in Moore, "Sacrifice,
Session, and Intercession."

hand. Christ's session is particularly salient in Heb. 10:11–14. The contrast drawn with the levitical priests is reinforced by a careful chiastic structure:

> And every priest **stands** *day after day* at his service,
>   offering *again and again* the same sacrifices that can never take away sins.
> But when Christ had offered a *single* sacrifice for sins,
> *for all time* "he **sat down** at the right hand of God." (10:11–12 NRSV modified)

The similarities are clear: Christ and the priests are cultic ministers, who offer sacrifices. The differences are also evident: Christ's offering was singular and perpetually effective, whereas the priests' sacrifices were repeated and did not remove sins. Most important for our purposes is the contrast in posture. The priests stood to serve, which is the correct cultic position. No earthly priest sat down when on duty, just as the angels in heaven dare not sit in God's presence.[68] One of the few mentions in the period of sitting in relation to sacrificial service comes from the Letter of Aristeas 94, where it is explicitly stated that "those who are relieved from duty" *sit* in a dedicated place away from the cultic service (καθίζουσιν οἱ διαναπαυόμενοι). Likewise, Christ sat down *after* having offered "a single sacrifice for sins" (μίαν ὑπὲρ ἁμαρτιῶν προσενέγκας θυσίαν, 10:12). Here as in 1:3 an aorist participle preceding the main verb indicates prior action. The inference is that, like the levitical priests, Christ was standing when he made his offering. This single, finished offering has perpetual effects, guaranteeing the sanctification and perfection of his followers (10:10, 14). Christ's singular offering and his session, just like his perfection for the priesthood, integrate recognition of process with emphasis on the finished aspect of his work:

> Singularity is to Christ's sacrifice what perfection is to his priesthood: both terms are evocative of a process . . . yet most importantly both stress the aspect of completion. Not only this, but [in Heb. 10:11–18] enthronement re-enters the picture as well. In the space of a few verses we find combined the messianic-priestly session of Ps. 110.1 with priestly-vocational perfection and historical-traditional singularity, together providing the supreme expression of the theological finality and all-sufficiency of the atonement, and the perpetuity of its effects.[69]

68. E.g., Dan. 7:10; Tob. 12:15; 4Q430; 1 En. 14.22; 39.12–40.2. Notably Metatron is punished for sitting in God's presence (3 En. 16.1–5), and the rabbis (y. Berakhot 1.1.18) hold that angels have no knees so that they cannot sit.

69. Moore, *Repetition in Hebrews*, 177.

Following his session, Christ no longer offers but instead awaits (ἐκδεχόμε-
νος, 10:13) his enemies becoming a footstool for his feet, continuing the citation of Ps. 110:1. This present period of waiting is not passive, however, but
involves active intercession for his people.

Intercession

When the author establishes Christ's superlative priesthood in Heb. 7, he
attributes Christ's ability to save completely to the fact that "he always lives
to make intercession for them" (ἐντυγχάνειν, 7:25; cf. Rom. 8:34). Notably
this action of prayer is separated from his single offering, which is mentioned
shortly afterward. The contrasts are eloquent. Unlike mortal priests who die
and thus do not continue in office, Christ's enduring resurrection life enables
him to pray for believers (7:23–25). And unlike sinful priests, who offer sacrifices daily, Christ offered himself once (7:26–27). The levitical priesthood
is unlike Christ both in its *failure* to persist (in relation to prayer) and in its
continued persistence (in relation to sacrifice). Moreover, Christ's seated posture is appropriate for the action of interceding in a way that it would not be
for sacrifice (see 2 Sam. 7:18; 1 Kings 2:19–21; 1 Macc. 10:63).

What is expressed through contrasts in Heb. 7 is expressed in terms of
continuity in Heb. 9. Earlier, I noted that Heb. 9:1–14 forms an extended
typological comparison of the old covenant's sacrificial place, personnel,
and process with those of the new covenant. It is fundamental to Hebrews'
argument that both sides of the twofold distinctions (outer/inner chamber;
priests/high priest; *tamid*/Yom Kippur sacrifices) within the levitical cult are
incorporated and fulfilled in Christ's ministry. I have argued above for what
may be the more controversial part of this contention, that Hebrews envisages
a united, unicameral heavenly sanctuary along apocalyptic and not (only or
primarily) Hellenistic lines. Here I return to the priestly service. The high
priest's offering on Yom Kippur is both singular and repeated, as something
that occurs "once a year" (9:7; cf. 7:27; 9:25). It is fulfilled and perfected in
Christ's offering "once for all" (ἐφάπαξ, 9:12). Yet this does not reflect a
predetermined opposition to repetition as something inherently negative or
as constitutive of ritual. Christ's sacrifice is, after all, the atoning rite par
excellence, and in any case repetition is but one way (and by no means the
only or a necessary way) to elevate ordinary action to the status of ritual.
In this regard, the ordinary twice-daily priestly service alluded to briefly in
9:6—offering animals, grain, and incense, and attending to the lampstand
and (once a week) the showbread—is not simply a negative foil for Christ's
once-for-all offering. Rather, it is a necessary feature of the old covenant

service, which ensured ongoing relationship with God. This feature is fulfilled in the "eternal redemption" of the new covenant (αἰωνίαν λύτρωσιν, 9:12), which is achieved only via the agency of the "eternal Spirit" (διὰ πνεύματος αἰωνίου, 9:14).

This typology is established in Heb. 9 but is already assumed in 7:25, where the perpetuity of Christ's risen, ascended life enables his intercession and therefore his ability to save forever, or perpetually, those who approach through him. The same notion undergirds 4:14–16. Here Jesus is portrayed as a high priest who has gone through the heavens and thus into the heavenly sanctuary. The addressees are urged to approach the "throne of grace," a reference to the ark of the covenant, which confirms that the most holy place is in view. They approach in order to "receive mercy and find grace to help in time of need" (λάβωμεν ἔλεος καὶ χάριν εὕρωμεν εἰς εὔκαιρον βοήθειαν, 4:16). Such heavenly help is *timely* because of Jesus's enduring presence and prayer. This is what it means for him to be a cult minister (λειτουργός) in the true tabernacle and mediator (μεσίτης) of a better covenant (8:2, 6; 9:15; 12:24).

Believers' Priestly Service

Christ's mediation and intercession lead us to our final area of interest: How are believers, from their earthly position, engaged in this heavenly cult? It is first worth noting that Hebrews' conception of the heavenly cult extends beyond Christ's priestly service. Angels serve and visit humans, including by delivering the old covenant (1:7, 14; 2:2; 13:2), but they are primarily engaged in heavenly worship. They worship Christ as firstborn when God brings him into the heavenly world (1:6).[70] An innumerable company of angels joins the feast (πανήγυρις) along with the "assembly of the firstborn" and the "spirits of the righteous made perfect" in the heavenly Jerusalem (12:22–24). Angels and the righteous offering worship in heaven is entirely in keeping with many of the texts we observed in chapter 2, though specific indications of the nature of the worship offered are lacking.

As for the faithful still on earth, it is striking that, in contrast to 1 Peter (2:5, 9) and Revelation (1:6; 5:10; 20:6), Hebrews nowhere describes them as priests.[71] Yet they are exhorted to perform priestly tasks such as "offer a sacrifice of praise to God, that is, the fruit of lips that confess his name"

---

70. I take οἰκουμένη here, as in 2:5, as denoting the inhabited *heavenly* realm, in contrast to its more common usage to mean the inhabited earthly realm. So Caneday, "Eschatological World." For a review of options and for arguments in favor of understanding the verse as referring to the parousia, see Stolz, "Einführen des Erstgeborenen."

71. See Kleinig's (*Hebrews*, 145–55) excursuses on this issue and on perfection as priestly ordination.

and likewise to do good and share possessions, which are also described as sacrifices pleasing to God (13:15–16). The offering of praise is enjoined "continually" (NRSV, translating διὰ παντός). As noted above, this term should be translated "regularly" and reflects the twice-daily *tamid* sacrifices. In 9:6 this was applied to the priestly service proper, whereas here it is applied to the audience. In chapter 6 we will see that the same term is used in Acts to denote prayer at the times of the daily sacrifices, whether corporately in the temple courts (Acts 3:1) or privately in a home (10:2–3). This means that, whether or not the Jerusalem temple was still standing at the time when Hebrews was written, its author urges his audience to offer regular praise in keeping with the times of the daily sacrifices. Indeed, even after the destruction of the temple, the rhythms of celestial worship continue, and believers on earth can continue to join in with it. The morning and evening sacrifices are correlated with the rising and setting of the sun at Qumran, reflecting the angelic liturgy.[72] Thus, just as the *tamid* has typological relevance for Christ's perpetual intercession, so it also forms the model for Christian sacrifices of praise.[73]

The injunction to join in with *tamid* prayers does not, however, make believers priests. All of God's people could share these times of prayer whether in Jerusalem or far from it, as is clear from a range of texts (Ps. 141:2; Dan. 9:21; Jdt. 9:1). One additional feature of Hebrews' argument, however, is suggestive that all Christians are considered priestly. Language of "approach" (προσέρ-χομαι) is used multiple times and reflects Pentateuchal usage. Roughly half of this verb's occurrences in the Pentateuch are cultic, relating either directly to the tabernacle or to Sinai, Passover, or the assembly of Israel.[74] The contexts of all seven occurrences of "drawing near" in Hebrews are also cultic.[75] Again, this does not in itself demonstrate that believers are priests, because at certain points the whole congregation of Israel is described as drawing near. But the verb has a yet more specific usage: it distinguishes priests from Levites in

72. Falk, *Daily, Sabbath, and Festival*, 246; Alexander, *Mystical Texts*, 65–66. In the B recension of the Testament of Abraham, "at the setting of the sun all angels worship God" (4.4), indicating the coordination of angelic worship with the *tamid*; cf. Apoc. Mos. 7.2; 17.1; Apoc. Paul 7.

73. Against the more antithetical construal of the contrast between old covenant sacrifice and Christian worship drawn by Hutchens, "Christian Worship." For an excellent typological approach to old covenant sacrifices in Hebrews, see Ribbens, *Levitical Sacrifice*.

74. Twenty-two of 47 occurrences. Tabernacle: Lev. 9:5, 7, 8; 21:17, 18, 21, 23; 22:3; Num. 17:5; 18:3, 4, 22. Wider refs.: Exod. 12:48; 16:9; 34:32; Lev. 10:4, 5; Num. 9:6; 27:1; Deut. 4:11; 5:23, 27. On προσέρχομαι in Hebrews, see Scholer, *Proleptic Priests*; Mackie, "'Let Us Draw Near'"; Moore, "'In' or 'Near'?"

75. Heb. 4:16; 7:25; 10:1, 22; 11:6; 12:18, 22. Hebrews 11:6 speaks of "the one who approaches"; God is the object of approach, and other exemplars of faith in the chapter offer sacrifice (Abel, 11:4; Abraham, 11:17). Note the related use of ἐγγίζειν in 7:19.

Num. 18:3, the latter group forbidden from approaching the vessels or altar. Similarly, any descendants of the priestly family of Aaron with a deformity may eat the holy food from the cult but may not approach to offer—which is to say, they may not serve as priests (Lev. 21:21–23). Thus "approach" can in specific circumstances denote an action that *only* priests may perform.

When we read Hebrews from this perspective, we see that this is exactly the kind of approach that is envisaged: Christians are to "approach the throne of grace" (that is, the ark of the covenant with its atonement cover, Heb. 4:16) and to approach the entryway to the most holy place (10:19–22). This is not the same as entering that space, both because it is the apex of sanctity for which still-sinful humans are in the process of being sanctified (10:14) and because it is a heavenly space that earthbound humans cannot access during this life.[76] But it does accord believers some level of privileged access—most fundamentally, proximity to the most holy place—that hitherto belonged only to the unblemished levitical priest. What believers draw near to offer is the sacrifice of praise (13:15), intimated earlier in the use of the word "boldly" (μετὰ παρρησίας, 4:16), which usually suggests not merely confidence per se but confidence issuing forth in speech.[77] I would also suggest that "seiz[ing] the hope set before us" (6:18) refers in part to prayer, given that such hope is like the rope or chain of an anchor that resides within the most holy place (6:19). The proximity that believers enjoy, coupled with the structural shifts discussed above, affords them one further privilege. Through the open entryway, past the drawn curtain, they can see Jesus (2:9). This reality serves as a source of assurance and also of encouragement, as they are exhorted to continue in the contest, looking to Jesus who is seated at the right hand of God (12:2).

Conclusion

Hebrews portrays a heavenly tabernacle. This much is relatively uncontroversial. What I have sought to do here, however, is offer a number of clarifications to this general observation. The heavenly sanctuary preexisted the earthly one, and (insofar as can be inferred) it was established at the creation of the world. It formed the model for Moses's tabernacle, which in turn foreshadowed the high priestly ministry of Christ. Both of the tabernacle's chambers,

---

76. Moore, "Heaven's Revolving Door?"

77. This is true both in classical usage more generally (e.g., Euripides, *Hippolytus* 422, referring to Athenians' freedom of speech; see LSJ, s.v. παρρησία, for further references) and in the NT (e.g., Acts 28:31; Eph. 6:19).

along with the priests who could enter them and the rites performed therein, are instructive for the inauguration of the new covenant in heaven. Christ's priesthood incorporates priestly and high priestly service, perfecting both the annual Yom Kippur rite and the twice-daily *tamid* rite. In his risen, bodily state Jesus entered heaven, offered himself before God, and sat down. His session acts as a hinge, bringing his offering to an emphatic close and beginning a period of ongoing intercession and waiting for his royal sovereignty to be fully recognized. Hebrews' overwhelming interest in the heavenly most holy place is not simply a consequence of its concern for the Day of Atonement but reflects a more fundamental shift at the end of the ages. In this "time of reformation," the first tent or outer chamber's function falls away as it is united with the most holy place, forming a single chamber. This is not because Hebrews conceives the universe as a temple, however, but because it combines the temple-as-heaven conceptualization with the end-times ministry of Jesus, leading to a unicameral sanctuary coextensive with heaven. The structural transformation is effected by the removal of the curtain at his ascension, which constitutes the inauguration of a permanent entryway. In this, Hebrews' vision of the present structure of the heavenly sanctuary is similar to Revelation's, although Hebrews speaks of a tabernacle, whereas Revelation prefers the language of temple. Believers can now see Jesus when they approach him in prayer, enjoying a degree of proximity that confirms their priestly status. The figure of Jesus and his relationship to heaven also lie at the heart of the evangelists' concerns as they construe both the figure and the place cultically. We next focus our attention on the Gospels and Acts.

5

Mark and Matthew

Heavens and Mountains

As we turn in the second half of this book to the Gospels and Acts, we move from the explicit heavenly sanctuary of certain Second Temple Jewish texts, Revelation, and Hebrews to cosmologies that are more subtle, allusive, or implied. A few comments are in order before we begin to read this rather different set of texts. First, knowing that there were clear and widely held temple-related understandings of heaven in the period, as has been amply demonstrated, should heighten our sensitivity to echoes of the heavenly temple in the texts we now examine. Second, as I mentioned in the introduction, my selection of texts takes its cue from explicitly cultic features and moves from these toward possible cosmic aspects, or from explicitly cosmic features toward cultic ones. Third, while possible heavenly temple features are explored in the light of a range of other texts, the text of the Gospels themselves (and Acts together with the Gospel in the case of Luke) serves as a control on my readings. Fourth, unlike in the previous chapters, the argument here is cumulative by nature of the texts studied. Any one point taken on its own may not persuade, but when taken collectively, there is good reason to believe that each evangelist draws on the notion of a heavenly sanctuary. Finally, the nature of the conclusions drawn is of necessity more limited and tentative, and we will not here see clear indications of the structure or contents of heaven-as-temple. Nevertheless, I argue that each evangelist engages the heavenly temple in his own unique way, even when using the same traditions, reflecting a range of overlapping and divergent ends.

The first half of this chapter focuses on Mark's Gospel and falls into two parts. First, we examine the baptism, transfiguration, and crucifixion scenes, where there are strong intimations that heaven is a cultic space. These heavenly openings constitute a cumulative revelation of Jesus's identity. Second, we explore the Jerusalem temple, which becomes prominent in the second half of the narrative as the setting for Jesus's intensifying dispute with the Jewish authorities, culminating in his trial and crucifixion (Mark 11–15). Throughout this section, there is anticipation of eschatological restoration, which many interpreters have identified as the transfer of temple functions to the church. Reading Mark's eschatology through the lens of the cosmology established in the three heavenly opening scenes, however, suggests that the new temple is to be identified as a heavenly one. Cosmology and eschatology coincide in the trial scene: here the sanctuary "not made with hands" (14:58) is where Jesus will take up office after his death (14:62).

In the second half of this chapter, we turn to Matthew. I work sequentially through four relevant features. First, Matthew has a strongly dualistic cosmology in which the heavens and divine throne are distinct from the earth. Yet, second, Matthew also reveals at several points that he shares the commonplace association of the earthly temple with heaven, not only as its mirror but also as a point of connection between heaven and earth. The ministry of Jesus as the one who mediates the divine presence—as Emmanuel who is with us always (Matt. 28:20)—fulfills a similar function. Third, this mediating role is heightened through the cosmic mountain setting of Jesus's testing, transfiguration, and commissioning of his disciples. Fourth and finally, Jesus's mediating role is also highlighted through Matthew's development of the apocalyptic framing of the crucifixion. In the person of Jesus, heaven and earth are reunited. Jesus's status as one "greater than the temple" (12:6), the very presence of God with us, enables him to bring in the kingdom of heaven as not only a royal but also a cultic reality.

Mark

A Cosmological Triptych

We begin by examining Mark's baptism, transfiguration, and crucifixion scenes. Some have argued that these episodes function structurally to bind the Gospel together, with the outer two forming an inclusio marking the beginning

**Table 4.1. Connections between Mark's Baptism,
Transfiguration, and Crucifixion**

Baptism (1:4–11)	Transfiguration (9:2–13)	Crucifixion (15:33–39)
heavens torn (σχίζω)		curtain torn (σχίζω)
heavens torn, voice comes from heaven (οἱ οὐρανοί)	garments whiter than anything earthly (ἐπὶ τῆς γῆς)	
dove descends (κατα-βαίνω), voice comes (ἐγένετο)	cloud comes (ἐγένετο)	darkness comes (ἐγένετο)
voice (φωνή) from heaven	voice (φωνή) from cloud	Jesus gives a great cry (φωνή)
Spirit on Jesus (πνεῦμα)		Jesus gives up his spirit (ἐκπνέω)
You are my beloved Son (σὺ εἶ ὁ υἱός μου ὁ ἀγα-πητός, cf. 1:1)	This is my beloved Son (οὗτός ἐστιν ὁ υἱός μου ὁ ἀγαπητός)	This man was God's Son (οὗτος ὁ ἄνθρωπος υἱὸς θεοῦ ἦν)
John the Baptist as an Eli-jah figure	Elijah appears with Jesus	Jesus thought to be calling Elijah

and end of Jesus's earthly ministry while also connecting to a prominent scene at or near its midpoint.[1] Whether or not one follows the structural proposals in their entirety, there are undeniable connections between the three scenes, which can be tabulated as in table 4.1.

These connections suggest that the three episodes are intended to be mutually informing. In particular, Mark's emphasis on Jesus's identity comes across clearly in all three, picking up the theme statement at the very opening of his Gospel.[2] We will take each episode in turn.

Baptism

The tearing of the heavens at Mark's baptism is a widely recognized allusion to Isa. 64:1 (63:19b MT, LXX): "O that you would tear open [לוֹא־קרעת/ ἐὰν ἀνοίξῃς] the heavens and come down."[3] The attention to the heavens in

1. Larsen, "Structure of Mark's Gospel," 146–52.
2. Taking υἱοῦ θεοῦ in Mark 1:1 to be original; even if not, it would constitute an addition by an early reader who had discerned the importance of this motif not least from these three sections.
3. Richard Hays (*Echoes*, 18) notes that σχίζω "offers a stronger allusion to the Hebrew text tradition of Isaiah 64:1 (63:19 MT)."

this section of Isaiah is laden with temple language. God's faithfulness during the wilderness years is recalled in Isa. 63:7–14, followed by an appeal to God to "look down from heaven and see, / from your holy and glorious habitation" (63:15). The term translated "habitation" here (זְבֻל), "elevation, height," is a circumlocution for God's lofty abode, house, or temple, and it is characterized as "beautiful" or "glorious" (תפארה).[4] Three verses further on, there is concern at the trampling of the earthly sanctuary (מקדש/τὸ ἁγίασμα, 63:18). The same thought is found in the oracle following 64:1, which mentions the burning and ruin of "our holy and beautiful house" (בית קדשנו ותפארתנו/ὁ οἶκος τὸ ἅγιον ἡμῶν καὶ ἡ δόξα, 64:11 [64:10 MT, LXX]). The appeal in Isaiah is thus for God to come forth from his heavenly dwelling place in response to the desolation of his earthly dwelling place.

Mark's use of this motif suggests that the request for God to intervene is answered in the ministry of Jesus. The likelihood that Mark is alluding to the source text's temple ideas is confirmed by his use of the verb "tear" (σχίζω) only here and in the tearing of the temple veil at the crucifixion. The verb is surprising or unusual with respect to "heavens," and Matthew and Luke change it to "open" (ἀνοίγω).[5] Mark's baptism and crucifixion scenes show numerous other connections: themes of spirit/expiring, a voice confessing Jesus's sonship, the rending of the heavens/curtain, and the Elijah connection.[6] Baptism is also linked to death via Jesus's response to James and John (10:38–39). The sending of the Spirit as a divine agent, his visionary appearance in the form of a dove, and the divine voice emerging from heaven all suggest divine emanation and combine to make this scene "thoroughly saturated with temple symbolism."[7]

Transfiguration

Mark's transfiguration scene is likewise replete with temple symbolism. One scholar describes this scene as "the unmistakable center of the whole

4. Cf. the glory language in Isa. 60:7, where we find "house of my glory" (בית תפארתי) rendered "my house of prayer" (ὁ οἶκος τῆς προσευχῆς μου) in the LXX. The LXX of 63:15 is "from your holy house of glory" (ἐκ τοῦ οἴκου τοῦ ἁγίου σου καὶ δόξης).
5. Ezekiel 1 is also evoked in the description of Jesus's baptism, and it is possible that Matthew's use of ἀνοίγω is due in part to a desire to strengthen the connection with Ezek. 1 and Isa. 64, both of which have this verb in the Septuagint. See Orlov, "Kavod on the River," 61–65.
6. See further Ulansey, "Mark's Cosmic Inclusio." In "Heavens Torn Open," Ulansey stresses the oddness of the verb. Orlov ("Kavod on the River," 75–80) identifies numerous allusions to divine glory in the scene as well as in early readings of it.
7. Hørning Jensen, "Temple 'before the Temple,'" 391–95. He suggests that the nearness of the kingdom of God in 1:15 is a further cultic allusion.

gospel."[8] Even if one does not adopt this view of the structure, the trans-figuration is clearly pivotal. Jesus chooses a select few disciples to go up "a high mountain" (ὄρος ὑψηλόν, Mark 9:2) with him, much as Moses was accompanied by Aaron, Aaron's sons, and seventy elders when he ascended Mount Sinai (Exod. 24). The exalted mountain is equally reminiscent of Mount Zion (e.g., Ps. 48:1–2). Recall that mountains, representing the cosmic center and the bond between heaven and earth, were privileged locations for divine encounters and theophanies in the ancient world. The transforma-tion of Jesus's clothes to a bright, otherworldly white is suggestive of the transfer to the heavenly realm and could also evoke the linen of the priestly garments, particularly the plain white clothes worn by the high priest when he entered the most holy place on the Day of Atonement.[9] Peter, James, and John's terror is reminiscent of Israel's response to the theophany at Sinai (Exod. 19:16; 20:18–20). A point relevant to this and the following chapter is the intimate relationship between Sinai and all other biblical theophanies. Sinai is "a touchstone for prior and subsequent glory theophanies in the Bible because the Sinai event was constitutive in Israel's history and crucial in salvation history."[10] This suggests that when we find theophanies in the Gospels, Sinai is likely in view, especially where multiple motifs from the Exodus account are present.

In addition to the Day of Atonement, another key annual gathering, the Festival of Booths/Tabernacles, is potentially in view in the transfiguration when Peter offers to build three tents (σκηναί, Mark 9:5). Although the sig-nificance of Peter's response is ultimately unclear (likely intentionally so), it is at least "a somewhat baffled attempt to respond correctly to the heavenly vision by drawing on the connection between tents and divine interaction."[11] The cloud is also a clear indicator of divine presence, and one that is pre-dominantly associated with cultic places.[12]

8. M. P. Scott, "Chiastic Structure," 18.
9. Second Peter 1:16–19 similarly mentions light in addition to the heavenly voice and holy mountain. For the view that the transfiguration foreshadows Jesus's becoming divine, see Burkett, "Epiphany or Apotheosis?" Giambrone ("Jesus' Transfiguration") argues that in Mark's and Matthew's transfiguration scenes, Jesus is cast as an eschatological high priest in the vein of Elijah, Moses, and Levi.
10. Niehaus, God at Sinai, 16. For Sinai's influence on the Gospels, see Niehaus, God at Sinai, 334–40. On Zion's assumption of some aspects of Sinai, see Levenson, Sinai and Zion, 206–9.
11. Hørning Jensen, "Temple 'before the Temple,'" 413.
12. Note the dark cloud at Sinai (Exod. 19:18), the cloud filling both the tabernacle and Solomon's temple at their inauguration (Exod. 40:34–38; 1 Kings 8:10–11), the cloud lead-ing the Israelites and settling over the tabernacle (Num. 10:11–12), and the cloud of incense smoke in the most holy place on the Day of Atonement (Lev. 16:2); cf. also Dan. 7:13; Isa. 4:5; 6:4.

This episode sets Jesus momentarily in a cosmic-cultic space where he is at home. It does so more explicitly and extensively than either the baptism or crucifixion scenes while being tightly bound to them. For Mark, then, the transfiguration enhances the heavenly temple allusions that are already present in the baptism and does so in order to clarify further Jesus's status as Son of God and his corresponding authority as one who is holy and intimate with God.

Crucifixion

The crucifixion scene in Mark is terse in its cultic allusions by comparison with the transfiguration, but it contains explicit mention of the Jerusalem temple curtain. The connections with Jesus's baptism and transfiguration have been detailed above. The three hours of darkness (Mark 15:33) may evoke the dark cloud of Sinai. The tearing of the temple veil (καταπέτασμα, 15:38) is striking: it interrupts the flow of the narrative with a glimpse of an event elsewhere in Jerusalem, and it is included without further comment, suggesting that Mark saw it as sufficiently self-interpreting at this stage of his Gospel.[13] It is debated whether the veil screening off the most holy place or the one at the entrance to the holy place is in view. Based on the lexical usage of καταπέτασμα in the Septuagint, the cosmic symbolism of the inner veil, and the narrative significance for the evangelists of the veil tearing, the inner veil is most likely intended.[14] As we have seen, for Josephus the curtain and its colored threads represent the firmament and the elements, respectively (J.W. 5.210–14), a notion grounded in the connections between the firmament and the veil in the OT. The rending of the temple veil thus images the rending of the heavens, as Mark intimates by using the same verb for both events.[15] This much is fairly widely acknowledged; what the tearing connotes is less certain. There are four broad possibilities: it is (1) a sign of the temple's obsolescence and/or destruction, (2) a symbol of mourning for the temple's and/or Jesus's demise, (3) the opening of a way into God's presence, or (4) an epiphanic revelation. These options are not mutually exclusive. In light of Jesus's interactions with the Jerusalem temple and predictions of its destruction, which we will look at below, it seems likely that at least something of that motif is portrayed by the rending of the temple veil. Yet the connection with the baptism and

13. For a detailed discussion of the veil tearing in the Synoptics in relation to the veil in Hebrews, see Moore, "'Once More unto the Breach.'"
14. For the outer curtain, see Ulansey, "Mark's Cosmic Inclusio"; Pelletier, "La tradition synoptique"; S. Motyer, "Rending of the Veil"; for the inner curtain, see Moore, "'Once More unto the Breach.'"
15. Gurtner, "Rending of the Veil," 303.

transfiguration and the centurion's response within the crucifixion narrative give strong support for the fourth option as well.

The centurion's statement might be taken as mockery, but within the Gospel it is only the third or fourth appearance of this phrase[16] and the first to be voiced within the narrative by a human character, and a gentile at that. It seems better, therefore, to take it as an authentic confession. The centurion's position "facing" Jesus (ἐξ ἐναντίας αὐτοῦ) could imply a cultic stance,[17] and the mirroring of the baptism might suggest that here it is the centurion who will receive the Spirit in response to Jesus breathing out (ἐξέπνευσεν, 15:39).[18] In narrative terms, the centurion's confession is a response to the veil tearing, which is therefore epiphanic, just as both the baptism and transfiguration revealed Jesus's divine identity to his companions.[19] The tearing of the veil is nevertheless more definitive than the tearing of the heavens, as the veil is rent completely in two, suggesting that the centurion's response is a paradigmatic first-of-many rather than a unique event of revelation to key figures like John the Baptist and Peter, James, and John.[20] Within Mark, these three scenes progressively build a picture of the heavenly temple, which is instrumental in revealing Jesus's identity, but they leave us with a definitive cosmological shift at Jesus's death, which indicates that this understanding is now permanently available to those who, like the centurion, have eyes to see.

Eschatological Expectation and the Jerusalem Temple

We now turn from these three interrelated scenes at the beginning, middle, and end of Mark to a series of episodes in the second half of the Gospel that are located in or have to do with the temple. The Jerusalem temple is largely absent from the Gospel until Mark 11–15, where it becomes prominent as the setting for Jesus's escalating dispute with the authorities.[21] The dispute does not pit Jesus (or Jesus and his followers) against the temple as a simple

16. Depending on the textual variation at Mark 1:1.
17. Chronis, "Torn Veil," 110.
18. S. Motyer, "Rending of the Veil."
19. So Chronis, "Torn Veil."
20. The christological potency of the motif of opening can be seen in the way the Gospel of Peter extends the motif to the resurrection (ἀνοιχθέντες τοὺς οὐρα[ν]οὺς . . . ὁ τάφος ἐνοίγη, 9.35–37), a scene "replete with points of contact with the scene of the baptism of Jesus," though we can only speculate as to whether a balancing baptism scene might have existed in the original text of this now incomplete Gospel. See P. Foster, *Gospel of Peter*, 400.
21. On the temple in Mark, see Juel, *Messiah and Temple*; Heil, "Temple Theme in Mark"; T. C. Gray, *Temple*. All argue that the Christian community replaces the temple. Hørning Jensen ("Temple 'before the Temple'") explores temple themes in the first part of Mark.

binary. Rather, it integrates dissatisfaction (primarily with Israel's current
authorities) with hope of eschatological restoration. My contention is that
this restoration includes the anticipation of a cosmic temple.

The Temple Clearing

Jesus's first encounter with the temple involves a brief entrance into the
temple complex[22] followed by his clearing the temple courts the next day and
intercalated with the account of the cursing of the fig tree (Mark 11:11–25).
Jesus's action in the temple courts prevents trade and the exchange of coinage. This appears to be primarily an economic protest although it must also
have implications for the sacrificial cult, given the mention of pigeon sellers
(11:15–16).[23] Jesus cites Isa. 56:7 and Jer. 7:11 to criticize the temple as failing
in some way to live up to its vocation as "a house of prayer for all the nations,"
having become instead "a den of robbers" (Mark 11:17). This term "robbers"
(λῃσταί) may allude to nationalist insurrectionists rather than simple criminals
as the usual English translations "robber" or "thief" tend to suggest,[24] though
this is harder to square with the presence of chief priests and scribes, who
were collaborators rather than revolutionaries. Jesus's action and charges are
commonly understood as presaging the destruction of the temple in judgment.
The sandwiched story of the fig tree is important for this interpretation: as
Jesus curses the fig tree and the disciples find it withered the next day, so the
temple is cursed and awaits its own withering.[25] For Mark, Jesus clearly does
expect that the temple will be destroyed (see 13:1–2), but judgment falls on the
temple authorities more than the temple itself, and cultic functions transfer to
an underspecified eschatological hope rather than to the Christian community.

The wider context clarifies that prayer and authority are the issues at
stake here (prayer: 11:14, 22–25; authority: 11:3–10, 27–33). Jesus's status
as Messiah is underscored in his triumphal entry as the Lord's emissary and
the heir of David (11:9–10) and in the implicit derivation of his authority,
like John's, from heaven (11:29–33). From the response to his teaching in the

22. Like other ancient Hellenistic Jewish authors, Mark is careful to use ἱερόν to refer to the
whole temple complex; he reserves ναός ("sanctuary") for the temple proper and uses it only in
the trial and crucifixion (14:58; 15:29, 38).

23. There were certainly economic grievances against the chief priestly families, and Caia-
phas may have opened a market. Nevertheless, changing coinage into the higher-grade silver
Tyrian shekel, the purchase of animals for sacrifice, and carrying cultic vessels through the
temple were all necessary components of the operation of the temple cult in the first century
AD, so T. C. Gray, *Temple*, 27–29. For a helpful guide to the historical issues, see Domeris,
"Enigma of Jesus' Temple Intervention."

24. So Wright, *Victory of God*, 294–304.

25. Key studies here are Telford, *Barren Temple*; Heil, "Temple Theme in Mark."

temple (11:18), it is clear that his authority trumps that of the chief priests. Similarly, Jesus's own prayer is effective, and he teaches his disciples how to pray, whereas the temple is not an effective place of prayer because of how it has been misused and mismanaged.

That it is the Jewish authorities that are being critiqued in the temple clearing is confirmed by two other considerations: First, imagery of trees bearing fruit usually applies to people, whether individually or corporately, and not to institutions (see, e.g., Ps. 1:3; Jer. 17:6; Matt. 7:16–20). Thus the fig tree represents the temple leadership, not the temple per se.[26] Second, the parable of the tenants, which immediately follows the controversy over Jesus's authority and John's baptism, depicts the nation as a vineyard with a tower. The tower is a characteristic way of depicting the temple within the nation (cf. 1 En. 89.50). The parable's point is not that the vineyard will be destroyed but rather that the rebellious, murderous tenants will be destroyed (Mark 12:1–11).

Eschatological expectation comes to the fore in two key places in these passages. Much attention has focused on the wider resonances of Jeremiah's temple sermon, which is quoted in Mark 11:17, and its implications for destruction (Jer. 7:1–15 and surroundings mention lack of figs, withered leaves, and cursed land).[27] Yet much less attention has been given to the other, longer citation, which expresses Isaiah's hope for eschatological restoration (Mark 11:17; see Isa. 56:1–7). Here foreigners and eunuchs come to the holy mountain, and their sacrifices are accepted.[28] In keeping with this forward-looking hope that the temple will once again be a "house of prayer for all the nations," Jesus identifies himself as the rejected stone that becomes the cornerstone at the close of the parable of the tenants (Mark 12:10–11, citing Ps. 118:22–23). No comment is given on the meaning of this citation, but in juxtaposition to the image of a vineyard with a tower, it suggests an anticipated future building project that will include a renewed, restored temple. The temple action and its near context therefore highlight eschatological hope and not only judgment.

The Little Apocalypse

Mark 13 stands out for its apocalyptic language and style and has elicited much debate over the precise referent of the predicted destruction. Is it of Jerusalem in AD 70, the end of the age, or some combination of the two? Jesus's prediction of the temple's destruction opens this section of teaching (13:1–2).

---

26. For more detail on this, see Wahlen, "Temple in Mark," esp. 261–63.
27. Hays, *Echoes*, 26–29.
28. See Guthrie, "Tree and the Temple."

The phrase "desolating sacrilege" (βδέλυγμα τῆς ἐρημώσεως, 13:14) is lifted directly from Daniel, where it refers to Antiochus IV Epiphanes's erection of an altar to Zeus in the Jerusalem temple in 167 BC and to the cessation of the regular offerings.[29] What exactly it refers to in Jesus's day is less clear, but there is no doubt that it marks "the beginning of the process which leads to the temple's destruction."[30] Yet the cosmic portents heralding the ingathering of the elect and the statement that "heaven and earth will pass away" (Mark 13:31; see vv. 24–27) indicate that more is at play here than simply the climactic events of the Jewish War.[31] Given its cosmic significance, the end of the temple portends the end of the age.[32] Alongside the overwhelming emphasis on destruction, we again find hope of restoration. Here it comes in the blossoming of the fig tree (13:28), which evokes the cursed fig tree on either side of the temple-clearing episode. Just as Isa. 56:7 balances Jer. 7:11 in the temple clearing, so the fig tree on the cusp of summer balances the fig tree out of season and without fruit.[33] Mark hints at the expectation of an eschatological temple, but the nature of that temple does not become clear until Jesus's trial.

The Trial

When Jesus is arrested in Gethsemane, he protests, "Day after day I was with you in the temple teaching, and you did not arrest me" (Mark 14:49). This focalizes the temple in anticipation of the first reported charge against him at the trial: "We heard him say, 'I will destroy this temple [ναός] that is made with hands [χειροποίητος], and in three days I will build another, not made with hands [ἀχειροποίητος]'" (14:58). Mark comments that this testimony is false and that the witnesses do not agree among themselves (14:57, 59). Yet it is not a complete fabrication. Within Mark, the same notion is found in the mocking comments of passersby at the cross: "You who would destroy the temple and build it in three days, save yourself, and come down from the cross!" (15:29–30). There is no suggestion that these passersby were at the trial, so the idea appears to have been generally known.[34] Moreover, as

29. Dan. 9:27; 11:31; 12:11. See also Diodorus Siculus, *Lib. Hist.* 34.1.4; 1 Macc. 1:59.
30. France, *Mark*, 520; for a review of the possibilities (Caligula's statue, Roman military standards, the Zealot takeover of AD 67–68), see France, *Mark*, 519–26.
31. On the cosmological and not (only) political import of this passage, see Adams, *Stars Will Fall*, 133–81.
32. T. C. Gray, *Temple*, 148–49.
33. Telford, *Barren Temple*, 216–17; for a skeptical outlook on the fig tree in Mark 13:28, see T. C. Gray, *Temple*, 147.
34. Matthew preserves the saying without the terminology of (ἀ)χειροποίητος (26:61). Note similar statements in John 2:19; Acts 6:14; on the potential connections between Mark and

we have seen, Jesus does predict the temple's destruction. The falseness of the charge is primarily a question of agency: Jesus claimed not that *he* would destroy the temple but simply that it would be destroyed.[35]

The same possibility should be entertained for the second part of the charge: Mark affirms the premise but not the ascription of agency. This is to say, Jesus spoke of a temple "not made with hands" in contrast to the one in Jerusalem that was "made with hands," but he did not claim that he would build it himself. The term χειροποίητος ("made with hands") often refers to idolatry in the Septuagint,[36] but this is not its basic or only meaning. In Philo, this and a similar form (χειρόκμητος) can denote human-made things, whether disasters or objects, and in two cases it describes the temple without any pejorative nuance.[37] The implication of the charges at the trial is borne out by Mark's earlier narrative: Jesus did predict the temple's destruction and spoke of being the cornerstone of a renewed temple, yet he did not claim that he himself would carry out the demolition. This is the misconstrual that makes the accusation false.

This reading gains plausibility from the indications in the baptism, transfiguration, and crucifixion that both Mark and Mark's Jesus know of a temple "not made with hands," heaven itself.[38] The idea is confirmed within the trial narrative in Jesus's only reply to the high priest's questioning. Asked whether he is the Messiah, he states "I am; and / 'you will see the Son of Man / seated at the right hand of the Power,' / and 'coming with the clouds of heaven'" (14:62). The combination of Ps. 110:1 and Dan. 7:13 underlines Jesus's messianic claim, as both texts locate him by the divine throne in the heavenly courtroom.[39] As we have seen, regal and cultic imagery in the ancient world are two sides of the same coin, and supremely so when related to God's dwelling place. Jesus expects to enter the heavenly temple after his death to take up a priestly position at the right hand of God.[40] This builds on the cosmology

John, see Rojas-Flores, "From John 2.19 to Mark 15.29." He argues that the idea of rebuilding is not historical but came to Mark via a hostile source.

35. T. C. Gray, *Temple*, 172–73.

36. E.g., Lev. 26:1, 30; Isa. 2:18; Jdt. 8:18; Wis. 14:8. It occurs in Dan. 5:4, 23; 6:28; Bel 1:5 with εἴδωλον and in Isa. 16:12 describing Moab's sanctuary.

37. Disasters: *Spec. Laws* 3.203; 4.154; *Embassy* 107; objects: *Unchangeable* 25; *Dreams* 2.118; temple: *Moses* 2.88; *Spec. Laws* 1.67.

38. Daniel 2:34 may be in play here as well: in Nebuchadnezzar's dream, a stone is cut out "not by human hands" (ἄνευ χειρῶν). It destroys the statue and becomes a great mountain filling the earth—none other than the cosmic mountain (2:35).

39. There is extensive debate over whether "coming on the clouds" refers to Jesus's exaltation or his return. The use of Ps. 110:1 implies the *duration* of Jesus's session and thus both its start and end, as argued by Smith and Vaillancourt, "Enthroned and Coming."

40. This case is well argued by Botner, "Sanctuary in the Heavens."

established at key epiphanic moments throughout the Gospel, accepts the premise of the false charge, and corrects it by demonstrating that Jesus will inaugurate the sanctuary "not made with hands." In this light, two other passages make complementary claims. In Mark 12:10–11, Jesus cites Ps. 118 to indicate that his rejection and death will lead, through his resurrection, to the foundation of a new temple in his very self. And in Mark 14:22–25, at the Last Supper with his disciples, Jesus aligns himself with Passover and identifies his death with the covenant inauguration ceremony of Exod. 24:4–8.[41] Jesus is thus priest, cornerstone, and sacrifice in the eschatological temple.

Mark assumes that as the dwelling place of God, heaven is a sanctuary. It is opened in Jesus's ministry to reveal and affirm his identity as God's Son and Messiah. In light of this cosmology, the lesser note of expectation of restoration (which accompanies the foreboding judgment and predicted destruction hanging over Jerusalem's temple) refers in part to the heavenly temple. This supposition is confirmed in the trial, where Jesus states that he will take up his place in heaven as Messiah and priest following his death and resurrection. The effect of this is reflected in the decisive opening signaled by the tearing of the veil, which prompts the centurion's confession and indicates that, once inaugurated by Jesus, the heavenly temple truly is a house of prayer for all the nations.

Matthew

As we read Matthew with Mark (his main source text) in mind, we see that he disrupts the careful structural parallelism Mark establishes between the baptism, transfiguration, and crucifixion scenes. He changes Mark's "tear" (σχίζω) at the baptism to "open" (ἀνοίγω), a more conventional term but one that weakens the connection with the crucifixion. The transfiguration is pushed later in a significantly longer text, and Matthew introduces a mini-apocalypse between the veil tearing and the centurion's confession, separating what Mark had juxtaposed. These changes are indicative of how Matthew, while largely following Mark's order, nevertheless charts his own course. Here I will show how Matthew conveys a strongly dualistic cosmology by his distinctive use of language of "heaven(s)," often paired with (and in contradistinction to) "earth." We then explore Matthew's assumptions about the Jerusalem temple's relation to God's heavenly dwelling, as a point

41. Shauf, *Jesus the Sacrifice*, 116–22.

of connection between earth and heaven. In this light, Jesus as Emmanuel, "God with us," can be seen to fulfill similar functions. This subtle temple Christology is strengthened by Matthew's use of mountains as settings for Jesus's ministry—especially the mountains of testing, transfiguration, and commissioning—as well as by the apocalyptic framing of the crucifixion. Like the temple, Jesus brings together spheres that would otherwise remain distinct and unbroachable.

Heaven and Earth

Matthew uses the term οὐρανός ("heaven") more than any other NT book.[42] He is distinctive among the Synoptic Gospels in his use of the plural (οὐρανοί) in the phrase "kingdom of the heavens" where Mark and Luke have "kingdom of God." In an important study, Jonathan Pennington has shown that this is not, as often assumed, a reverential circumlocution for the divine name. Instead, Matthew observes a careful distinction between "heavens" as the invisible dwelling place of God and "heaven" as the visible sky above.[43] (This is in contrast to the opposite usage in contemporary English of singular heaven and plural heavens, with the singular referring to God's dwelling and the plural to the starry sky.) The one significant exception to this pattern is the use of the singular "heaven" in tandem with "earth" to signify the totality of the created order.[44] This pairing emphasizes a basic cosmological dualism, in keeping with the simpler forms of temple-related cosmology that we have observed in a range of Second Temple Jewish texts.

At Jesus's baptism, the heavens are "opened" (rather than "torn," as in Mark) and a voice comes from the heavens. Matthew heightens the focus on the opening and the voice with his characteristic "and behold" twice (καὶ ἰδού, 3:16, 17) and makes the event more public with a general declaration: "This is my Son, the Beloved" (rather than Mark's "You are . . ."). The significance of the baptism remains theophanic, and it constitutes Jesus's commissioning by God from the heavens. The connection with the transfiguration and

---

42. The term appears 82× in Matthew, almost a third of all NT occurrences; Revelation has the next highest number at 52×.

43. Pennington, *Heaven and Earth*, 125–61.

44. The plural/singular distinction is not without exception. Some cases are borderline, as with the twofold tradition regarding binding and loosing on earth and heaven, where we have both the earth/heaven pairing (singular, as in 18:18) and reference to God's ultimate dwelling place (hence the plural found in 16:19, also influenced by "kingdom of the heavens" in the same verse). Exceptions include 21:25; 22:30; 23:22 (implicit contrast with earth?); 24:31. See discussion in Pennington, *Heaven and Earth*, 143–49.

crucifixion scenes, although changed from Mark, remains, as we will see below, and this strengthens the cultic connotations.

Another Matthean distinctive is his recurrent use of the phrases "Father in the heavens" (ὁ πατὴρ ὁ ἐν τοῖς οὐρανοῖς, e.g., Matt. 7:11; 16:17) and "your/ my heavenly Father" (ὁ πατὴρ ὑμῶν/μου ὁ οὐράνιος, e.g., 5:48; cf. 23:9) to refer to God. These terms emphasize God's heavenly location and dwelling place, his otherness from creation, and his close association with the king-dom of heaven.[45] The stress is primarily on God's kingly status, and this is reinforced by the association of heaven with God's throne. In connection with oaths, Jesus at one point forbids swearing by heaven "for it is the throne of God" (5:34), and at another warns that whoever swears by heaven "swears by the throne of God and by the one who is seated upon it" (23:22). The other references to thrones point to the eschatological judgment: the Son of Man will sit on his throne when he comes to judge, and his twelve disciples will also sit on twelve thrones to judge God's people alongside him (19:28; 25:31; cf. 20:21). This is royal imagery with military and juridical nuances, and it likely denotes an earthly judgment rather than a heavenly one (cf. 1 En. 1.1–7). The image of the throne is nevertheless readily related to earth and heaven, palace and court, as indicated by Matthew's easy move in 23:21–22 from the sanctuary and its inhabitant to the heavens, God's throne, and its occupant. The heavens are where God is and, by implication, where humans are not and cannot be.

Temple Presuppositions

In light of Matthew's starkly dichotomous cosmology, it is significant that he at several points (and almost incidentally) reveals common Second Temple presuppositions about the temple's relationship to heaven. In critiquing the practice of the scribes and Pharisees, Jesus restores the order of sanctity: the sanctuary (ναός) is greater than its gold, and the altar greater than the gift offered on it (23:16–19). Whoever takes an oath invoking the Jerusalem sanctuary swears by "the one who dwells in it," and whoever swears by heaven "swears by the throne of God and by the one who is seated upon it" (23:20–22).[46] The main point is to refute the Pharisees' casuistry, but in the process Matthew's Jesus reveals the shared assumption that God dwells in the temple

45. Pennington, *Heaven and Earth*, 231–51.
46. Matthew's material on oaths emphasizes his "special concern" for the temple and "stresses the sanctity of the altar and the sanctuary's shrine, that is, God's presence there" (Regev, *Temple in Early Christianity*, 145).

and that his ultimate dwelling place is the heavenly throne room of which the earthly most holy place and ark are reflections.

The same point emerges in an earlier passage on oaths. In the Sermon on the Mount, Jesus instructs his hearers not to swear at all, "either by heaven, for it is the throne of God, or by the earth, for it is his footstool, or by Jerusalem, for it is the city of the great King" (5:34–35). This alludes to Isa. 66:1, but as we have seen, the "footstool" in the OT is most commonly a reference to the temple or specifically the ark within it as the footrest or model throne corresponding to the heavenly throne (1 Chron. 28:2; Pss. 99:5; 132:7). An allusion to the temple in Matt. 5 is made more likely both by the specific temple connections of the later passage on oaths and by the mention of Jerusalem in 5:35, which suggests that attention is focused not on the earth in general but on the holy city and on the mountain and temple that make it holy.[47] Only in connection with the temple and Jerusalem can heaven and earth be aligned, because like heaven the temple is God's dwelling place, as indicated by the ark, his throne or footstool within it.

Given that Matthew shares these assumptions about the temple's relation to God and heaven, his portrayal of interactions with the temple makes perfect sense.[48] The temple complex is a sphere for Jesus's teaching and healing (Matt. 21:14, 23; 26:55), and while the temple tax may not be compulsory for the king's children, it is still paid (17:24–27).[49] Jesus assumes that his hearers participate in the temple cult (5:23–24). This teaching about leaving one's gift at the altar prioritizes reconciliation, but it also shows that Jesus regards sacrificial observance as normal and important to fulfill (cf. 8:4). The same can be said of the necessity of tithing alongside attending to weightier matters of the law (23:23). Equally, as the priestly service takes priority over the sabbath regulations, so mercy takes priority even over sacrifice (12:1–8). This is not to reject the sabbath but to set it in its due legal priority.[50]

At the same time, a relativization of the Jerusalem temple is implied by the designation of Jesus as one "greater than the temple" (12:6). This places him, like the practice of mercy, above the sacrificial system in importance, and most importantly, it intimates that Matthew has a temple Christology. This suggestion is amplified by the notion that God's presence is found in Jesus.

47. They are "inseparably linked with God as his dwelling and possession" (France, *Matthew*, 215).

48. On Matthew's positive view of the temple, see Cohen, "Matthew and the Temple." For a contrasting view, that Jerusalem becomes an image of rebellion and deceit, see Verseput, "Jesus' Pilgrimage to Jerusalem."

49. There is debate over whether "children" here represents Israelites in general or Jesus's followers/Matthew's community in particular.

50. Regev, *Temple in Early Christianity*, 136–39.

He is named at the outset as Emmanuel, "God with us" (μεθ' ἡμῶν ὁ θεός, 1:23; cf. Isa. 7:14), and reiterates his enduring presence with his disciples in his teaching (Matt. 18:20) and after the resurrection: "I am with you [ἐγὼ μεθ' ὑμῶν εἰμι] always" (28:20).[51] The notion of divine presence is by no means the only way in which Matthew articulates his Christology, but it is highly significant and is reinforced by its association with another Matthean motif, the mountain.

Mountains

Matthew often uses and draws attention to mountains as a setting for events in his Gospel.[52] The theological importance of mountains has been well established, and we have encountered the idea of the cosmic mountain in both ancient Near Eastern and Greco-Roman mythology, which is also reflected in the significance assigned to Sinai and Zion in the OT. Matthew's first mountain is the site for the third of Jesus's temptations, immediately after the devil takes Jesus to the "pinnacle of the temple" (τὸ πτερύγιον τοῦ ἱεροῦ, Matt. 4:5). The Scripture passage that the devil cites is from Ps. 91:11–12 (Matt. 4:6), a psalm that just two verses before describes the Lord as a dwelling place (מעון, Ps. 91:9; cf. 90:1).[53] This Hebrew word often refers to heaven and is also used of the temple,[54] and the argument of the psalm is that the one who makes God a refuge and dwelling place will know his protection. If a wider metaleptic allusion is at play here, then Jesus in 4:7 refuses a crass testing of this principle with appropriate reverence for God and his dwelling place in a way that is true to the individual described in Ps. 91.

In the very next verse, the devil takes Jesus to "a very high mountain" (ὄρος ὑψηλὸν λίαν, Matt. 4:8) from where he can see all the kingdoms of the world. This is reminiscent of Balaam and Balak's vantage point in Numbers (e.g., 23:13–14; 24:2) but surpasses it in its supernatural and visionary access

51. "The Messiah's abiding presence with his people constitutes a deliberate editorial clasp around the Gospel as a whole" (Bockmuehl, "Being Emmanuel," 3). On connections between Jesus's presence and the Jerusalem temple, see Bockmuehl, "Being Emmanuel," 7–8. On the distinctly Matthean aspects of this presence motif, see Kupp, *Matthew's Emmanuel*; Hays (*Echoes*, 162–75) goes further than Kupp in affirming that "Jesus is the embodied presence of God" (175).

52. See Donaldson, *Jesus on the Mountain*.

53. The temple setting for the second temptation suggests that interpreters are not limited to the Deuteronomic background of Jesus's responses but should look for other parallels (Donaldson, *Jesus on the Mountain*, 93–94).

54. For heaven, see Deut. 26:15; 2 Chron. 30:27; Jer. 25:30; Ps. 68:5 [68:6 MT]; Zech. 2:13 [2:17 MT]; for temple, see 2 Chron. 36:15; Ps. 26:8.

to a field of vision that is not physically possible.[55] The devil requests Jesus's worship as a shortcut to gaining the glory of all these earthly kingdoms. The emphatic description of the mountain's exalted status, in combination with the salience of worship and glory, carries all the connotations of holy mountain ideology, and this evocation is reinforced by Jesus's response that God alone is to be worshiped and served. Here he cites Deut. 6:13 but changes "fear" (φοβέομαι) to "worship" (προσκυνέω), answering the devil's question directly and reinforcing the cultic connotation of "serve" (λατρεύω, Matt. 4:10).

The next mountain of interest for our purposes is found at the transfiguration.[56] Here, as in Mark, Jesus takes his disciples "up a high mountain" (εἰς ὄρος ὑψηλόν, Matt. 17:1). The brightness of the transfiguration, the whiteness of Jesus's garments, the overshadowing of the cloud, and the response of fear all intimate the Sinai theophany,[57] as outlined for Mark's account above. Jesus's face shining like the sun (17:2) echoes and surpasses the brightness of Moses's face.[58] As Terence Donaldson states, "Apocalyptic mountains of revelation combined the biblical pattern of divine theophany with the cosmic notion of the mountain as the point of entry into the heavenly realm."[59] The words of the divine voice are once again a public declaration, precisely like in Matthew's version of the baptism (17:5; cf. 3:17), thus tightening the connection between the scenes. Matthew further enhances the apocalyptic nature of the transfiguration by highlighting the disciples' fear as they fall down on their faces (17:6) and the need for reassurance (17:7), as well as by referring to the event as a "vision" (τὸ ὅραμα, 17:9).[60] He heightens the connections between the transfiguration and Daniel's Son of Man by framing the passage within an inclusio that mentions the Son of Man four times and alludes to Dan. 7 (see Matt. 16:27, 28; 17:9, 12).[61] Additionally, the verb προσέρχομαι ("to approach") carries a potential cultic nuance with Jesus as subject (17:7). In three-quarters of the instances of this verb in Matthew, Jesus is the object; here in a cultically charged setting he becomes the subject, reassuring and

55. France, *Matthew*, 132.
56. Mountains are also the location of Jesus's teaching (Matt. 5:1; 24:3) and its subject (the city on a hill is presumably Jerusalem, 5:14; and the house built on rock might intimate the temple, 7:24–27) as well as sites for prayer and for healing and feeding miracles (8:1; 14:23; 15:29).
57. On the specifics, see France, *Matthew*, 644–51.
58. Davies and Allison, *Matthew*, 2:685–87. They draw out the Moses and Sinai connections.
59. Donaldson, *Jesus on the Mountain*, 142.
60. Donaldson, *Jesus on the Mountain*, 137–55; Moses, *Matthew's Transfiguration Story*, 86–89.
61. Moses, *Matthew's Transfiguration Story*, 85–113, esp. 91–103.

empowering the disciples with his presence (cf. 28:18, Matthew's only other use of the verb in this way).[62]

The Mount of Transfiguration, like the mount of teaching (Matt. 5:1), identifies Jesus as one "greater than Moses"—not only a teacher of God's people who ascends to meet with God and reflects his glory but one who himself bears God's glory.[63] The significance of the transfiguration extends to encompass the Gospel as a whole: it connects with the baptism and crucifixion scenes, as in Mark, but also, via the mountain motif, with the temptation (4:1–11) and the commissioning (28:16–20).[64]

On this final mountain of commissioning, after the resurrection, Jesus is worshiped (προσκυνέω, 28:17), and he declares his possession of "all authority in heaven and on earth" (28:18)—authority that is literally of "cosmic proportions."[65] This pairing of "heaven" and "earth" in Matthew usually denotes the cosmological split between the two spheres, but here they are reunited in the risen Jesus.[66] The passage is of great importance for the structure of the entire Gospel. The presence of Father, Son, and Holy Spirit forms a link with the baptism scene, where the Spirit is explicitly present and distinct from the divine voice, and also with the divine voice at the transfiguration. Jesus's closing proclamation "I am with you [ἐγὼ μεθ' ὑμῶν εἰμι] always, to the end of the age" (28:20) reprises and fulfills his naming as Emmanuel, "God with us" (μεθ' ἡμῶν ὁ θεός, 1:23). The affirmation of God's presence in Jesus on a mountain specifies both his identity and the outcome of his entire ministry, death, and resurrection in terms of divine emanation.[67] As one "greater than the temple" he overcomes the distinction between heaven and earth.

The Crucifixion and a Mini-apocalypse

The final scene in Matthew that calls for attention is the crucifixion. As noted above, Matthew disrupts Mark's tightly knit association of the moment of Jesus's death and the temple veil-tearing with the centurion's confession by

62. Edwards, "Use of ΠΡΟΣΕΡΧΕΣΘΑΙ."

63. On Matthew's Moses typology, which establishes Jesus as "more than a successor to Moses," see Hays, *Echoes*, 143–45.

64. "On these three mountains Matthew has depicted for us in bold but economical fashion the whole pattern of the path of obedient Sonship and its outcome" (Donaldson, *Jesus on the Mountain*, 155); so also Moses, *Matthew's Transfiguration Story*, 241–42.

65. Kupp, *Matthew's Emmanuel*, 240.

66. Pennington (*Heaven and Earth*, 345) further suggests that Matt. 28:16–20 forms a grand inclusio with Gen. 1:1, bringing heaven and earth back together in the person of Jesus just as God created them together at the beginning.

67. For the Sinai resonances here, see Kupp, *Matthew's Emmanuel*, 201–19.

inserting material that is unique to him: an earthquake, opening of tombs and resurrections, and the appearing of the raised to many in Jerusalem (27:51–53).[68] Daniel Gurtner characterizes the veil tearing as "an apocalyptic opening of heaven whereby the following material is conveyed as a heavenly vision depicting the sovereignty of God despite the tragic event of Jesus' death."[69] There are certainly strong apocalyptic overtones, including a possible allusion to the saints possessing the kingdom in Daniel 7:18–22 (cf. 12:2). The veil's association with the heavenly firmament is also salient here, just as it was in Mark. For Gurtner, the veil's tearing signifies the end of its shielding function, opening the way to visible and physical access to God and re-enabling access to Eden.[70] This is a maximal reading of the veil, but in the light of its cosmic symbolism and Matthew's baptism and transfiguration scenes, Gurtner is at least right to interpret it as a heavenly opening.

Yet this mini-apocalypse is not characterized as a heavenly or future vision,[71] unlike the transfiguration, which Matthew explicitly refers to as such. While these events are triggered by the heavenly phenomenon of the veil tearing "in two, from top to bottom" (27:51), they proceed from the earthly phenomenon of the earthquake (27:51, 54), which is "a symbol of the cosmic power of Jesus as the Son of God."[72] In place of Mark's lone centurion who makes an immediate confession, Matthew portrays others with the centurion and describes their observation of the earthquake and their great fear (ἐφοβήθησαν σφόδρα, 27:54) before their confession of Jesus's identity as Son of God. The sequence of earth shaking and rocks splitting, which prompts a corporate response of fear followed by confession of divine identity, evokes the Israelites' response to the theophany at Sinai (Exod. 19:16–25).

The resurrection scene bears similarities both to the mini-apocalypse (an earthquake, caused by an angel descending from heaven, 28:2) and to the transfiguration (white clothing, 28:3), and fear is an appropriate response to all three portents (28:4–5).[73] In Matthew's portrayal, the crucifixion and

68. The dead appear in Jerusalem only after Jesus's resurrection, but in narrative terms their raising is associated with Jesus's death. Davies and Allison (*Matthew*, 3:639) characterize these verses as "an explosion of the supernatural."

69. Gurtner, *Torn Veil*, 138. It is equally possible to see the events following the veil tearing as happening *due to* rather than *in spite of* Jesus's death. Regev (*Temple in Early Christianity*, 149) associates the veil tearing with new life.

70. Gurtner, *Torn Veil*, 186–93. Contrast Theophilos (*Abomination of Desolation*, 227–28), who reads the veil tearing as judgment foreshadowing the final consummation.

71. *Pace* Gurtner, *Torn Veil*; Waters, "Temporal-Spatial Collapse."

72. Regev, *Temple in Early Christianity*, 149.

73. Numerous commentators (e.g., France, *Matthew*, 1081–83) deal with the awkwardness of the location of the mini-apocalypse by situating it chronologically at the resurrection.

resurrection together (like the baptism) become a more public and general, indeed a cosmic, revelation of divine glory.

Conclusion

Neither Mark nor Matthew gives a detailed account of the structure or contents of heaven, its population, or the activities that take place within it. Yet both, in different ways, testify to a shared notion of heaven as temple. For Mark, heaven is the sanctuary "not built with hands." It is opened in an abrupt way at the outset of Jesus's ministry and in a similar fashion, but definitively, at its climax on the cross. The opening of the heavenly sanctuary reveals Jesus's identity, at first to privileged individuals—John the Baptist and three of the disciples—but then to an unnamed gentile centurion as a representative of all believers. Jesus not only experiences the opening of heaven in his baptism and a proleptic ascent in the transfiguration but also expects that he will in the future ascend as priestly Messiah to take up his place on the divine throne. In this light, Mark's hints at eschatological restoration in connection with the temple should not be taken only as intimations of cultic function passing to the church. Rather, they are associated with this cosmic sanctuary that is also an end-times temple.

For Matthew, the heavens are utterly distinct from the earth. The Jerusalem temple, as an earthly mirror of heavenly space, is the only place to overcome this separation. Matthew is thus aware of the scale of the cosmic breach necessary for the kingdom of the heavens to come fully on earth, and like Mark he holds that such a breach occurs in Jesus's baptism, transfiguration, and crucifixion. While Matthew does not follow Mark's structural parallelism, he heightens the apocalyptic resonances in these scenes and the connections with Israel's archetypal cosmic mountain, Sinai. The significance of mountains is extended as they become settings for pivotal moments in Jesus's ministry. Combined with the affirmation that Jesus bears God's presence, Matthew hints at a temple Christology in which heaven and earth are decisively reunited in Jesus, the one "greater than the temple." Temple Christology and temple cosmology find a related yet distinctive expression in Luke's two volumes, to which we now turn.

6

Luke and Acts

Ascension and Mission

Luke displays extensive interest in the Jerusalem temple and Jewish cultic and legal matters throughout his Gospel and Acts.[1] He also makes striking use of geography, tracing Jesus's movement to Jerusalem in the Gospel and then the expansion of the Way from Jerusalem to the ends of the earth in Acts. This geographical interest has often led commentators to see divine presence as passing from the Jerusalem temple to Jesus, the church, or both as the agents of this universal mission.[2] To focus only on the earthly plane, however, does not do Luke justice. At the center and hinge of his two volumes stands Jesus's ascension into heaven, the goal of the Gospel and the precondition for all that takes place in Acts. Thus Luke's use of motion cannot be treated on a horizontal plane alone, nor can it be regarded as a set of binaries (to or from Jerusalem; from temple to Jesus; from temple to church). Instead, it must be triangulated in relation to heaven. Only when we take into account heaven, including its cultic framing, can we make full sense of Luke's portrayal of Jerusalem, the earthly temple, Jesus, and the church's expansion.

1. There is consensus about the authorial unity of Luke and Acts, but their literary unity has recently been questioned. I take the two books as deliberately shaped with respect to one another, even if quickly separated in their early reception, but note Parsons and Pervo, *Rethinking the Unity*; and the essays in Gregory and Rowe, *Unity and Reception*.
2. For a review of scholarship and critique, see Moore, "'He Saw Heaven Opened,'" 38–40.

This chapter falls into two unequal parts. I first explore, relatively briefly, three temple themes: (1) the importance of the Jerusalem temple as a setting in Luke and Acts; (2) the significance of visionary experience and angelic visitations, especially in connection with the temple, for Luke's narrative across both volumes; (3) the subtle temple Christology, which emerges in Luke alongside the anticipation of ascension as a cultic inauguration and not only a royal exaltation. These thematic features set up the second, longer portion of the chapter. Here I lay out my key thesis, that Jesus's return to heaven effects a decisive shift: the openness of heaven as a sanctuary, and Jesus's action from within it, enables the universal mission. This dynamic is traced sequentially through Luke's two volumes in a series of events in which the boundary between heaven and earth is traversed: Jesus's trial and crucifixion; his ascension; the coming of the Spirit at Pentecost; Stephen's speech and vision; Paul's Damascus Road experience; and Cornelius's conversion. Recognition of the significance of these events as the re-establishment of a sanctuary that now embraces gentiles is cemented at the Jerusalem Council in Acts 15, consideration of which rounds off the second part of the chapter.

Temple Themes in Luke and Acts

Operation of the Temple Cult

Luke demonstrates a good knowledge of the temple system.[3] The Gospel's opening scene depicts Zechariah on duty with his priestly division (ἐν τῇ τάξει τῆς ἐφημερίας, Luke 1:8), chosen by lot to make the daily incense offering at the appointed time (1:9–10). Jesus is circumcised on the eighth day and later taken up to the temple for the purification offering (2:21–24).[4] Here the family encounters the righteous and prophetic individuals Simeon and Anna, for whom the temple is the apt location for prayer, fasting, and awaiting Israel's consolation. With his family, Jesus attends Passover in Jerusalem on an annual basis (2:41–51), and he describes the temple as "my Father's house" (2:49). The temple is a place where Jesus teaches and is the location for his confrontation with the Jerusalem authorities.[5] In part this conflict arises from Jesus's words and actions presaging the temple's destruction (19:41–48;

---

3. On Luke's treatment of the Jerusalem temple, see Bachmann, *Jerusalem und der Tempel*; Chance, *Jerusalem, Temple and the New Age*. Monier (*Temple and Empire*) argues that Roman respect for ancestral customs accounts for Luke's positive portrayal.

4. On Luke's familiarity with Second Temple Jewish purification practices here, see Thiessen, "Parturient Impurity."

5. Teaching: 19:47; 20:1; 21:1, 5, 37; confrontation: 19:45–20:8, 19–20, 27, 40, 45–47.

21:5–6, 20–24).[6] Nevertheless, Jesus presumes that appropriate sacrifices will be made and will have their effect, as with the healed leper whom he instructs to make a cleansing offering (5:14) and the tax collector's plea for atonement in the parable (18:9–14).

Like other Hellenistic Jewish authors we have encountered, Luke is careful to distinguish between the sanctuary proper (ναός or οἶκος)[7] and the temple complex (ἱερόν) in which it is situated. The temple courts are the location for prayer during the daily sacrifices, observed both in Jerusalem and at the same hour elsewhere (Luke 1:10, 21–22; Acts 10:2–3). Here it is worth recalling that the phrase in Acts 10:2 often translated "continually" (διὰ παντός) really indicates *regularly*—that is, twice-daily observance.[8] Followers of the Way after Jesus's ascension also join in with these observances, whether the *tamid* or the fulfillment of specific vows (Acts 3:1; 21:17–26), and the temple courts serve as the obvious venue in Jerusalem for the nascent Jesus movement to gather (Luke 24:53; Acts 2:46; 5:12–13). Luke's attitude to the temple is on balance positive, and he displays extensive familiarity with cultic matters.

Visionary Experiences

Where Matthew characterizes angelic visitations as dreams, Luke lays particular emphasis on visionary or ecstatic experiences of angelic figures or voices or, on several occasions, heavenly openings.[9] This expectation is established at the outset of the Gospel, during Zechariah's service in the outer chamber of the sanctuary: the angel Gabriel appears at the right side of the incense altar, near the veil to the most holy place (Luke 1:11), and tells him to expect a son who will be a prophet. The encounter is later described as a "vision" (ὀπτασία, 1:22). Zechariah's incredulity at Gabriel's message incurs a rebuke and loss of his faculty of speech.[10] The content of Gabriel's rebuke is noteworthy: he has been sent to give this message as one who stands before

6. Luke 13:35 reads "your house is left to you," though some manuscripts add "desolate" which would sharpen the critique (compare Matt. 23:38). For a full treatment of Jesus's (and Stephen's) destruction sayings in Luke-Acts, see S. Smith, *Fate of the Jerusalem Temple*.

7. Note that where Luke 11:51 speaks of the prophet Zechariah perishing between the altar (θυσιαστήριον) and the house (οἶκος), Codex Bezae has altar and sanctuary (ναός). The ναός denotes the entire sanctuary building, not just the most holy place, *pace* Lanier, "Luke's Distinctive Use," 435.

8. See chap. 4 above and Hamm, "Tamid Service in Luke-Acts."

9. Matthew characteristically speaks of messages or visitations occurring κατ' ὄναρ (1:20; 2:12, 13, 19, 22; 27:19), where Luke uses language of ὅραμα (Acts 7:31; 9:10, 12; 10:3, 17, 19; 11:5; 12:9; 16:9, 10; 18:9), ὀπτασία (Luke 1:22; 24:23; Acts 26:19), and ἔκστασις (Acts 10:10; 11:5; 22:17).

10. On the tension between these characters and their thematic function in opening the Gospel, see Cocksworth, "Zechariah and Gabriel."

God (1:19). This verse highlights the parallelism between Gabriel's current posture, standing by the most holy place (ἑστώς, 1:11), and his usual heavenly posture, standing before God's presence (ὁ παρεστηκὼς ἐνώπιον τοῦ θεοῦ, 1:19). Standing is the posture of active priestly service.[11] At the same time, the statement "I was sent" (ἀπεστάλην) emphasizes the *distance* between the earthly temple and heaven. Thus a parallel is implied between Gabriel and Zechariah along with an acknowledgment of the distinction between their heavenly and earthly spheres of service.

The temple is the setting for one other visionary experience, Paul's "trance" (ἔκστασις) in the temple courts (ἱερόν) during a period of prayer after his Damascus Road encounter with Jesus, as related to the crowd from the garrison steps in Acts 22:17. Aside from these two visions, Luke (unlike Matthew) does not directly correlate the Jerusalem temple with heaven, although there is an indirect connection in the parable of the pharisee and the tax collector. Standing far off—that is, further back in the temple courts—the tax collector "would not even look up to heaven" while he prayed (Luke 18:13). This evokes the tight link between heaven and the temple that is made, for example, in Solomon's prayer of dedication (1 Kings 8:30; 2 Chron. 6:21).[12]

Other visions and angelic visitations in Luke's narrative have multiple cultic resonances. For the most part, these will be covered in the specific episodes examined below, but one other early angelic encounter is worth mentioning here. After Jesus's birth, an angel suddenly "stood before" (ἐπέστη) shepherds in fields near Bethlehem (Luke 2:9).[13] There is no language of vision, but it is clearly a visitation.[14] Military features are present, but cultic aspects abound. For instance, the glory of the Lord shines around the shepherds, and they are appropriately fearful in response. Further, the many angels are an "army" (στρατία), but one that praises God, a feature mirrored in the shepherds' praise after finding the holy family (2:9–10, 13–15, 20). After praising God in the highest, the angels return to their heavenly point of origin (2:15). Alongside Gabriel's visit to Mary (which I discuss below), Luke opens his Gospel with

11. See esp. Let. Aris. 94, where priests sit only when off duty, and for further references and discussion, Moore, "Sacrifice, Session, and Intercession," 536.

12. Note also the language of heavenly bodies and powers shaking and of heaven and earth passing away in Jesus's apocalyptic discourse in Luke 21:25–26, 33.

13. Wilson (*Embodied God*, 257) notes that ἐφίστημι is "a favorite word of Luke's," which often "occurs in reference to the visual manifestation of heavenly characters."

14. Luke does not sharply differentiate the two, in that Gabriel's physical appearance to Zechariah can later be characterized as a vision; only in Acts 12:9 is a clear distinction drawn, where Peter thinks that he is merely seeing a vision, but an angel is actually present, leading him out of prison. Bifurcations between vision and physical encounter are in any case problematic because "visions are not viewed as 'subjective' or discounted as lesser forms of visual evidence in many ancient texts (especially of the religious variety)" (Wilson, *Embodied God*, 266).

three angelic appearances, the first in the temple and then two away from it but still within the confines of Israel. This may be an early intimation of the outward movement that will become pronounced in Acts: one that begins at the temple and spreads far abroad, but only via heavenly intervention.

Temple Christology

Numerous features throughout Luke's Gospel indicate that he casts Jesus as God's visitation of his people. When Gabriel is sent from God to Mary to announce the birth of Jesus, his initial message presents the child as a Davidic king. But in answer to Mary's question "How can this be?" (1:34), Gabriel answers, "The Holy Spirit will come upon you, and the power of the Most High will overshadow you" (1:35). The verb "overshadow" (ἐπισκιάζω) is used in all three Synoptic accounts of the transfiguration, but only Luke uses it more than once. It occurs only four times in the Greek OT, including at Exod. 40:35, where it describes the cloud of the Lord's glory filling the tabernacle (translating שָׁכַן ["to dwell"], cognate with הַמִּשְׁכָּן ["the tabernacle"]).

The theme is carried forward in language of visitation in Zechariah's song, which speaks of the Lord visiting (ἐπισκέπτομαι) and redeeming his people (Luke 1:68) and again of "the dawn from on high" visiting those who sit in darkness (same verb, 1:78–79). Zechariah's son will go before the Lord, preparing the way for this visitation (1:16–17, 76–77), evoking Mal. 3:1, which prophesies a messenger preparing the Lord's return to his temple.[15] For Luke, this pattern is fulfilled in the ministry of John the Baptist preparing a way for Jesus, and he thus equates Jesus with the Lord. Building on the Malachi allusion, when the infant Jesus is taken into the temple, Simeon's blessing over him states that he has seen God's salvation, "a light for revelation to the Gentiles" (compare the "dawn from on high," 1:78) and "glory to your people Israel" (2:32). When Jesus raises a young man back to life, those present exclaim that *God has visited* his people (ἐπισκέπτομαι, 7:16).

Luke's baptism scene is rather attenuated compared with Mark's, let alone Matthew's, but the core elements we saw in those Gospels remain: a heavenly opening, the descent of the Spirit, and the heavenly voice of affirmation and commissioning (3:21–22).[16] Luke's transfiguration engages themes similar to those in Mark and Matthew but with his own twist, which in a different way highlights temple themes. Jesus takes the three "up on the mountain" (9:28;

15. For a fuller treatment of the OT background of visitation, see Lanier, "Luke's Distinctive Use," 447–51.
16. On temple resonances in the baptism and transfiguration scenes, see Lanier, "Luke's Distinctive Use," 451–53.

not a "high" mountain, as in Mark and Matthew) for the explicit purpose of prayer (neither Mark nor Matthew specifies why they go). The topic of Jesus's conversation with Moses and Elijah is briefly indicated: "his departure," literally "his exodus" (τὴν ἔξοδον αὐτοῦ, 9:31). His death is about to take place in Jerusalem, but the resonances of *departure* (to heaven) and of *the* exodus are unmistakable and can only serve to highlight the Sinai setting, which Matthew also does, but via a different route. Moses and Elijah's appearance is "in glory" (ἐν δόξῃ, 9:31), and the sight of Jesus's "glory" causes the disciples to awake fully (9:32),[17] a striking double use of a theophanic term, which neither Mark nor Matthew uses here. The cloud and fearful response are shared with the other Gospels, but as noted above, Luke has already made careful use of "overshadow" (ἐπισκιάζω, 9:34; cf. 1:35) to describe the process of Jesus's conception in Mary, and the verb evokes the cloud filling the tabernacle and first temple at their consecration.

If Luke's Jesus represents the divine presence, can there also be room in his narrative for a notion of heavenly temple? I touched on this question in relation to Matthew in the previous chapter, and we will encounter it at its sharpest in relation to John in the following chapter. It is part of a wider issue, which I will revisit in the book's conclusion: Is temple imagery a zero-sum game? In what follows I argue that the heavenly temple becomes particularly prominent in the trial and crucifixion scenes in anticipation of the ascension. As the hinge for Luke's two books, the ascension represents the return of the divine presence in Jesus to its heavenly dwelling place, and as such marks a decisive shift in the availability of heavenly space. The ascended Jesus intervenes decisively from the heavenly temple to ensure the universal progress of the Way, with the church becoming the primary location for God's earthly presence by the Spirit.

Ascension, Cult, and Mission

Trial and Crucifixion

Luke's account of Jesus's trial is brief and omits the false charge regarding temple destruction.[18] While Jesus avoids the question as to whether he is the Messiah, his response to the high priest offers a combination of Dan. 7:13 and Ps. 110:1: "From now on the Son of Man will be seated at the right

17. Or "stay awake" (διαγρηγορήσαντες, so NRSV).
18. The charge is present in Acts 6:14. The omission from Luke's trial account is perhaps because it is not the ultimate grounds for Jesus's conviction and therefore unimportant; so Bock, "Son of Man," 183.

hand of the power of God" (Luke 22:69). Two features are noteworthy. First, Luke omits Mark's introductory "you will see" and the phrase "coming on the clouds of heaven" from Daniel. These omissions reshape the saying into a statement of Jesus's objective position and status. They reduce the emphasis on human experience and redirect the focus toward Jesus's resurrection and ascension rather than his eschatological return.[19] This balances Jesus's earlier statement that "they will see 'the Son of Man coming in a cloud' with power and great glory" (21:27), which relates to his return.[20] The use of the singular "cloud" (νεφέλη; contrast Mark 13:26; Matt. 24:30; Dan. 7:13 LXX, which all have the plural) connects this verse with Acts 1:9, where a cloud (also singular) hides Jesus from sight. The angels' comment that Jesus "will come in the same way as you saw him go into heaven" (1:11) indicates that his ascension and his return mirror each other. This mirroring is present in the Gospel as well: Jesus's earlier statement anticipates a heavenly location from which he will return in epiphanic glory, and his statement at the trial anticipates his imminent transition to that place.

Second, at the trial Luke adds the phrase "from now" (ἀπὸ τοῦ νῦν, 22:69), which further modifies the temporal situation of Jesus's exaltation. His heavenly location is a proleptic reality—not fully inaugurated until his ascension (and even then, hidden from many on earth)—but one that is presaged and demonstrated at his trial and, as we shall see, at the crucifixion.[21] What is more, the reference to a heavenly throne is evocative of the temple in general and the most holy place in particular. This episode, for Luke, sets up the significance of heavenly sacred space as Jesus's location even before the narrative reaches the ascension.

Turning to Luke's account of Jesus's crucifixion, at first sight this would seem to have less connection with heavenly temple than either Mark's or Matthew's account. Luke removes any verbal connection to the opening of the heavens at the baptism by not using "tear" (σχίζω) there and by changing the centurion's confession at the crucifixion to "a righteous man" rather than "Son of God." Nevertheless, Luke's passion has features that establish both cosmic and cultic associations.

Luke's account of the second criminal's exchange with Jesus includes the promise that "today you will be with me in Paradise" (23:43). "Paradise"

19. Johnson, *Luke*, 359–60.

20. This passage in Luke speaks not of geopolitical events but "entirely of cosmic events" (Johnson, *Luke*, 330).

21. So Franklin, "Eschatology of Luke-Acts," 192. Martin Bauspieß ("Überlegungen zur lukanischen Eschatologie," 139) makes this point more fully, tracing connections between Jesus's trial and Stephen's.

(παράδεισος) in the Greek OT refers to gardens, preeminently the garden
of Eden (e.g., Gen. 2:8; Isa. 51:3), but here it clearly transfers to a heavenly
realm (cf. 2 Cor. 12:4; the two senses coalesce in Rev. 2:7). This would appear
to intimate Jesus's imminent heavenly destination. The various symmetries
between Eden and the tabernacle or temple were noted in chapter 1, and we
will see below a further cosmic connection in Luke's crucifixion account.

Immediately after this scene, Luke recounts Jesus's death. He omits the
cry of Ps. 22:1 that appears in Mark and the associated confusion and offering of a drink. The effect of this is to bring the timing of the darkness (from
the sixth to the ninth hour) much closer to the veil tearing and Jesus's death.
These timings are mentioned by Mark and Matthew, but only in Luke and
Acts is the significance of the ninth hour elucidated as the hour of prayer, as
mentioned above.[22] Luke recounts the veil tearing before Jesus's death, rather
than after as in Mark and Matthew. This turns Jesus's cry of commending
his spirit (which is unique to Luke) into a response to the veil tearing—a response that is a prayer to God, a "communion at the last moment before his
death with the Father."[23] The centurion responds by praising God, and the
crowds beat their breasts, a sign of repentance. Praise is an activity that has
clear links with temple worship, and breast beating is an action that Luke has
elsewhere portrayed in Jesus's parable as the appropriately humble, penitent
response of the tax collector *in the temple*, an attitude that results in justification (18:13–14; note also 23:27).

Luke's juxtaposition of the evening hour of sacrifice and prayer with
the tearing of the temple veil in the context of an emphasis on heavenly
phenomena suggests that the cosmic sanctuary is in view. The three hours
of darkness are common to all three Synoptics, but Luke spells out an additional entailment of this statement: the sun stopped shining (a genitive
absolute, τοῦ ἡλίου ἐκλιπόντος, 23:45). This is highly uncharacteristic of
Luke, who normally removes redundancies from Mark's account rather
than introducing them, especially temporal and meteorological markers.[24]
More is going on here than mere naturalistic explanation or reduplication.
In Luke 22:53, darkness is symbolic of evil and is contrasted with Jesus's
teaching openly *in the temple*. Equally, while the sun can be simply a natural phenomenon for Luke (Luke 4:40; Acts 27:20), signs relating to the sun
portend the eschaton (Luke 21:25; Acts 2:20), and on the third telling, Paul's
vision of Jesus is described as "a light from heaven, brighter than the sun"

22. Sylva, "Temple Curtain," 245.
23. Sylva, "Temple Curtain," 243.
24. Compare Mark 1:32 (ὀψίας δὲ γενομένης, ὅτε ἔδυ ὁ ἥλιος) with Luke 4:40 (δύνοντος δὲ
τοῦ ἡλίου), and note Luke's omission of the timing of the crucifixion mentioned in Mark 15:25.

(Acts 26:13; cf. the brightness of the transfiguration scene, Luke 9:29, 31, 34–35).

Focusing on the sun's absence during the period of darkness highlights the fact that at the ninth hour, concurrent with the veil tearing, *the sun begins to shine again*.[25] The hour of the evening sacrifice, the rending of the sanctuary veil, and the transition in the heavens that allows the sun's light through once more are simultaneous events.[26] Collectively, they prompt Jesus's response of commending his spirit to God as he dies. Here Jesus's statement at his trial concerning his heavenly location "from now on" is salient: in Jesus's commending his spirit into heaven, Luke alludes back to the trial and forward to the ascension. The veil tearing functions as a narrative device to elucidate the cosmic phenomena surrounding Jesus's death, and it elucidates them in cultic terms. In connection with Jesus's expectation of his own bodily location in heaven after his ascension, his crucifixion and death offer an interim picture of a heavenly opening and revelation cast in temple terms, in which Jesus's spirit and that of the thief are proleptically received into God's garden-sanctuary.

Ascension to the Heavenly Sanctuary

Uniquely among the evangelists, Luke narrates the ascension of Jesus, and he does so twice: at the end of his Gospel and at the beginning of Acts.[27] In Luke 24:50–53, Jesus blesses his disciples (εὐλογέω), and while he is blessing them he withdraws from them and is carried up into heaven.[28] The disciples worship him (προσκυνέω) and then return to Jerusalem.[29] Here they are continually in the temple, blessing God (εὐλογέω; some manuscripts have "praising," αἰνέω, instead of or as well as εὐλογέω). As noted above, "continually"

---

25. For this reason, the veil tearing should be associated more closely with Jesus's death than with the darkness since it coincides with the *end* of the darkness. So Sylva, "Temple Curtain," 242–43; contra Brown, *Death of the Messiah*, 1103–6.

26. Compare Gospel of Peter 6.22, which makes explicit the sun's shining again at the ninth hour. It disrupts the synchronization by placing this after the veil tearing and Jesus's removal from the cross.

27. Though note that the later "longer ending" of Mark includes the ascension (16:19). Mikeal Parsons (*Departure of Jesus in Luke-Acts*, 189–99) accounts for Luke's reduplication in narrative terms as deliberate redundancy allowing variation and contextual connections rather than representing different sources. For Greco-Roman parallels to "a cloud-borne ascent to heaven," see Litwa, *How the Gospels Became History*, 187–93.

28. The twofold indication of movement is odd (active, possibly horizontal, withdrawal; passive, vertical, ascension) and is therefore the harder reading. Codex Bezae omits "and was carried up into heaven."

29. The mention of worship (the verb indicates prostration) in 24:52 *following* Jesus's ascent could be incongruous, and again Codex Bezae omits this phrase. Parsons (*Departure of Jesus in Luke-Acts*, 36–37, 49–52) opts for the shorter reading of both verses.

(διὰ παντός, 24:53) should be read not as "constantly" but as indicating the regular, twice-daily prayer times synchronous with the morning and evening sacrifices. The ascension itself receives little attention, and the Gospel offers no details about how it took place. The narrative perspective remains with the disciples, and no journey or ascent narrative is given. The ascension takes place in a context of blessing and worship, and two parallels are noteworthy: between Jesus and God as objects of worship, and between heaven and temple as settings for worship.

Acts offers a fuller account. The book opens with a prologue, harking back to Luke's first work. As is often noted, by describing his Gospel as an account of what Jesus *began* to do and teach (Acts 1:1), Luke implies that this second volume will be an account of his *continued* activity through the apostles and the Holy Spirit.[30] The first volume covered the period until "the day when he was taken up" (1:2). The passive form "he was taken up" (ἀνελήμφθη) is a clear spatial reference to his ascension, and it connects back to the key directional statement in Luke 9:51, which speaks of the days of Jesus's being "taken up" (the cognate noun ἀνάλημψις in its only NT occurrence). In Luke 9:51, Jesus sets his face to go to Jerusalem, and the choice of the wording "taken up" rather than a less ambiguous reference to death alone suggests that Luke is referring to his death, resurrection, and ascension together.[31]

The apostles gather together (συνέρχομαι, Acts 1:6), a word that can indicate gathering for worship (16:13; 1 Cor. 14:26). Following a brief dialog, Jesus is "lifted up [ἐπήρθη], and a cloud took him out of their sight" (Acts 1:9). I noted above that the singular "cloud" constitutes a link with Jesus's saying about his return in Luke 21:27, given that in Acts the "men in white robes" announce to the disciples that Jesus "will come *in the same way* as you saw him go into heaven" (Acts 1:11).[32] These verses are replete with verbs of sight describing the apostles' actions: looking, staring, seeing ([ἐμ]βλέπω, ἀτενίζω, θεάομαι, 1:9–11). Various epiphanic elements that are by now familiar are present here: vision, ascent, angels, bright clothing, and the cloud. These recall the transfiguration and resurrection scenes in Luke.[33]

30. E.g., Bruce, *Acts*, 30.

31. Parsons, *Departure of Jesus in Luke-Acts*, 133.

32. Rick Strelan's ("Ascension as a Cultic Experience," 229–32) reading of the cultic aspects of the ascension complements mine, though he regards Jesus's "coming" as visionary appearances to early Christians in worship, whereas with most commentators I take 1:11 as a reference to his parousia. Of course, this need not exclude the possibility of early Christian visionary experience.

33. Hay ("Moses and Elijah") argues that the phrase "and behold, two men" (common to Luke 9:30, 24:4, and Acts 1:10) implies that Moses and Elijah are present at the resurrection and ascension. This would further strengthen the connections between the three scenes.

While the verb describing the angels' presence (παρίστημι) is not in itself a technical term, in Luke-Acts it is used several times of angelic visitation and in connection with the temple or priests, and it denotes a standing position appropriate to worship, just as we saw in Luke 1 with Gabriel.[34] The echo of that earlier passage extends further: angels are present at the outset of each of Luke's volumes, in or near Jerusalem, in order to commission key protagonists (Zechariah, Mary, and the apostles). The location of the ascension is not initially specified, but in Acts 1:12 the apostles return to Jerusalem from Mount Olivet, which is just outside the city.[35] In the OT, this hill has cultic and eschatological associations (Ezek. 11:23; Zech. 14:4), and in later rabbinic tradition it is counted as part of the temple for ritual purposes.[36]

In all, Luke's ascension scenes are framed with epiphanic and cultic notions, but they do not offer a vista into heaven itself, which is obscured by the cloud. For this we need to look back to the vision of Jesus on the cross and forward to the vision of Stephen. The ascension is the essential stage, taking us from the former to the latter, and indeed forms the basis for all of the heavenly interventions in Acts that we turn to consider now.

Pentecost: The Coming of the Divine Presence

The coming of the Holy Spirit at Pentecost in Acts 2 fulfills a promise that has been repeatedly presaged (see Luke 3:16; Acts 1:5, 8). Numerous elements of the account evoke divine theophany, with allusions to Sinai.[37] The Holy Spirit is the emanation of God "from heaven" (Acts 2:2) and manifests as a "rushing, violent wind" (AT; like πνεῦμα ["spirit"], πνοή can also indicate breath) and as "tongues, as of fire."[38] Wind and fire occur together with an earthquake as part of the theophany to Elijah on Mount Horeb in 1 Kings 19:11–18. Fire as the complement of cloud is the visible representation of divine presence with the Israelites in the wilderness, going before them while

34. Angels: Luke 1:19; Acts 27:23; temple/priests: Luke 2:22; Acts 23:2, 4.
35. The village of Bethany (the site of the ascension in Luke 24:50) is on Mount Olivet. James Scott (*Geography in Early Judaism*, 57) regards this location as indicating that "Jerusalem is the omphalos connecting heaven and earth, a veritable *axis mundi* of intersecting horizontal and vertical planes."
36. See m. Parah 3:6; Ben-Eliyahu, "Mount of Olives," 29–31.
37. This has been argued extensively by Beale, "Pentecost: Part 1"; "Pentecost: Part 2." I refer the reader to the evidence he presents, though I do not think Pentecost represents the *extension* of the heavenly temple to the church but rather their *connection*, bringing the church into line with other earthly sanctuaries. For a judicious if ultimately skeptical assessment of specific Sinai correspondences, see Butticaz, *L'identité de l'Église*, 98–103.
38. Compare God's tongue "like a devouring fire" in Isa. 30:27–30; see also 5:24–25; Pss. 18:12 [18:13 MT]; 29:7–9.

journeying but settling on the tabernacle when at rest (Exod. 13:21–22; 40:34–38; Num. 9:15–23), and both are present at Sinai (Exod. 19:16–18; 24:15–18).[39] Closer still to Pentecost, fire emerges from the tabernacle at the consecration of Aaron and his sons as priests, when "fire [אֵשׁ/πῦρ] came out from the LORD and consumed the burnt offering and the fat on the altar" (Lev. 9:24). In Acts, the Spirit fills (πληρόω) not just the individuals but the house (οἶκος) where they are staying (2:2), intimating that God's presence in the apostles is equivalent to his presence at the inauguration of the tabernacle and temple (מלא/[ἐμ]πίμπλημι, Exod. 40:34; 1 Kings 8:10; 2 Chron. 5:13). The apostles themselves are also filled (πίμπλημι, Acts 2:4) with the Holy Spirit, at which point tongues of fire become tongues of speech (the same word, γλῶσσα, in both cases). Peter identifies the timing of these phenomena as the third hour (2:15), which is the time of the morning *tamid* sacrifice. As we have already seen, and will see again, the hours of the twice-daily sacrifices bear heightened significance for Luke as moments that are particularly susceptible to divine revelation.

When Peter explains to the crowd what is happening, he quotes from Joel, which describes the day of the Lord in terms that include heavenly portents.[40] The sun turning to darkness before the day echoes Luke's distinctive presentation of the darkness at the cross, which climaxes in the sun shining again, heralding the start of the day of the Lord. The terms for "sun" (ἥλιος) and "darkness" (σκότος) are common to both (cf. Acts 2:20, citing Joel 2:31, with Luke 23:44–45). Moreover, Peter's explanation highlights Jesus's agency as the one exalted to the right hand of God in line with Ps. 110:1, who from there gives the Holy Spirit (Acts 2:33–35). Some have suggested that Acts 2:33 echoes Ps. 68:18: "You ascended the high mount, . . . receiving gifts from people." This verse is widely associated with the ascent of Moses at Sinai in Jewish tradition.[41]

In its wider context, Pentecost alludes to the story of the Tower of Babel, seen most clearly in the Septuagint version (Gen. 11:1–9).[42] Wind is not mentioned in Gen. 11 but is often mentioned in retellings of Babel.[43] In Genesis,

39. Later Jewish tradition identifies Pentecost with the giving of the law at Sinai (e.g., Jub. 6.17–22; b. Pesahim 68b). Sejin Park (*Pentecost and Sinai*, 208–9) argues extensively for a Pentecost-Sinai connection in Acts, noting numerous similarities: divine descent, morning setting, the great sound and voices. He further notes (*Pentecost and Sinai*, 210–13) the many parallels between Philo's account of Sinai (*Decalogue* 33–47) and Luke's account of Pentecost.

40. Beale, "Pentecost: Part 1," 93–99.

41. E.g., in the targum; see Beale, "Pentecost: Part 2," 69–72. Compare Eph. 4:8–10, discussed briefly in chap. 8 below.

42. Beale, *Temple and the Church's Mission*, 201–3.

43. Jub. 10.26; Sib. Or. 3.101–3; Josephus, *Ant.* 1.118; Epiphanius, *Pan.* 2.11; see J. Scott, *Geography in Early Judaism*, 65nn134–35.

God "confounds" the people, just as the Jews gathered in Jerusalem for the festival are confounded (συγχέω, Gen. 11:7, 9; Acts 2:6). And the "divided tongues" of fire evoke the division of languages at Babel, a point reinforced by Luke's use of "tongues" (γλῶσσα) to refer to both flames and languages (Acts 2:3–4; cf. 2:8). The notion that Babel's divisions—which spread human beings over the "face of the whole earth" (ἐπὶ προσώπου πάσης τῆς γῆς, Gen. 11:4; cf. vv. 8–9)—are undone at Pentecost is reinforced by the gathering of Jews "from every nation under heaven" (ἀπὸ παντὸς ἔθνους τῶν ὑπὸ τὸν οὐρανόν, Acts 2:5).[44] What is more, scholars identify the Tower of Babel as an ancient Mesopotamian ziggurat, a temple built to imitate the cosmic mountain and so connect heaven and earth.[45] In this light, Babel's sin is not simply political hubris; there is also a religious transgression, the erection of an unsanctioned temple. Its reversal at Pentecost involves the divine Spirit coming down from heaven in a manner that is initiated and sanctioned by God to establish and inhabit a cultic place on earth. The way back to God is opened by divine initiative, as at Sinai and in the tabernacle, rather than by human initiative, as at Babel. The scattering of Babel (διασπείρω, Gen. 11:4, 8, 9) is reversed in both the gathering and the understanding of diaspora Jews, and later in Acts by the renewed scattering (διασπείρω) of those who have the divine Spirit (Acts 8:1). As we will see several more times in Acts, the spread of the universal mission is instigated by the action of the ascended Jesus from the heavenly sanctuary.[46]

Stephen: A Vision of Jesus's Priestly, Heavenly Service

We turn next to Stephen's trial, speech, and execution in Acts 6–7. In its setting in Acts, Stephen's speech seeks to answer the charges laid against him: that he blasphemes against Moses, God, "this holy place" (the temple), and the law (6:11–14).[47] In the course of his speech, Moses is vindicated and honored, God is portrayed as a transcendent agent, and the law is described as living oracles ordained by angels. Stephen's accusers, by contrast, are the ones who persecute the prophets (including Moses, see 7:37), oppose the Holy Spirit, and have not kept the law (7:51–53).

44. A further contrast is highlighted by the οἰκ- morpheme in the diaspora Jews' gathering to "dwell" (κατοικέω, Acts 2:5), as opposed to humanity's gathering to "build" (οἰκοδομέω, Gen. 11:4, 5, 8).

45. E.g., Wenham, *Genesis 1–15*, 236.

46. As Anderson ("Lukan Cosmology and the Ascension," 186–93) notes, Luke's "story is driven, in significant measure, by heaven" (186).

47. Following Stanton, "Stephen in Lucan Perspective"; so also Sylva, "Acts 7:46–50."

By comparison, the temple receives an apparently cooler reception. Some suggest that the static temple built by Solomon is condemned in favor of the dynamic, movable tabernacle (cf. Acts 7:44 with vv. 47–48).[48] The statement that "the Most High does not dwell in houses made with human hands" (7:48) uses a term that elsewhere in biblical literature denotes idols (χειροποίητος).[49] This coheres with the condemnation of the wilderness generation's idolatry (7:39–43).[50] However, the notion that God does not live in earthly dwellings applies equally to the tabernacle, which is described as instituted by God (7:44, alluding to Exod. 25:9, 40). This notion is supported by a scriptural quotation (Isa. 66:1–2), and it is a sentiment expressed by Solomon himself at the institution of the temple (1 Kings 8:27–30).[51] Further, there is no clear contrast in Acts 7:47 between the mention of the temple (introduced by δέ) and the tabernacle that preceded it (compare the strongly disjunctive ἀλλά in 7:48).[52] It seems clear, then, that Stephen's countercharge is not so much against the temple itself as against the people's attitude toward it and toward the God whose presence it represents.[53]

What is more, it is precisely the nature of heaven as sanctuary that Stephen stresses. This emphasis builds through the speech, and alongside a consistent focus on heaven is a more ambivalent stance toward the land and Jerusalem. God's glory appears to Abraham outside the land but directs him toward the land (7:2–3). Alongside the prediction of his descendants' slavery in Egypt comes the promise that "they shall come out and worship me in this place" (7:7). This citation of Exod. 3:12 has "this place" (Zion/the temple) rather than "this mountain" (הר/ὄρος; i.e., Horeb). Instead of an exclusive focus on Judea and Jerusalem, Egypt receives heavy emphasis, as does Shechem as the final resting place of Jacob and the ancestors (7:9–16). Moses's ministry begins when he receives a vision at Sinai (7:30–33), and he later receives living oracles from angels, also at Sinai (7:38). The people turn to idolatry precisely at the point when Moses is up the mountain (7:42–43). God institutes the tabernacle,

48. Marguerat ("Du temple," 306) tilts in this direction when he claims that "Luke takes the divine mode of presence with Israel during the exodus and the conquest of Canaan, and elevates it as a canonical model" (AT; "Luc érige ainsi en modèle canonique le mode de présence divine à Israël durant l'exode et l'entrée en Canaan."). See the opinions cited and counterargument mounted in Larsson, "Temple-Criticism and the Jewish Heritage," 388–94.

49. E.g., Lev. 26:1, 30; Isa. 2:18; 46:6; cf. Acts 17:24. Note also the discussion of this term in Mark's trial scene in chap. 5 above.

50. Sylva ("Acts 7:46–50," 269–72) argues that Stephen is refuting the charge that Jesus will destroy the temple made by hands.

51. Sylva ("Acts 7:46–50," 265–67) establishes this connection at greater length.

52. Sylva, "Acts 7:46–50," 263–65.

53. So, e.g., Witherington, *Acts of the Apostles*, 275. Contra Koester, *Dwelling of God*, 80–81, 98–99.

based on a heavenly pattern (7:44), and it travels with the people and is replaced by the temple under Solomon (7:47). That God's actual dwelling is in heaven, which Stephen elucidates by quoting Isa. 66:1–2, is not surprising; this is, after all, the God who has appeared and given revelation from heaven throughout Israel's history. What becomes more explicit in this quotation is the specifically cultic nature of heaven. It is God's throne, and the earth is his footstool, language that has royal as much as cultic connotations but that is further determined in temple terms by the use of "house" and especially "resting place" (7:49).[54]

This construal of heaven as sanctuary sets up the close of the speech. Stephen looks into heaven and sees God's glory and Jesus at God's right hand (7:55). There are clear echoes of the theophanies experienced by Abraham and Moses (7:2, 30–33, 38, 44) and also of the combination of Dan. 7:13 and Ps. 110:1 found in all three Synoptic Gospels.[55] When Stephen reports this vision to the crowd, he adds, "I see the heavens opened" (τοὺς οὐρανοὺς διηνοιγμένους, 7:56; cf. ἀνεῳχθῆναι τὸν οὐρανόν, Luke 3:21). The parallels with Jesus's death in Luke have been widely noted: both commit their spirits to a heavenly figure, their deaths follow immediately and are described similarly (τοῦτο εἰπὼν ἐκοιμήθη, Acts 7:60; τοῦτο δὲ εἰπὼν ἐξέπνευσεν, Luke 23:46), and they are buried by just men (Acts 8:2; Luke 23:50–53).[56] Given the cosmic significance of the veil tearing in Luke's passion, in both cases their final words are prompted by a heavenly opening. For Luke, these two episodes belong together: the cultic and cosmic aspects of Stephen's death reinforce those of Jesus's death and vice versa.

In addition to the use of Isa. 66 at the climax of Stephen's speech, two further details cement the cultic understanding of his vision. First, God's glory (7:2, 55) is a key term for explaining how God as a heavenly being might dwell in an earthly sanctuary. Israelites down the ages recognized the issue that Stephen highlights and circumvented it by reference to the Name, the Shekinah, and so forth as representations of God's presence.[57] Second, an

---

54. For "resting place" (מנוחה/נוח; ἀνάπαυσις/κατάπαυσις), see 2 Chron. 6:41; Ps. 132:8, 14 [131:8, 14 LXX].

55. Matt. 22:44//Mark 12:36//Luke 20:42; Matt. 26:64//Mark 14:62//Luke 22:69. Note that Ps. 110:1 also mentions a "footstool," a potential resonance with Isa. 66:1.

56. Sylva, "Temple Curtain," 243–45. Recognition of these parallels apparently led to their reinforcement in early textual transmission by the insertion of a prayer of forgiveness for enemies into Jesus's crucifixion on the model of Stephen's (cf. Luke 23:34 with Acts 7:60).

57. Esler, *Community and Gospel*, 153. His conclusion that Acts 7:48 is "outside the mainstream of Jewish opinion" overreaches, as Stephen's statement is qualified by his recognition of divine ordinance behind the tabernacle and of the importance of place earlier in the speech (as, e.g., Koester, *Dwelling of God*, 85, recognizes).

unusual detail, repeated twice, is that Jesus is *standing* at the right hand of God (7:55–56). This does not fit Ps. 110:1, in which an exalted Lord is invited to *sit* at YHWH's right hand, nor can it be found in any other allusion to Ps. 110:1 in the NT. This is the most frequently cited or evoked OT verse across the NT, and it is often quoted or paraphrased using terminology of sitting, being, or exaltation but nowhere else with "standing." Commentators are often baffled by this and suggest that perhaps Jesus is standing ready to receive Stephen's spirit,[58] to testify for him as a court witness, or to judge those who deny him.[59] A more convincing and coherent explanation, however, lies in the fact that standing is the appropriate posture of a priest and, indeed, of the angels in heaven in their priestly function. Jesus is thus presented as a priest standing in the heavenly sanctuary in service of God Most High.[60]

Stephen's speech, then, calls attention to the heavenly sanctuary as the true dwelling place of God and of Jesus, the Son of Man now exalted to priestly service. This transcendent perspective condemns the limited vision of his hearers and their attachment to the Jerusalem temple in an idolatrous and disobedient way. Yet this is not so much to point completely away from the temple toward the presence of God in Jesus and the community.[61] Rather, it points away from the supposed sufficiency of the Jerusalem temple and toward the heavenly sanctuary as the abode of God and of the risen, ascended Lord Jesus. The opening of this sanctuary to Stephen may pertain specifically to his martyrdom, but it is consonant with his proclamation of heaven as God's dwelling.[62] In the narrative of Acts, Stephen's killing "serves as a catalyst of mission" (8:1–3),[63] scattering believers from their gathering in Jerusalem in a way that simultaneously parallels and reverses Babel. Yet God's transcendence is not directly correlated with universal mission.[64] Rather, in Stephen's speech Luke highlights God's localization in the heavenly sanctuary, which is accessible in myriad places and not only in "this place"—that is, Jerusalem and its temple. Stephen's survey of salvation history demonstrates that God's

---

58. E.g., Sylva, "Temple Curtain," 244n13.

59. Peterson (*Acts*, 267) outlines these possibilities and opts for the last.

60. So Moffitt, "Atonement at the Right Hand," esp. 564–65.

61. E.g., for Peterson (*Acts*, 263n69), Stephen's teaching points "Jews away from the temple to the presence of God in the person of Jesus and in the Spirit-filled community created through faith in him."

62. Sleeman (*Geography and the Ascension*, 165) describes Acts 7:55–56 as "the culmination of what 7:49–50 projected, the heavenly 'house' not built by human hands that resolves debate concerning the cultic and cosmic dimensions of God's presence raised in these earlier verses."

63. Peterson, *Acts*, 268.

64. As Marguerat ("Du temple," 316) suggests, "His [God's] radical transcendence serves the cause of divine universality" (AT; "Sa radicale transcendence [*sc.* de Dieu . . .] est mise au service de l'universalité de Dieu.").

presence was, by divine ordinance, accessed in tabernacle and temple and that it has also always been available at his initiative in other ways, times, and places. It is to this latter theme that Luke increasingly shifts the emphasis as his narrative progresses.

Paul: A Vision of Jesus's Glory

Paul's striking Damascus Road experience carries such weight for Luke that he tells it three times, once directly as part of his narrative and twice in Paul's own words in public addresses (Acts 9:1–19; 22:6–21; 26:12–19).[65] Here I take all three tellings together in order to highlight the epiphanic and cultic aspects of Jesus's visionary appearance, which turns Paul from opponent of the Way to foremost protagonist of the gentile mission.

The timing of the event is not clear in the first telling but is specified in Paul's words as "about noon" (περὶ μεσημβρίαν, 22:6) and "midday" (ἡμέρας μέσης, 26:13). This time is not correlated with the morning or evening sacrifice, but it is the time at which Peter prays and receives his vision (10:9). A thrice-daily prayer pattern coordinated with the daily sacrifices with the addition of a prayer at noon is attested in the Second Temple period alongside the twice-daily pattern.[66] It is therefore an auspicious time for a vision, despite Paul's own disposition, which is far from prayerful ("breathing threats and murder," 9:1), unlike other recipients of visions in Luke and Acts.

There is a light from heaven (ἐκ τοῦ οὐρανοῦ, 9:3; 22:6; οὐρανόθεν, 26:13), which is amplified in the retelling from simply a light, to a great light, to a light brighter than the sun. Internally and across all three visions, there is a deliberate interplay of sight, hearing, and inability to see and hear. In Acts 9, Paul hears a voice/sound (Luke plays on the polyvalency of the term φωνή) and speaks with Jesus, while his companions hear a voice/sound but see nothing. Paul's encounter is later described by Barnabas as seeing the Lord (εἶδεν τὸν κύριον, 9:27). In Acts 22, Paul hears a voice/sound, and his companions see the light but do not hear the voice/sound. Paul is to become a witness to what he has seen and heard (ὧν ἑώρακας καὶ ἤκουσας, 22:15). And in Acts 26, Jesus states that he has appeared to Paul, and Paul is to testify to what he has seen and to what Jesus will show him (ὧν τε εἶδές [με] ὧν τε ὀφθήσομαί σοι, 26:16). In this final telling, the companions have all but disappeared from

65. For a narrative rather than source-critical approach to the retellings, see Witherup, "Functional Redundancy." The Damascus Road encounter is better characterized as a "call" rather than a "conversion" (see Fredriksen, "Paul the 'Convert'?"), so long as space is given for a significant change in his core orientation, as both Luke and Paul himself relate it. On this, see Du Toit, "Was Paul a Christian?"
66. See, e.g., Dan. 6:10; Ps. 55:17; and Beckwith, "Daily and Weekly."

view. It is noteworthy that at Sinai the Israelites are said to have *seen* God's *voice* (Exod. 20:18 in both MT and LXX; cf. Ps. 29:7).[67] The play on seeing and not seeing fits the characterization of Paul's experience as a "heavenly vision" (οὐρανίος ὀπτασία, Acts 26:19) to which others both were and were not party in that they knew it was taking place but did not directly experience either the sight or the speech of Jesus.

We have already noted that Paul has a further vision while in the temple precincts, which is reported rather than narrated (22:17). This coheres with what we saw in the Gospel, that both the temple and other places are possible and appropriate locales for visionary encounters. In the same speech, Paul describes the intense light of Jesus on the Damascus Road in terms of glory: he could not see "because of the glory of that light" (ἀπὸ τῆς δόξης τοῦ φωτὸς ἐκείνου, 22:11 AT; "brightness" NRSV). The superlative terms in which Paul expresses his vision of Jesus indicate his heavenly and divine status as one worthy of worship and of address as "Lord."[68] Following the vision, Paul immediately sets to proclaiming Jesus, in particular to the gentiles (9:15; 22:15, 21; 26:17, 20, 23). By divine orchestration, Paul is first unwittingly the instigator of a new diaspora as persecutor (8:1) and then actively engages in the mission to the gentiles as an apostle. It is the heavenly intervention of the glorified Jesus that turns him from one to the other.

Cornelius: Gentile Participation in Heavenly Worship

Luke records one further and decisive series of heavenly interventions, which enable the shift toward gentile mission and thus the fulfillment of the programmatic statement of Acts 1:8. Here again my concern is to emphasize the oft-overlooked cultic framing of these events. Cornelius is introduced as devout and God-fearing, committed to almsgiving and to regular prayer (Acts 10:2). As we have seen, the term "regular" (διὰ παντός; "constantly" NRSV) is a technical term in the Septuagint for the *tamid*, the regular, twice-daily sacrifices in the tabernacle and temple. In a striking confirmation of this point, Cornelius's vision occurs at "the ninth hour" (Acts 10:3 NASB): it is during his time of prayer, coordinated with the afternoon *tamid* sacrifice, that he receives an angelic visitation. Readers of Luke-Acts already have reason to see the ninth hour as a time of day particularly susceptible to

67. For rabbinic texts attesting the *visibility* of divine speech or Torah, see Haynes, "Voices of Fire," 37–43. There is a further similarity to Sinai in that the experience of Moses's companions differs from his own (Exod. 24:9–15), although, like the three disciples in Luke's transfiguration, their experience is fuller and more privileged than that of Paul's companions.

68. On the veneration of Jesus as divine in Acts, see S. Walton, "Jesus, Present and/or Absent?"

divine action (Luke 23:44–48; Acts 3:1–10), precisely because it is an hour of prayer.

The angel's words to Cornelius affirm his piety and inform him that his prayers and almsgiving "have ascended as a memorial before God" (Acts 10:4). The term "memorial" (μνημόσυνον) occurs in Leviticus to describe offerings of grain (translating אזכרה, from the root זכר, "to remember"; Lev. 2:2, 9, 16; 5:12; 6:8) and in Sir. 45:16 in association with Aaron's incense offering (the *tamid* is mentioned in 45:14). There are also parallels between Cornelius and Zechariah: both are upright figures (Zechariah is righteous and blameless, Cornelius devout and God-fearing) and receive an angelic visitor who informs them that their prayers have been heard.

The scene moves to Peter in Joppa, who is also engaged in prayer, at the sixth hour (i.e., midday, Acts 10:9). As we saw with Paul above, this is also a privileged time for prayer and visionary experience. Peter receives a vision that explicitly involves the opening of heaven (Acts 10:11; cf. 7:56; Luke 3:21). Heaven is the source of the lowered sheet containing animals in Acts 10:16 and is emphasized in the retelling in 11:5. It seems likely that the giver of the vision is Jesus and not God: Peter addresses the one who speaks to him as "Lord" (10:14), the voice refers to God in the third person (10:15), and Peter argues, refusing to comply *three times* (10:16; cf. Luke 22:34, 56–62).[69] Just as Cornelius's vision joins an array of angelic visitations throughout Luke-Acts, so Peter's vision joins a series of heavenly openings with (since the ascension) Jesus at the right hand of God.

Peter sees the forbidden animals and is instructed to kill and eat. In response, he protests that he has never eaten anything "common" (κοινός) or "impure" (ἀκάθαρτος). These are technical terms, referring to what is profane (as opposed to holy) and ceremonially unclean (as opposed to ceremonially clean), and while they relate to the kashrut food laws, these are basically a derivation and extension of the purity laws surrounding levitical worship.[70] Peter does not, so far as Luke relates, kill and eat.[71] Instead, the vision's meaning and purpose become clear to the reader once Peter reaches Cornelius's house two days later (10:23–28), though for Peter it seems to have been clear from the moment he decided to go with Cornelius's emissaries (see 10:29; 11:12). Cornelius falls down to honor Peter but is quickly corrected (10:25–26). The verb describing

69. So Sleeman, *Geography and the Ascension*, 226.
70. A key study here, supportive of the non-abrogation or anti-abolitionist reading, is Moxon, *Peter's Halakhic Nightmare*.
71. Indeed, the Jerusalem Council's decision in Acts 15 would seem to insist that gentiles observe certain purity regulations, though not the full kashrut. While *distinctions* between gentiles and Jews are not entirely effaced, any *divisions* that these might potentially cause are removed.

Cornelius's actions, προσκυνέω, is typically translated "worship" (so NRSV) but can also indicate other forms of reverencing. Cornelius's error is curious: though he did not attempt to worship the angel in his vision, he appears to mistake Peter for an angel or some other heavenly being.[72] Whatever the reasons for it, this action fronts questions of worship and not only of purity.

Peter explains that, although it is "unlawful" (ἀθέμιτος) for him to associate with gentiles, nevertheless God has shown him that he should not call any *person* (ἄνθρωπος) common or unclean (10:28). He associates the same purity terminology (κοινός and ἀκάθαρτος) from his vision with human beings and not with animals or food. Significantly, both in the narrative and in Peter's account to the Judean believers, the Spirit twice tells Peter not to make a distinction (μηδὲν διακρινόμενος, 10:20; μηδὲν διακρίναντα, 11:12; cf. 15:9). In the second case, Peter is explicitly prohibited from distinguishing "between persons," and the same meaning holds for the first.[73] The verb διακρίνω has a wide semantic range but does not in the Septuagint translate key "division" terms (such as the hiphil of בדל, which occurs in Gen. 1:6–7; Exod. 26:33; Ezek. 42:20). However, it can evoke the dividing function of the priests and the sanctuary veil or wall, as is notably indicated by its use to describe the discerning or judging function of the priests in Ezekiel's eschatological temple, which occurs immediately after their didactic role in teaching the people to distinguish holy from common and clean from unclean (Ezek. 44:23–24). Peter again applies cultic language to people when he responds to Cornelius's account of his vision by describing all who fear God and practice righteousness as "acceptable" (δεκτός) to God (Acts 10:35).[74] While Peter is still in mid-flow, the Holy Spirit is poured out on his hearers, a divine passive made explicit in the retelling (cf. Acts 10:44–45 with 11:15–18). The Spirit's descent at Pentecost is explicitly said to have originated from heaven (2:2); here it suggests that Cornelius and his associates are considered forgiven and pure.[75]

The whole Cornelius episode, then, is a challenge to the regulations governing association with gentiles, but it is the result of a reconfiguration of the more fundamental and prior distinctions in operation in the Jerusalem temple. Cornelius is portrayed in terms befitting a devout Jew and receives

72. Peterson, *Acts*, 333. This is potentially something of a type scene, given the parallel later in Acts where the people of Lystra mistake Paul and Barnabas for Hermes and Zeus (Acts 14:11–18).

73. Contra NRSV, which translates 10:20 as "without hesitation"; this is a possible meaning of διακρίνω but is overridden by the context of Acts 10–11, where partiality (10:34) and distinctions between peoples are in view.

74. See, e.g., the LXX of Exod. 28:38; Lev. 1:3; Isa. 56:7; cf. Phil. 4:18; Sleeman, *Geography and the Ascension*, 239.

75. Moffitt, "Atonement at the Right Hand," 560–62.

benefits that hitherto in Luke-Acts only privileged Jews have received. These benefits, moreover, have strong associations with both the temple and Jerusalem. Yet Cornelius has not become a proselyte but remains a God-fearing gentile. Are we then to conclude that "the Temple has not been opened up to non-Jews; it has been replaced"?[76] This conclusion might seem reasonable, but it fails to take account of the place of heaven in the narrative and the consistently careful and positive use of cultic categories and terminology. The evidence considered above strongly suggests that Cornelius is engaged in temple-shaped worship of God in heaven, and the events that unfold vindicate this worship and incorporate him fully into the people of God. The transition, then, is not from the Jerusalem temple to the new community via Jesus. Rather, it is a transition from the temple to a refocalization on what the temple was always and only imaging, the heavenly sanctuary. This transition validates cultic categories and at the same time expands them in a way that partially undoes their instantiation in the Jerusalem temple in the era of Israel. The heavenly temple is accessible to Jews and gentiles alike in a way that the Jerusalem temple never was. The distinction of peoples no longer obtains *precisely because* access to the celestial sanctuary through Jesus and the Spirit enables all people everywhere to worship Israel's God.

James: Rebuilding David's Fallen Tabernacle

One further episode in Acts forms an apt final stop in the argument of this chapter. The Jerusalem Council does not involve a heavenly opening, intervention, or vision. Yet for Luke it represents the reaching of a consensus that enables Paul's missionary work among gentiles to continue all the way through to his arrival in Rome. Following a summary of the position of the circumcision party (15:1–5) and then of Peter's position (15:7–12), James speaks. His verdict includes a conclusion (God has visited the gentiles, 15:13–14) and conditions (observing four basic purity requirements rather than the full law, 15:19–21). Between these two elements, James offers scriptural support for his decision, citing Amos 9:11–12 (Acts 15:15–18). These verses refer to "all other peoples" and "all the Gentiles" seeking the Lord, but this occurs only and directly as a result of rebuilding "the fallen tent of David" (τὴν σκηνὴν Δαυὶδ τὴν πεπτωκυῖαν, AT) and restoring[77] its ruins (τὰ κατεσκαμμένα, Acts 15:16).[78]

76. So Esler, *Community and Gospel*, 162.
77. The verse uses a series of words beginning with αν- (ἀναστρέψω, ἀνοικοδομήσω, ἀνορθώσω), which has much the same meaning and effect as the prefix *re-* in English (return, rebuild, restore).
78. This substantive participle comes from a verb (κατασκάπτω) that in the Septuagint often refers to the tearing down of altars or temples (e.g., 1 Kings 19:10; 2 Macc. 14:33; Jdt. 3:8).

Richard Bauckham argues that "tent" should be understood not as Davidic dynasty or sovereignty[79] but as the eschatological temple—that is, the church.[80] This is in keeping with the identification of James, Cephas, and John as "pillars" (Gal. 2:9) and with community-as-temple imagery elsewhere in Paul and at Qumran. This reading of Acts 15 becomes clearer in light of the differences from Amos: in place of the Hebrew "on that day I will restore," the citation in Acts opens "after these things I will return and rebuild" (Acts 15:16 AT). "After these things" (μετὰ ταῦτα) alludes to Hosea 3:5, which has other echoes in the Acts citation: Hosea's context is the postexilic restoration of the temple.[81] Bauckham argues in detail that this passage offers halakhic justification for the decision that James hands down, including not only the incorporation of gentiles but the specific purity restrictions required of them.[82] Bauckham's case is convincing and coheres with the cultic connotations of the Spirit's presence at Pentecost and with Cornelius. Yet it need not exclude reference to a heavenly sanctuary in addition to the restored earthly one, given the close interrelationship between the two. This is precisely what we find in the context of the Amos citation.

Amos 9 contains an oracle against the idolatrous temple of Bethel in which the Lord visits and destroys the sanctuary and pursues the false worshipers to the ends of the earth (9:1–10). As part of this oracle, God identifies himself as "one who builds his upper chambers in the heavens, / and founds his vault upon the earth" (Amos 9:6). The Hebrew "his stairs" (מעלותו in the consonantal text) is often amended to "his upper chambers" (עליתו) as in the NRSV, though either reading makes sense of the building imagery, given the prominence of steps as a feature of ziggurats and other temples.[83] In response to an idolatrous temple, God affirms his status as creator of the whole universe as his temple. In this context, the reference to David's "tent" in the singular (סכת דויד/τὴν σκηνὴν Δαυίδ, Amos 9:11), while it could denote the Festival of Booths/Tabernacles or the city of Succoth,[84] could also be read as a tabernacle, a possibility heightened by language of "seeking" and the divine

79. Many commentators note the oddness of "tent" instead of "house" in Amos 9:11 but read it as "house/dynasty" all the same (e.g., Bruce, *Acts*, 294; Hubbard, *Joel and Amos*, 253–55).

80. Bauckham, "James and the Jerusalem Church," 452–62.

81. Jeremiah 12:16 and Isa. 45:21 are also in view (Bauckham, "James and the Jerusalem Church," 454–55).

82. The purity restrictions derive from the four instructions for those "in the midst of" (בתוך, Jer. 12:16) God's people in Lev. 17–18.

83. Sweeney, *Twelve Prophets*, 1:270–71. The LXX seems to confirm the MT here, translating "ascent" or "stairs" (ἀνάβασις). Note too the presence of steps at least in the second temple (m. Middot 2.5; m. Sukkah 5.4).

84. So, respectively, Sweeney, *Twelve Prophets*, 1:273; Stuart, *Hosea-Jonah*, 395–99.

name (Amos 9:12).[85] Whether or not David restored a sanctuary is beside the point;[86] the language of breaches and ruins is suggestive of the temple building that replaced the tabernacle through David's planning and preparations (1 Chron. 22:2–5), and Amos's oracle promises that *God*, not David, will restore the fallen tent. While the oracles of Amos 9 may have originated separately, in the final form of the book their juxtaposition is suggestive: we move from condemnation of an idolatrous temple, to the heavenly temple, to a promised restoration of Israel's sanctuary in which the gentiles will be able to join in worship.

With this movement in mind, Amos's oracle serves as a concise summary of the dynamic traced repeatedly in this chapter. Jesus's ascension to the heavenly sanctuary and his outpouring from there of the Spirit as the locus of God's presence on earth leads to renewal, including the gentiles seeking God. This is what happened with Cornelius, as Peter has reminded the council, and it is what James as presiding elder now confirms from Scripture.

Conclusion

Luke has great respect for the Jerusalem temple and its associated regulations. Yet he recognizes that its function was only ever derivative from the heavenly sphere that it represented. In Jesus's life and ministry, Luke sees God's renewed visitation of his people; in Jesus's trial and death, Luke intimates the cultic nature of heaven. Unlike the other evangelists, Luke not only anticipates but twice narrates the return of Jesus to the heavenly realm. In his second volume, we see the consequences of this relocation. The priority of the heavenly sanctuary, as the location of the presence of God in Jesus and the departure point of the Holy Spirit, forms the essential presupposition for the universal mission. As Steve Walton puts it, "Heaven is now 'open for business' on a permanent basis."[87] While this is true, it is also the case that at certain junctures the gentile mission makes critical advances only via specific heavenly interventions of the glorified Jesus, interventions that are correlated with the celestial rhythms of temple worship. A binary, horizontal framing of Luke's two volumes is thus insufficient. God's place and presence is not now everywhere instead of exclusively in Jerusalem or

---

85. Amos 9:11–12 likely has an origin different from the earlier parts of Amos 9, but their occurrence together in the final form of the text invites the reading "tabernacle."

86. Keener (*Acts*, 2255–57) is unconvinced by the temple reading on these grounds.

87. S. Walton, "Heavens Opened," 68.

the temple. Rather, it remains preeminently in heaven. Yet through Jesus this place is now accessible from every place by the agency of the Spirit present in a renewed people of God, both Jew and gentile. Universal access to heaven through worship in Spirit is also a concern of John's Gospel, to which we now turn.

7

John

Emanation and Dwelling

It is widely held that in John's Gospel, Jesus is the temple. This connection is made explicitly at one point and is supported by strong intimations in other places, which cumulatively build toward a temple Christology. John also speaks of the Jerusalem temple at several points, and the annual festivals are particularly important for the progression of his narrative and his Christology. A point of special interest (and difficulty) for studies of the historical Jesus is John's location of a temple-clearing incident at the outset of Jesus's ministry rather than at its climax as the preeminent cause for his death, as in the Synoptic Gospels.[1] In and among this dual focus on the Jerusalem temple and Jesus-as-temple, there seems to be little interest in the church or Johannine community as temple, though some have suggested otherwise.[2] The crucial point for this book, however, is that there is apparently little or no interest in the heavenly temple. Moreover, scholarship has often tended to view temple imagery as a zero-sum game: if Jesus is identified with the temple, then neither the building in Jerusalem nor heaven can be such, and the church can be a temple only by identification with the body of Jesus. In this chapter, I wish to contest both the apparent absence of the heavenly temple

1. On which, see McGrath, "'Destroy This Temple.'"
2. Mary Coloe (*God Dwells with Us*) sees the temple identity transferring to the Johannine community following Jesus's departure.

148 The Open Sanctuary

and this zero-sum approach. Despite the absence of key scenes that we have studied in the previous two chapters—Jesus's baptism, transfiguration, and the veil tearing at the crucifixion—the Fourth Gospel's interest in the temple does extend to heaven. My thesis in this chapter can be simply stated: John's temple Christology both presupposes the notion of a cosmic sanctuary and is in turn reinforced by it.[3]

The chapter is divided into six parts, each of which treats a passage of particular relevance, proceeding through the Gospel in narrative sequence. We begin with the Prologue, where the Logos is the emanation of divine Wisdom tabernacling now in flesh. We then consider the evocation of Jacob's Bethel vision at the end of John 1, which I argue portrays Jesus as fulfilling the functions of a patriarchal cult place. Next we turn to the temple clearing, where Jesus's body is explicitly identified with the temple. This is consonant with the emerging picture but also prepares the multivalent sense of the "Father's house," which is picked up later in the Gospel. The fourth passage of interest is the encounter with the Samaritan woman, where Jesus relativizes the importance of earthly cult places while reaffirming the necessity of the Spirit's presence in order to access God in heaven. I then examine the shepherd and sheepfold imagery of John 10 in the light of 1 Enoch, arguing that there may be intimations of an eschatological temple in the "sheepfold-courtyard" language. Finally, we arrive at John 14, a passage that in popular imagination has often suggested the heavenly temple or, due to the KJV's unfortunate use of "mansions," perhaps a heavenly Mayfair or Beverly Hills. Here, against recent arguments that the "house" is Jesus and the "dwellings" are solely relational, I argue that the heavenly temple is indeed in view. Jesus, who throughout John's Gospel is multiply portrayed as an earthly sanctuary of varying sorts, thus gives access to the Father's house in heaven.

The Emanation of Wisdom as the Word

One of the climactic phrases in John's Prologue describes the incarnation as the Word becoming flesh and living, or dwelling, among us (1:14).[4] The Greek verb "to dwell" (σκηνόω) is linked to the word for "tent" or "tabernacle"

---

3. Joseph Greene ("Jesus as the Heavenly Temple") makes a similar case from many of the same texts. He does not distinguish the Word as divine emanation or presence from heavenly temple as location. This may partly explain his omission of John 14:1–6, where the two are clearly distinct. See also Kinzer ("Temple Christology," 454–57), who connects John's temple Christology with heaven.

4. Behr (*Paschal Gospel*, 264) describes this as "the verse that has reverberated most profoundly and forcefully across all later theological reflection."

(σκηνή). To translate "the Word tabernacled among us" might nevertheless seem tendentious were it not for the immediate context.[5] The Prologue uses several terms associated in other Jewish literature with the emanation of the divine presence and power, whose significance is primarily to be sought in Wisdom traditions.[6]

Proverbs emphasizes Wisdom's presence and role in creation, before the primordial cosmic features such as depths, springs, mountains, heavens, and fountains of the deep were formed (8:22–31; cf. 3:19–20). There is a possible temple allusion in Wisdom's building her house (בֵּיתָהּ/ἑαυτῇ οἶκον, 9:1), with its seven pillars matching archaeological discoveries of temple remains in the Near East. This likelihood is enhanced by the contrast with Folly, who is portrayed as a cult prostitute (7:10, 14, 21–23) with a house of her own (בֵּיתָהּ, 7:27). This need not imply that Wisdom is a distinct goddess (Folly, by contrast, might bear comparison to the Canaanite goddess Astarte).[7] Rather, Wisdom dwells in a temple as an instantiation of God's presence. These cultic connections are more developed in later wisdom writings.

Wisdom of Solomon describes Wisdom as "a breath [ἀτμίς] of the power of God, / and a pure emanation [ἀπόρροια] of the glory [δόξης] of the Almighty; / . . . a reflection of eternal light [φωτὸς ἀϊδίου]" (7:25–26),[8] who excels the sun, stars, and all natural light (7:29; cf. 17:20–18:2). Wisdom was present and active in creation (9:1–2, 9) and is sent forth to make humans wise (e.g., 7:27; 8:9; 9:4). However, Wisdom's function is not only to make individuals wise as Torah, instruction, and divine word. Her presence with God is in "the holy tent [σκηνῆς ἁγίας] that [God] prepared from the beginning [ἀπ᾽ ἀρχῆς]" (9:8), and she is sent forth "from the holy heavens [ἐξ ἁγίων οὐρανῶν], / and from the throne of [God's] glory [ἀπὸ θρόνου δόξης σου]" (9:10; cf. 9:4). It is thus by Wisdom that the temple and altar are built on Zion as a copy (μίμημα) of the heavenly sanctuary (9:8).[9]

Similar resonances can be found in Sirach, where Wisdom dwells (κα-τεσκήνωσα) in the highest heavens and has a throne in the cloud (24:4). She seeks a resting place (ἀνάπαυσις, 24:7) and God "causes [her] dwelling [or tabernacle] to rest" in Israel (κατέπαυσεν τὴν σκηνήν μου, 24:8 AT, which NRSV renders "chose the place for my tent"). Likewise, in Bar. 3:28–37 [3:28–38 LXX], Wisdom is not found by the giants but does ultimately appear on earth

5. See Macaskill, *Union with Christ*, 172–74.
6. So Meeks, "Man from Heaven," 46.
7. E. Davis, *Proverbs, Ecclesiastes, and the Song of Songs*, 71.
8. Winston (*Wisdom of Solomon*, 184) describes this as emphatic and "very bold language" for emanation.
9. Winston (*Wisdom of Solomon*, 203–5) expands on the heavenly temple connections here.

and live among humans (συναναστρέφω, 3:38 LXX). In Sirach, Wisdom was created before the ages, from the beginning (ἀπ' ἀρχῆς, Sir. 24:9; cf. 1:1–10). She ministered "in the holy tent" (ἐν σκηνῇ ἁγίᾳ) and was thus established in Zion (24:10).[10] As noted in chapter 2, the "holy tent" here could refer to the earthly tabernacle, but verse 9's description of Wisdom's eternality makes it more likely that this is the heavenly tabernacle where Wisdom served before being established in Zion. Once rooted in the holy city, Wisdom grows like a whole variety of plants, including a palm tree (24:12–17; cf. Ps. 92:12–13), and overflows like the various major rivers of the region and also like the Gihon (Sir. 24:25–27). This minor spring below the temple mount holds cosmic significance in its association with the primordial waters and with the land of Eden. Wisdom is also equated with the law (24:23), but this is a minor note in a chapter that abounds with temple imagery.

The same notion, though with a more pessimistic outlook, is found in 1 En. 42. Here Wisdom cannot find a place to dwell, and instead a place is found for her "in the heavens." Although she tries to dwell with humanity, she finds no dwelling place and ultimately settles permanently among the angels (1 En. 42.1–2). Language of "dwelling" and "place" is, as we have seen, closely connected with the temple.

All of these texts demonstrate that Wisdom is rightly associated with Torah as the means par excellence by which God instills wisdom in those humans who are ready to receive it. Wisdom is also described as light, glory, and word. Yet we find Wisdom described more extensively in temple terms: heaven is her ultimate dwelling place with God, and she helped to found the earthly sanctuary as heaven's mirror, and (in some texts) for some time at least, she made her home there on earth as God's agent and emanation.

These texts are well known to interpreters of John's Prologue, but their clear and extensive temple imagery is often overlooked. The Prologue opens by asserting the existence of the Word, its presence with and distinction from God, and its identity with him (John 1:1–2). It is instrumental to creation and contains life, which is also described as light (1:3–5), motifs familiar from the Wisdom of Solomon.[11] Verses 6–8 proleptically describe John's testimony to this light, while verse 9 describes the true light's coming into the world.[12]

---

10. Those who are wise likewise "pitch their tents near her" (Sir. 14:25).

11. The use of Gen. 1 may also suggest connections with the heavenly temple theme as identified in chap. 1.

12. The apparent intrusion of John the Baptist's testimony along with explicit reference to incarnation and Christ are features that have inclined some scholars to regard the Prologue as a preexistent Logos hymn that John modified, whereas others regard it as a Johannine composition. See the summaries in Behr, *Paschal Gospel*, 245–46; Brown, *John I–XII*, 21–23. On either view, the Wisdom connections are undeniable.

This I take to be a reference not to the incarnation but to the prior coming, or possibly comings, of the Word into the world.[13] As in 1 Enoch, the Word is not recognized or received by "the world" or "his own."[14] Those who receive the Word become not merely "friends of God and prophets" (Wis. 7:27) but God's children (John 1:10–13). In this light, 1:14 describes a *further* tabernacling of the Word in his becoming flesh. This dwelling entails a revelation of divine glory, grace, and truth. At this point John's testimony is given in chronological sequence and in his own words (1:15). We have received grace upon grace from the Word's fullness (πλήρωμα), a term that like ἀπόρροια in Wis. 7:25 denotes divine emanation (John 1:16). That is, grace and truth are now received in Christ, the climactic coming of the Word, on top of the grace of the law given through Moses, both of which made God known (1:17–18).

Like Wisdom, the divine Word's dwelling is with God in heaven. Part of what it means for him to have been sent forth into the world is his dwelling in the tabernacle and temple, which mirror the heavenly realm. The newness of the incarnation consists precisely in the Word's coming into flesh (σάρξ), not in his "tabernacling" on earth per se. The accompaniments of this enfleshment include glory, grace, truth, light, and fullness, all of which are ways of describing the divine emanation associated with the temple. Thus Jesus is the ultimate and climactic instantiation of God's presence on earth, the revelation of the Father by the one who has come from his heavenly dwelling.

Stairway to Heaven

At the climax of the calling episodes in John 1:35–51, Nathanael comes to Jesus at Philip's invitation. Jesus's knowledge of Nathanael's character and his past impresses Nathanael sufficiently to elicit the confession, "Rabbi, you are the Son of God! You are the King of Israel!" (1:49). In response, Jesus says that Nathanael will see "greater things" and adds, "Very truly, I tell you, you will see heaven opened and the angels of God ascending and descending upon the Son of Man" (1:51).

13. This reading is close to that of Daniel Boyarin (*Border Lines*, 93–105), who relates Wisdom/Word primarily to Torah, but as I have shown, Torah and temple are not mutually exclusive. Those who take 1:9–13 as referring to Jesus's incarnate state point to the connection between phraseology here and later in the Gospel, an allusion to the virginal conception in 1:13, and the fact that comparable christological texts such as Phil. 2 and Col. 1 make no mention of Christ's presence in the world before his incarnation, among other arguments. See, e.g., Brant, *John*, 31–34; Brown, *John I–XII*, 28–30; Morris, *John*, 92–102. Behr (*Paschal Gospel*, 245–49) charts his own path by relating the entire prologue to the passion.

14. "His own" could denote the Jewish people or all humanity; the former seems more likely in light of the reference to "the world" in 1:10 (Brown, *John I–XII*, 10).

The saying alludes to Jacob's vision at Bethel (Gen. 28:10–22) in which he dreams of a ladder bridging earth and heaven, with angels moving up and down on it. God reiterates his promises to Jacob, who upon awaking declares, "Surely the LORD is in this place—and I did not know it!" and in his fear adds, "This is none other than the house of God [בית אלהים /οἶκος θεοῦ], and this is the gate of heaven [שער השמים/ἡ πύλη τοῦ οὐρανοῦ]" (Gen. 28:16–17). He sets up a pillar, pours a libation of oil on it, and names it the house of God, *Beth-El* (28:18–19, 22).[15]

Some scholars are skeptical of whether John is in fact alluding to this episode in Jesus's short saying to Nathanael,[16] but several shared features dispel any doubt. The phrase "angels of God" and the same verbs in the same unusual order (ascending first, then descending) occur in the Greek of Gen. 28:12. It also seems likely that John is playing on Jacob's names: as Jacob he is the deceiver (he came to Isaac "with deceit," μετὰ δόλου, Gen. 27:35; cf. 25:26; 27:36), yet as the one who strives with God he becomes Israel (32:22–32), just as Nathanael is "truly an Israelite ['Ισραηλίτης] in whom there is no deceit [δόλος]" (John 1:47).[17] Some commentators note that the ladder, a key feature of the vision, is missing.[18] The angels' ascent and descent "on the Son of Man" (ἐπὶ τὸν υἱὸν τοῦ ἀνθρώπου) could imply that Jesus takes the place of Jacob, but given that in Gen. 28 they ascend *on the ladder* (ἐπ' αὐτῆς)[19] and that in John 1, Nathanael and the other disciples are those who *see*, it makes better sense to understand Jesus as in the place of the ladder and the disciples in the place of Jacob.[20] If so, this is not a statement of the Son's future or de facto heavenly location[21] but instead describes the period of his earthly ministry.[22]

15. For a detailed discussion of the Genesis connections here, establishing the Son of Man as the link between heaven and earth, see Reynolds, *Apocalyptic Son of Man*, 89–103, esp. 96–99.
16. E.g., Michaels, *John*, 136–39.
17. Neyrey ("Jacob Allusions," 589) sees these as "a secondary addition."
18. Neyrey ("Jacob Allusions," 589–90) sees Jesus as the Shekinah, with "no need for a ladder to mediate between heaven and earth"; cf. Neyrey, "Jacob Allusions," 605.
19. The Septuagint is forced to clarify because κλίμαξ is feminine, whereas the Hebrew בו could refer to either the ladder or Jacob; see the rabbinic discussion of which is meant in Gen. Rab. 69.3. The change to accusative instead of genitive with ἐπί does not indicate that the angels descend "toward" Jesus; ἐπί occurs in John with both cases to mean "on" (Reynolds, *Apocalyptic Son of Man*, 97n47).
20. So also Kerr, *Temple of Jesus' Body*, 164; Kanagaraj, *"Mysticism,"* 192; Morgen, "Promesse de Jésus à Nathanaël," 21; Richir, "Jacob à Cana?," 71; Hoskins, *Jesus as the Fulfillment*, 125–35. Kanagaraj also references the appearance "like a human form" on the throne in Ezek. 1:26.
21. Contra Neyrey, "Jacob Allusions," 597–600.
22. So Zumstein, *Jean (1–12)*, 91. Rowland ("John 1.51") rightly stresses the earth-bound location of God's revelation in Jesus but wrongly denies the possibility of access to heaven. The whole purpose of Jesus's earthly presence construed as cultic space is heavenly access.

The equation of Jesus with a ladder is a rather strange image and appears to be without parallel until we realize that we are dealing here not with a wooden ladder (though these were not unknown in the ancient world, in domestic settings as well as in siege warfare)[23] but with a ramp or stairway. "The object described [in Gen. 28:12] is probably a *ramp* rather than the conventional 'ladder.' It refers to something like the Mesopotamian ziggurat, a land mass formed as a temple through which earth touches heaven."[24] This identification makes sense in the ancient Near Eastern context, and the cultic aspects embedded in the narrative of Gen. 28 are developed in ways more in keeping with Israelite and Jewish worship in later sources. Bethel is attested as a cultic site for the worship of YHWH in the form of a calf under Jeroboam after the kingdoms divided, which attracts southern condemnation (1 Kings 12:29–13:34).[25] Philo of Alexandria (*Dreams* 1.144) identifies the ladder with the air, connects it with the Israelites' request for mediation at Mount Sinai (Exod. 20:19), and applies the image to the individual soul, which should aim to become a house of God, a holy temple, a most excellent dwelling (θεοῦ οἶκος . . . , ἱερὸν ἅγιον, ἐνδιαίτημα κάλλιστον, *Dreams* 1.149). The evidence from rabbinic texts is late but represents an extension of cultic elements in the text. Genesis Rabbah connects the ladder standing on the earth with the altar of earth from Exod. 20:24 and thus interprets Gen. 28:12–13 to mean that God stands on an altar and that this altar is Mount Sinai (Gen. Rab. 68.12–13). Targum Pseudo-Jonathan's expansion of Gen. 28 has Jacob praying in "the place of the house of the sanctuary," seeing "the Glory of the Lord's Shekinah" and the "sanctuary of the Name of the Lord . . . founded beneath the throne of glory."[26]

On a minimal interpretation of John 1:51, then, Jesus is identified as a cult place; maximally, he is a temple.[27] It matters little that this is not the tabernacle or the Jerusalem temple,[28] as the Jacob episode comes from the patriarchal

---

23. In Neh. 3:15; 12:37, κλίμαξ denotes steps onto the city wall, and it refers to siege ladders in 1 Macc. 5:30; Josephus, *Ant.* 12.338; *J.W.* 3.257.

24. Brueggemann, *Genesis*, 243. Note the stepped mountain feature described as "the Ladder of Tyre" in Josephus, *Ant.* 13.146; 1 Macc. 11:59; and the Talmud.

25. Haran (*Temples and Temple-Service*, 28–31, 52) states that the Bethel temple's antiquity is "unquestionable" but sees Gen. 28 as the establishment of an open cultic place. Open cultic sites are nevertheless likely locations for the later founding of temples.

26. Targum translations by Etheridge, *Targums of Onkelos and Jonathan Ben Uzziel on the Pentateuch*. See also Morgen, "Promesse de Jésus à Nathanaël," 14–15; Neyrey, "Jacob Traditions," 427–28.

27. Kerr (*Temple of Jesus' Body*, 140–66) is thus too cautious when he concludes that there is "not sufficient evidence to see a Temple allusion in 1.51" (166).

28. The Jerusalem temple had no steps, though Ezekiel's temple has some between its courts (e.g., Ezek. 40:22), like Herod's temple (κλίμακες, Josephus, *J.W.* 5.198).

history, before the divine institution of either, and was interpreted in relation to these sanctuaries in later tradition. Jacob establishes a cultic center, which he names both "house of God" and "gate of heaven" (a non-Jerusalem cultic site thus receiving tacit approval through its inclusion in the Genesis narrative) and John draws on this to reinforce his portrayal of Jesus as the locus of God's presence.

Jesus is thus cast as a cult place. As we have seen, the ancient Near Eastern world regarded temples as imaging the cosmos and connecting heaven and earth. Implicitly, in Jacob's vision, heaven is open, at least for the angels who come and go from it via the sacred mountain-sanctuary. John makes this explicit (adding "opened," ἀνεῳγότα, to "heaven," τὸν οὐρανόν, from Gen. 28:12), implying a fulfillment of Jacob's vision in the person and ministry of Jesus. He, more truly than Bethel, is the house of God and gate of heaven through which (or whom) access to the heavenly dwelling of God is assured.[29]

Jesus the Temple Building

The one explicit reference to Jesus as temple comes in John 2:13–22 in one of John's frequent narrative asides. Jesus goes up to Jerusalem in preparation for Passover and begins to throw out the sellers from the temple courts (ἐκ τοῦ ἱεροῦ, 2:15; indicating the whole temple complex). As he does so, he says, "Stop making my Father's house [τὸν οἶκον τοῦ πατρός μου] a house of merchandise [οἶκον ἐμπορίου]" (2:16 AT). Unlike the Synoptic Gospels, John gives no indication of the proper usage of the temple (as a house of prayer), but he does identify it as the Father's house, a phrase that emphasizes God's presence there and prepares for the use of a similar phrase in 14:2. I will argue below that this is a reference to heaven, and thus the phrase here suggests that the Jerusalem temple holds a mirroring function vis-à-vis heaven, a notion that by now is familiar to us.

Following this incident, Jesus is in contention with the "Jews" and, in answer to their request for a sign, states: "Destroy this temple [τὸν ναὸν τοῦτον], and in three days I will raise it up" (2:19). The incredulity of the "Jews"—Herod's temple-building project has been underway for forty-six years and counting (2:20)—receives no narrative resolution, but the narrator's comment ensures that the reader is left in no doubt. Jesus's saying refers to the temple of his body (2:21), and this is a post-resurrection insight (2:22; cf. 2:17). This explicit

29. The writing called the Ladder of Jacob (dating perhaps from the early second century AD) elaborates Jacob's vision with a heavenly throne and temple, drawing elements from Isa. 6 and Ezek. 1.

identification of *Jesus's* body as a temple is in itself unique, but the notion that an individual human body constitutes a temple is not without parallel.[30] It is therefore not immediately clear that this connection means that Jesus *replaces* the temple, despite the assertions of many commentators.[31] The confusion between the two is understandable and fits John's liking for double entendre: Jesus clears out (part of) the temple complex (ἱερόν), which he identifies as his Father's house, and then talks about destroying a temple building (ναός). Only further revelation following the resurrection makes his meaning clear: the temple building is *not* the Jerusalem temple but his own body. This parallelism-with-difference between Jesus's body and the Jerusalem temple suggests that we might see his body as the locus for the Father's dwelling too (cf. 14:10–11, 20; 17:21). It may also explain the absence of the "house of prayer" motif when compared to the Synoptic Gospels: it is not Jesus-as-temple who will become the place of prayer. Instead, anywhere can be a place of prayer so long as it is done in spirit and truth, as John 4 will show. The temple-clearing incident contains the first and only explicit statement in John that Jesus is *the* or *a* temple, but as we have seen, the idea has already been prepared for even at this early stage in the Gospel. Moreover, it is only in light of other temple references that John's readers can understand what it means for Jesus's body to be a temple.

The Relativization of Earthly Cult Places

John 4 relays Jesus's meeting with a Samaritan woman at Jacob's well near Sychar.[32] Questions of worship arise in the third part of their discourse, but we will begin with the ritual connotations of water in the material preceding the encounter and opening the dialogue. The scene is prompted by the Pharisees' awareness of Jesus's growing influence through his disciples' baptismal ministry; he needs to leave Judea and takes the direct route through Samaria (4:1–4). This continues a focus on baptism and the ministry of John, whose disciples have been in dispute with "a Jew" concerning purification (περὶ

30. See, e.g., 1 Cor. 6:19; Ign. *Eph.* 15.3. For Philo (*Dreams* 1.215) the individual soul is a temple.
31. E.g., Gary Burge ("Territorial Religion," 389) states that "John's christology replaces Holy Spaces with Jesus Christ." Bill Salier ("Temple," 134) speaks more cautiously of "gracious replacement and fulfilment." Kåre Fuglseth (*Johannine Sectarianism*, 126–28, 160, 176) contests an overly quick and confident tendency to make this connection, preferring terminology of reinterpretation, transference, and "critical acceptance/loyalty." So also Regev, *Temple in Early Christianity*, 218–21.
32. Sychar is thought to be modern-day Askar, within a mile of a deep spring next to Shechem (Tell Balatah; Michaels, *John*, 235–36). Haran (*Temples and Temple-Service*, 49–52) details three open cultic places near Shechem.

καθαρισμοῦ, 3:25). Baptism is a matter of purity and as such an extension of
the purity requirements of the temple cult (note the large numbers of ritual
bathing pools, *mikvaot*, identified around the temple mount). Water fronts
the dialog between Jesus and the Samaritan woman as well: he asks to drink,
she is surprised that a Jewish man would ask a Samaritan woman for a drink
(again highlighting questions of purity), and Jesus states that he can give her
living water (ὕδωρ ζῶν, 4:10). This is an important phrase. In the period, it
meant running water, water that is suitable for ritual purity and safe to drink
and therefore life-giving in both senses. It is susceptible to being understood
as a dead metaphor, which is how the woman at first takes it: Where's your
bucket? How will you get this water? Jesus presses his point. The one who
drinks his water, he says, will never thirst again, and it will become a spring
overflowing to eternal life (4:14). The water spring (πηγή) evokes the primordial water beneath the ancient Near Eastern temple reflected in Jewish ideology in the Gihon emerging from below the temple mount in Jerusalem.[33] This
connection is made more plausible by the connection with Jacob, given that the
previous allusion to Jacob presents him as founder of a cult place: it is entirely
appropriate that such a cult founder would also uncover a primordial spring.[34]

A later passage is relevant here. In John 7:37–39, on the last day of the
Festival of Booths, or Tabernacles,[35] Jesus invites the thirsty to come to him
and drink by believing in him, for "as the scripture says, 'Out of his belly shall
flow rivers of living water'" (ὕδατος ζῶντος, 7:38 AT).[36] The imagery is apt,
as the festival involved drawing water from the pool of Siloam each day and
carrying it through what became known as the Water Gate before pouring it
out as a libation. A libation represents the foregoing of a liquid one would use
for drink or food as an offering to the deity. This rite was a petition for water
supply, a celebration of the temple as a source of cleansing water, and also
a symbol of the eschaton, connected with Zechariah's and Ezekiel's visions
(Zech. 14:8, 16; Ezek. 47:1–12).[37] Alongside the temple-purity connection, the

33. On the background to the water imagery here, see Um, *Temple Christology*, 15–67. For
his reading of John 4 in this light, see Um, *Temple Christology*, 147–66.

34. Genesis does not speak of a well sunk or owned by Jacob, but the targums of Gen. 28
connect him with Beersheba and relay a tradition that his well overflowed (Neyrey, "Jacob
Traditions," 421–23).

35. The imagery of light was also connected with the Festival of Booths, where, according to
m. Sukkah 5.2–4, four golden candelabra were lit in the Court of the Women. This is important
context for understanding Jesus's statement "I am the light of the world" (John 8:12), which
is also set during this festival and in the temple (8:20). This may not connect with John 4 but
does align with the use of light in 1:4–13.

36. Against the NRSV, I take "his" to be a reference to Jesus. On this point and on temple
connections in this passage more generally, see Greene, "Jesus as the Heavenly Temple," 338–41.

37. Behr, *Paschal Gospel*, 162; Jones, *Symbol of Water*, 151.

narrator identifies this water as the Spirit, whom believers are at this stage of the narrative yet to receive (7:39), mirroring the earlier elusive reference to being born "of water and Spirit" in Jesus's words to Nicodemus (3:5). I take the scripture of uncertain provenance in 7:38 to be a reference to Jesus, from whom living water flows, both because this explains how he is able to give drink to those who come to him and because water flows from his side at the crucifixion (19:34). Jesus as a water source coheres with his status as temple.

Returning to John 4, the conversation proceeds with a discussion of the woman's marital status, culminating in her astonishment (just like Nathanael) at his knowledge (4:19). This induces a question about the correct place (τόπος) to worship: Is it "on this mountain"—that is, Gerizim, quite possibly visible from where they were talking—or "in Jerusalem" (4:20)?[38] Neither Jerusalem's status as a mountain nor the temple itself is directly mentioned, reflecting the Samaritan perspective. Mount Gerizim remained a place of worship, although the temple that once stood on it had been destroyed by John Hyrcanus in ca. 112/111 BC, and its remains were removed by the Romans in AD 70.[39] Jesus's answer points in two directions. He affirms that Jewish worship is in accordance with knowledge and thus implicitly affirms Jerusalem as the correct place for worship (4:22). Yet his statement is framed on either side with a description of the hour when the Samaritans will worship "neither on this mountain nor in Jerusalem." Instead, "true worshipers will worship the Father in spirit and truth" (4:21, 23). As Jesus is speaking to a Samaritan, his statement in 4:21 need not imply that *everyone*, Jews included, will cease worshiping in Jerusalem, but it certainly relativizes all earthly places of worship. By the time the Gospel is written, its author and readers know that no sacrificial cult is currently operating in either place.

The implications of worshiping "in spirit and truth" are not spelled out, although the phrase is repeated and resonates with other statements in the Gospel. Many commentators take "spirit" as a reference to the Holy Spirit, and truth is elsewhere connected with Jesus (cf. 1:14, 17; 14:6), which would be consistent with notions of Jesus as the temple and the Spirit as the emanation of divine presence as in the temple.[40] The preposition "in" (ἐν) with spirit and truth likely indicates means rather than location and should not be overread. Yet the connection of spirit with water in John 3 and 7, mentioned

38. This question is "at the center of the meaning of the narrative and of Jesus' activity in it" (Boers, *Neither on This Mountain*, 175).

39. On the Gerizim temple, see Haran, *Temples and Temple-Service*, 47–48. It gains legitimacy in the Samaritan Bible through the commandment to build an altar on "Gerizim" rather than "Ebal" (cf. Deut. 27:4–5). On the date of its destruction, see Chalmers, "Samaritans."

40. So, e.g., Zumstein, *Jean (1–12)*, 155–56; contrast Morris (*John*, 270–71), who relates it to the human spirit.

above, suggests that we remain in the cultic-purity territory of baptism, the Festival of Booths, and Jacob's well. The key grounds given here are found in John 4:24: because "God is spirit," worshipers must worship in spirit. The logic is not spelled out but can be articulated as follows: since God is spirit and can be present with people in all places, he can therefore be worshiped in all places but only in and through spirit. This is not a denial that heaven is God's primary dwelling place or location, which John elsewhere assumes (see 1:32; 12:28; 17:1). The universal possibility of worship in spirit and truth must therefore be assessed as ultimately an extension of a reality that has long been demonstrated by earthly sanctuaries. John 4 on its own gives little sense of either Jesus or heaven as temple, yet in the context of the Gospel, it presupposes both.[41] God is spirit and sends Jesus to give the living water of his Spirit, which in turn enables spiritual worship. This guarantees access to the Father in heaven even as it downgrades other, geographically located cultic places, through universal availability of the true primordial water source.

The Gate to the Court

In John 10, Jesus uses the well-established biblical imagery of the shepherd to articulate his messianic role. First, the gate to the sheepfold establishes the legitimacy of the shepherd, to whom alone the gatekeeper will open (10:1–3). Then Jesus identifies himself as the gate through which the sheep who are to be saved will enter and exit (10:7–9). He is the good shepherd, who has other sheep from another sheepfold whom he will combine with these sheep to form a single flock (10:11, 16). It is not initially obvious that there is any temple imagery here, but a text from 1 Enoch suggests otherwise.

The imagery of God's people as sheep, drawn from the OT, is employed in the Animal Apocalypse at the end of the Enochic Book of Dreams (1 En. 83–90).[42] A house is built for the sheep in the desert, symbolizing the tabernacle (89.36). Once the sheep are in the land, the house becomes "great and spacious" with a tower "elevated and lofty," and here the sheep are "offered a full table" before the Lord (89.50). The sheep then abandon the house, and it is destroyed (89.54, 66–67) before being rebuilt but in an impure state (89.73). The eschatological hope for a new temple is expressed with the image of a new house being brought following the judgment and the sheep entering this house (90.28–29). All the sheep are invited, but they are so numerous that the house cannot contain them all (90.34). The distinction between a house

---

41. For an extended argument for temple Christology in John 4, see Um, *Temple Christology*.
42. On the use of Ezekiel in this part of 1 Enoch, see Manning, *Echoes of a Prophet*, 89–96.

and its tower appears to reflect the distinction between the temple proper and the temple complex with its courts.[43] Although there is condemnation of the second temple, the eschatological temple is continuous with the Solomonic temple in its spaciousness and elevation. It surpasses Solomon's temple and becomes a home for the sheep even as its extent remains limited. Four possible connections with John's use of sheep imagery can be noted.[44]

First, the term "sheepfold" (αὐλή, John 10:1, 16) denotes an enclosure of any sort and thus can refer to a pen for animals, the courtyard of a house (as in 18:15), a royal court (Josephus, *Ant.* 12.106, and by extension the members of that court, e.g., *Ant.* 12.47), or a court around a temple.[45] It is therefore appropriately translated "sheepfold" in John 10, but English readers miss a potential allusion. The same word is used to refer to the inner court of the temple by Josephus (ἡ ἔνδον αὐλή, *J.W.* 5.227) and the court around the temple in Rev. 11:2 (τὴν αὐλὴν τὴν ἔξωθεν τοῦ ναοῦ, i.e., the court outside the temple proper).[46] The material from 1 En. 89–90 shows that it is entirely conceivable to place God's people *as sheep* within the court of his temple. In this light, Jesus's statement that he has other sheep who are not from *this* "enclosure" (αὐλή, John 10:16), which is commonly taken to refer to the gentiles, could represent a Johannine take on Eph. 2:14, the removal of the dividing wall so that sheep from two distinct temple enclosures (αὐλαί) can become one flock.[47]

Second, the discourse in John continues with the Festival of Dedication (John 10:22–39), where Jesus is surrounded by "the Jews" precisely in the temple courts. This is the only place in John where the location "in the portico of Solomon" is specified, locating Jesus on the east side of the temple complex in the court of the gentiles (10:23). This may be a hint that Jesus is already looking for his other sheep from another enclosure before the Greeks come looking for him in 12:20.

43. For a detailed discussion of the relationship of house and tower to temple in the later parts of 1 Enoch, see Suter, "Temples and the Temple," 207–9; Himmelfarb, "Temple and Priests," 228–31. Suter identifies the house as the city and leaves open the question of whether this is coextensive with temple as in Rev. 21–22.

44. Manning (*Echoes of a Prophet*, 100–131) explores the influence of Num. 27 and Ezek. 34 on John 10. In his comparison of 1 En. 89–90 with John 10 (*Echoes of a Prophet*, 132–35), he makes little of the temple imagery.

45. Sheep also enter God's courts in worship in Ps. 100:1–4. The term αὐλή is roughly synonymous with περίβολος, denoting an enclosing wall or precinct, including for the temple (e.g., Ezek. 40:5; Sir. 50:2), but περίβολος is rarer in biblical Greek and not used at all in the NT.

46. Manning (*Echoes of a Prophet*, 110) notes that the Septuagint usage is predominantly for tabernacle or temple courts, counting 141 occurrences against 45 generic. He sees this as polemical against the temple council but does not explore temple connections further.

47. On the oneness motif here and its background in Ezek. 34 and 37, see Byers, *Ecclesiology and Theosis*, 134–36.

Third, Jesus's self-designation as the gate for the sheep (θύρα, 10:7, 9) marks him as the means of entrance into the enclosure (αὐλή).[48] This function of access is, as we have seen, closely associated with the temple in its purpose of making heaven accessible, and it finds further expression in a closely parallel saying in John 14, where Jesus describes himself as the way (ἡ ὁδός, 14:6), a passage we will examine below. Alongside the access afforded by the gate and its guard, the sheepfold is identified as a place of security (10:9–10), just like the temple complex. The temple complex served as a treasury for public and private wealth and formed the last fortress within Jerusalem in case of attack.[49]

Fourth, John's vocabulary choices establish an intertext. The only other occurrence of "enclosure" (αὐλή) in the Gospel is in 18:15, where it refers to the high priest's courtyard, followed by "gate" in 18:16 (θύρα, elsewhere only in 20:19, 26). Similarly, "gatekeeper" (θυρωρός) appears in 10:3 and again in John only in 18:16–17. In John 18, this word refers to the doorkeeper whom the beloved disciple knows and who therefore grants Peter access. The word is not common in antiquity but usually refers to the guard for a door or gate of a permanent structure. In Josephus, three of four occurrences refer to the Levites as gatekeepers in the temple (*Ant.* 11.108, 128, 134).[50] Immediately following Peter and John's entry to the courtyard, Jesus is questioned by the high priest and points back to his open teaching "in synagogues and in the temple, where all the Jews come together" (18:20). Among other functions, this later passage serves as a narrative enactment of what John 10 describes figuratively, and it does so in a way that emphasizes the high priest and the temple.

Jesus's depiction of himself as the gate to an enclosure for sheep may therefore allude to the security offered by the temple. I make no claim that this is the primary meaning of John 10. Yet there is enough evidence within the Gospel to see a temple connection here, albeit in a different configuration. It is eschatologically oriented, with the timing of the fulfillment of the promise of a unified flock left unspecified. We find Jesus as the point of access into an eschatological temple complex open to Jew and gentile. He is identified with a part of the temple structure or with a function of the earthly temple, rather than with the temple as a whole. This should not surprise us, as it is another variation on a Johannine theme that has taken us from tabernacle to cult place to second temple and beyond.

48. Draper ("Temple, Tabernacle and Mystical Experience," 282–83) connects 10:1–16 with the temple on the basis of the door motif alone.
49. For the treasury (and its divine protection) see 2 Macc. 3:4–15; 4 Macc. 4:4–11. Note the integration of the temple into the defenses of Jerusalem, as described, e.g., by Josephus, *J.W.* 5.244–45 (the temple complex itself is described in 5.184–247).
50. LSJ, s.v. θυρωρός. The only other Greek Bible occurrence is Mark 13:34.

Dwellings in the Father's House

The final passage of interest, John 14, is well known as a reading at funerals and is widely understood to refer to heaven, although in recent decades several scholars have argued against this interpretation.[51] The KJV's rendering of verse 2 as "In my Father's house are many mansions" is a somewhat unfortunate legacy from the Vulgate: *mansio* in Latin means simply "room" or "hostel." The imagery is not of private palaces but of a heavenly temple.[52]

The passage forms the beginning of Jesus's Farewell Discourse (John 14–17). In the context of the meal and foot washing of John 13, Jesus is preparing and consoling his disciples ahead of his imminent departure. He exhorts them to calm their hearts and to renew their trust in God and himself. He then states, "My Father's house has many rooms" (ἐν τῇ οἰκίᾳ τοῦ πατρός μου μοναὶ πολλαί εἰσιν, 14:2a NIV). This phrase echoes the only other use of "my Father's house" (τὸν οἶκον τοῦ πατρός μου) in the Gospel, to denote the Jerusalem temple in 2:16. The reference matches: Solomon's and Herod's temples had rooms built onto their north and south sides as well as various other buildings within the temple complex, as does Ezekiel's visionary temple.[53] These rooms were for cultic use and not for permanent dwelling, although there was provision for the priests on watch or coming on duty the following day to sleep in certain chambers.[54] In John 14:2, it immediately becomes apparent that the "Father's house" is not the earthly temple, however, as Jesus speaks of going away to prepare a place for his disciples before coming to take them to be with him (14:2b–3).

A significant current in scholarship has argued that the "many dwellings" of John 14:2 should be interpreted as "a variety of interpersonal relationships between the Father, Jesus, Paraclete, and believers."[55] This is in view of John's only other use of the noun "dwelling" (μονή) in 14:23 to denote the relationship between the Father, Jesus, and the believer, and the extensive use of the

51. Coloe, *God Dwells with Us*; summarized in Coloe, "Temple Imagery in John"; Kerr, *Temple of Jesus' Body*; Neyrey, "Spaces and Places," 68–69; Rab, "Christ as Church."

52. So Bammel, "Farewell Discourse," 109; Bryan, "Eschatological Temple in John 14." I agree with Bryan that the theme is certainly eschatological, but cosmology has the upper hand here; so Zumstein, *Jean (13–21)*, 61. For a similar take, see Draper, "Temple, Tabernacle and Mystical Experience."

53. 1 Kings 6:5–10; Ezek. 40:38, 44–47; 41:5–11; 42:1–14; 11QT^a XLIV, 3–16. See further references in Bryan, "Eschatological Temple in John 14," 190.

54. Note Nehemiah's anger at Tobiah using a temple chamber for profane purposes (Neh. 13:4–9). It was forbidden to sleep while on watch, and the sleeping quarters within the fire chamber were on nonholy ground. There was also provision for ritual bathing in the case of emission of semen; see 1 Chron. 9:17–34; m. Middot 1.1–9; m. Tamid 1.1.

55. Coloe, *God Dwells with Us*, 162.

cognate verb "to dwell" or "abide" (μένω) in the Gospel to describe mutual indwelling. It is also suggested that the differing terms for "house" (οἶκος, 2:16; οἰκία, 14:2) reflect a shift in nuance from structure to household.[56] I agree that the wider context of the Gospel displays a strong interest in the relational and familial nature of dwelling or abiding, but I suggest that this reading of 14:1–6 founders on the passage's irreducibly spatial nature. Spatial ideas can of course be employed figuratively, and the relational motif is certainly predominant in the Farewell Discourse as a whole. But the particular form of the argument here requires that space not be classified as only symbolic, and thus 14:1–6 stands in some tension with the predominantly relational idea.[57] Three points are relevant here.

First, the phrase "to prepare a place" (ἑτοιμάσαι τόπον, 14:2; cf. 14:3) is a temple allusion, referring to the site prepared for the ark and temple in Chronicles. David "prepared a place for the ark" (יכן מקום/ἡτοίμασεν τὸν τόπον, 1 Chron. 15:1) and prepared the place of the threshing floor for the temple Solomon built (2 Chron. 3:1).[58] More generally, "place," "resting place," or "holy place" is a widely used term for the temple, including in John 4:20 and 11:48.[59] Jesus is not preparing a place *distributively*, one for each disciple, but rather *collectively*: he is preparing the place of the heavenly temple for all of them.[60]

Second, the notion of a journey is fundamental to the thought.[61] Jesus is going away, a reference to his death, which is the primary means by which he prepares a place (cf. 16:16–28). Yet he does not return to be or dwell with the

---

56. Coloe, *God Dwells with Us*, 160–62. On this distinction, see more fully Fischer, *Die himmlische Wohnung*, 58–68. Of the four other occurrences of οἰκία in John, two have a structural sense (11:31; 12:3), and two denote a household (4:53; 8:35).

57. McCaffrey (*House with Many Rooms*, 246–55) reads John 14 on two levels as denoting both the heavenly temple and Jesus, distinct now but to be united in the eschaton; similarly Gundry, "'Many Μοναί,'" 72. Yet in 14:1–6, a present relational sense cannot coexist with a future spatial sense. For a critique of McCaffrey, see Hoskins, *Jesus as the Fulfillment*, 12–15. Klauck ("Himmlisches Haus und irdische Bleibe," 20–27) expresses the tension well: "It could be that in a similar way, logically contradictory yet mythically-metaphorically consistent, he envisages both the present and future of this community, without simply removing one of these two poles" (AT; "Es könnte sein, dass er in ähnlicher Weise, logisch widersprüchlich, aber mythisch-metaphorisch vermittelbar, Gegenwart und Zukunft dieser Gemeinschaft zusammen sieht, ohne einen der beiden Pole einfach aufzulösen," 27).

58. See also 1 Chron. 15:3, 12; 2 Chron. 1:4. Coloe (*God Dwells with Us*, 164–67) points to evidence of "prepare" used of God's people, but nowhere in the OT is God said to prepare his people *as a place*.

59. Cf. τόπος to mean place of judgment seat (19:13), of crucifixion (19:17, 20, 41), and within the tomb (20:7).

60. In view of this language and that of the "Father's house," it is surprising to see Regev (*Temple in Early Christianity*, 212) conclude that 14:1–6 "does not contain hints of a Temple or its attributes."

61. Kanagaraj, "*Mysticism*," 208–13.

believers directly; rather, he comes in order to "take you to myself, so that where I am, there you may be also" (14:3). The pattern is quite distinct from the use of "dwelling" (μονή) in 14:23. That later passage makes no reference to Jesus going away; instead, Jesus and the Father *come* to make their dwelling (ἐλευσόμεθα καὶ μονήν ... ποιησόμεθα) with the believer, where making a dwelling is a circumlocution for abiding (μένω).[62] Here, by contrast, Jesus goes away and comes back and then in a further step *takes* the disciples to himself (παραλήμψομαι, 14:3).[63]

Third, the idea of "the way" (ἡ ὁδός) is important, and the term occurs three times. Jesus states, "You know the way," eliciting the (astonished, frustrated?) response from Thomas: "We do not know where you are going. How can we know the way?" Jesus responds, "I am the way, and the truth, and the life" (14:4–6). There are significant formal similarities to the gate saying in John 10. Both form "I am" statements and affirm that it is "through me" (δι' ἐμοῦ, 10:9; 14:6)[64] that one must enter (ἐάν τις εἰσέλθῃ, 10:9; ἔρχεται, 14:6), whether to the court or to the Father whose house one is entering (εἰς τὴν αὐλήν, 10:1; πρὸς τὸν πατέρα, 14:6).

In both passages, Jesus has become the point of access to the rest of the temple building or complex. He is the gate of one of the courts in John 10 and the way into the temple complex with its chambers in John 14. The imagery in John is certainly fluid, but it is also readily understandable in terms already available in one of the core functions of the temple on earth: as the gate of heaven, it is the way to God's cosmic abode. The chief innovation here is not the idea of heaven as a temple or the idea of a point of access on earth. Rather, it is the notion that the temple's many rooms are to become permanent dwelling places for the people of God where they will enjoy relationship with Jesus, the Spirit, and the Father in all its fullness.[65] In this we find a soft echo of the idea of the martyrs safe under the altar and the people of God dwelling in the most holy place of the New Jerusalem in Revelation.

62. Meeks ("Man from Heaven," 65) suggests that 14:23 "'corrects' the commonplace notion of an ascent to heaven after death which was suggested by vss. 2–3," before adding "though of course the two are not mutually exclusive." This last point is important. For the reasons stated here, I do not see 14:23 as controlling or even correcting the reading of 14:1–6. Rather, the extensive use of "abiding" shows that space matters as a context for relationship. This fits with my discussion of spatial theory in the introduction.

63. "Neither the equation of the Father's house to Jesus' body nor to the community of disciples makes sense of Jesus' promise to receive his followers into the house" (Bryan, "Eschatological Temple in John 14," 196).

64. This phrase does not occur elsewhere in John.

65. Fischer (*Die himmlische Wohnung*, 73) stresses the abundance and permanence of the dwellings. Note that the temple chambers were for human use (e.g., Ezek. 40:44–46) but not human residence.

Conclusion

In his article on John 14, Steven Bryan writes, "Neither use of the Temple imagery should be dissolved into the other; it is entirely possible that John views the concepts of heavenly sanctuary and Jesus' glorified body as entirely harmonious."[66] I agree with Bryan in rejecting the zero-sum game; these concepts are harmonious rather than in competition. Yet this chapter has sought to demonstrate more than this: they are intimately connected and mutually informing. John's symbolism is certainly rich and fluid. He develops a multi-layered motif of Jesus as temple and not only as such but also as tabernacle, patriarchal cult place-cum-ziggurat, primordial water source, and the gate and way to the temple complex. I suggest that these images presuppose the idea that heaven too is a cultic place: as the originating locus of the divine emanation of the Word, as the place connected to earth in Jesus who is the ladder of Jacob, as the true cult center that relativizes all earthly cult centers, and as the temple complex and the Father's house to which Jesus gives access.

Part of the concern of commentators such as Mary Coloe and Alan Kerr is to fit John 14:1–6 into the context of the Farewell Discourse and the Gospel as a whole. This accounts for their opposition to seeing reference to a heavenly temple here. Yet the implicit presence of a heavenly temple in earlier passages means that John 14 is not an outlier or an unexpected intrusion into a text that is otherwise interested in identifying Jesus alone (or Jesus and church) with the temple. Instead, the idea of God's heavenly dwelling place and Jesus's journey from there to earth to bring his people back there with him is pre-echoed several times before reaching its most overt statement at the very point when Jesus is preparing to go away.

Moreover, the motif of Jesus as temple, which John develops more extensively than any other early Christian text, is reinforced and elaborated by this reading of John 14. In granting access to his Father's house, Jesus fulfills the function of the earthly temple. The same is true of the other Jesus-temple connections and highlights three key functions: revelation of eternal realities, divine presence, and heavenly access. The Prologue's eternal perspective is rooted in the history of Israel by its use of Wisdom traditions: the Word dwells in Jesus as God dwelt in Israel's sanctuaries, both continuous with them and yet a greater kind of revelation in flesh and surpassing fullness. In the closest John comes to the Synoptic Gospels' heavenly openings at the baptism, transfiguration, and crucifixion, the divine presence is broken open in Jesus's earthly ministry. In the destruction and raising of Jesus-as-temple, God will

---

66. Bryan, "Eschatological Temple in John 14," 197.

create a permanent and undefiled means of access to himself. As source of light and living water, Jesus brings the presence of God to all on earth who have the Spirit so that earthly cultic places can be relativized without impeding access to heaven. And as gate, he offers a sure and legitimate means of access to God's courts in which a renewed, united people of God will dwell in the last days. The potency and multivalency of temple imagery that John's Gospel so richly attests is also found across a range of other early Christian texts, as the final chapter will demonstrate.

8

Other Early Christian Texts

Altars and Ascents

In this final chapter, we turn to consider other early Christian writings that engage the notion of the heavenly temple. I have selected a range of demonstrably Christian texts from the first three centuries AD where this motif is present, even if only in passing, without regard to later canonical status. This survey demonstrates the continuing trajectory of early Christian reflection on the heavenly temple. It is not a comprehensive treatment, and inevitably the division of texts between this chapter and chapter 2 might appear arbitrary. Some of the texts examined in that earlier chapter are arguably Christian, at least in their preservation and (in some cases) also in their final form, just as debates continue over possible Jewish sources for texts examined here (especially the Ascension of Isaiah). Nevertheless, the arrangement is sufficient for the purposes of this study, and this chapter should be read in conjunction with chapters 1 and 2 as setting the context for the more detailed study of the intervening chapters. Just as those first chapters demonstrated that heavenly temple was a shared ancient and Second Temple Jewish notion that Christianity inherited, so the present chapter aims to explore some ways in which such a notion found its way into the developing stream of early Christian thought. As we shall see, the presence of a heavenly sanctuary is less extensive than was found in texts such as 1 Enoch, Revelation, and Hebrews—even as texts frequently assume that this motif will make sense to early Christian

167

audiences without explanation or elaboration. Further, the theme is employed to a significant variety of ends across a range of texts and genres.

The chapter is divided thematically into two parts, with the texts within each part arranged broadly chronologically. The first part explores texts in which the church or believers are likened to a temple, where there are potential cosmological associations (Ephesians, Shepherd of Hermas, Barnabas, Ignatius, and 2 Clement). These associations are found to be more or less substantial depending on the text in question. The second part turns to texts where a more direct association or identification of heaven with temple is discernible (1 Clement, Polycarp, Irenaeus, Ascension of Isaiah, Epistula Apostolorum, and Apocalypse of Paul). The more extended focus on heavenly temple in a text such as the Ascension of Isaiah and the passing references to the heavenly altar or temple in several of the other texts speak eloquently of the enduring importance of this motif.

Church as Heavenly Temple

The Letter to the Ephesians

Ephesians is both quintessentially Pauline and also widely regarded among scholars as pseudepigraphal. The question of its date is closely bound up with that of authorship, but neither question need detain us here: its presence in this chapter is due to the sporadic occurrence of potential heavenly temple motifs in the traditional Pauline corpus rather than any judgment about the origins of Ephesians. Like 1 and 2 Corinthians and 1 Peter, it offers developed reflection on the church as a temple, but unlike these texts (which are not directly studied in this book) it also displays a sustained interest in the heavenly status, significance, and even location of the church. I take these two themes in turn.

The church is "one new humanity," created by the reconciling of Jews and gentiles into a single group (Eph. 2:15–16). This unification is dramatically symbolized as breaking down "the dividing wall" (τὸ μεσότοιχον τοῦ φραγμοῦ, 2:14). This is likely a reference to the wall in the Herodian temple that divided the Court of the Gentiles from that of Israel (cf. Josephus, *Ant.* 15.417).[1] This interpretation gains in plausibility when we see the church further described as

1. So, e.g., Bruce, *Epistles*, 296–98.

citizens with the saints and also members of the household of God [οἰκεῖοι τοῦ θεοῦ], built upon the foundation [ἐποικοδομηθέντες ἐπὶ τῷ θεμελίῳ] of the apostles and prophets, with Christ Jesus himself as the cornerstone [ἀκρο-γωνιαίου]. In him the whole structure [πᾶσα οἰκοδομή] is joined together and grows into a holy temple [εἰς ναὸν ἅγιον] in the Lord; in whom you also are built together [συνοικοδομεῖσθε] spiritually into a dwelling place [εἰς κατοικητήριον] for God. (Eph. 2:19–22)

Relational concepts (citizenship, family) are connected with organic motifs (joined, growing) and with structural indications. The structure is explicitly named as a temple in 2:21, reinforced by the notion of God's dwelling in 2:22.[2] Temple imagery continues to inform the portrayal of the church in Paul's prayer for the church in Eph. 3, where language of dwelling (κατοικῆσαι) coincides with that of foundation (τεθεμελιωμένοι, 3:17). In this light, the dimensions of "breadth and length and height and depth" in 3:18 reinforce the sense of a temple structure, and this culminates in being filled with the fullness of God (3:19; cf. 1:23; 4:10).[3] Ephesians 4 is more focused on the church as body motif, yet here too we find structural language:[4] the different gifts equip the saints for "building up" (εἰς οἰκοδομήν, 4:12) the body of Christ, and the body builds itself up in love (εἰς οἰκοδομὴν ἑαυτοῦ, 4:16).[5]

Alongside this portrayal of the church as temple, Ephesians contains a strong emphasis on cosmology. It is similar to Colossians in this regard but emphasizes more strongly the spatial aspect of Christ's heavenly location and, in Christ, the heavenly location of the church. The phrase "in the heavenly places" (ἐν τοῖς ἐπουρανίοις) is distinctive to Ephesians in biblical Greek, occurring five times and in each case having a spatial reference.[6] In Christ, believers have "every spiritual blessing in the heavenly places" (1:3), where Christ is seated at God's right hand (1:20; cf. Ps. 110:1). In a striking statement that displays some of the most realized eschatology in the whole NT, God "raised us up with him and seated us with him in the heavenly places in Christ Jesus" (2:6). This verse directly echoes 1:20: as God *raised* (ἐγείρας) Christ from the dead and *seated* (καθίσας) him in heaven, so he has *co-raised* (συνήγειρεν) and *co-seated* (συνεκάθισεν) us with him. At some level this must be a hidden or proleptic reality, but it is not sufficient to relate it to the point

2. Note the argument for a preexistent hymn about cosmic peace reworked to fit the theme of Jew-gentile reconciliation, in Sanders, "Hymnic Elements in Ephesians 1–3."
3. See more fully R. Foster, "'Temple in the Lord.'"
4. And vice versa; note that the participle of συναρμολογέω is used in 2:21 as in 4:16.
5. On the particular configuration of church, temple, and body (of Christ), see Macaskill, *Union with Christ*, 149–54.
6. Eph. 1:3, 20; 2:6; 3:10; 6:12; see Lincoln, "'Heavenlies' in Ephesians."

of death only.[7] Rather, it brings out in the strongest terms the implications of Ephesians' emphasis on the Spirit and union with Christ: "The Church terrestrial is at the same time included in heaven with the Church celestial by virtue of its union with the heavenly Christ."[8] The final two references draw Christ's and the church's heavenly location together in the frame of God's purposes: it is *through* the church that God makes known his wisdom to heavenly rulers and authorities (3:10), and the church's fight is against the evil powers in such realms (6:12).[9] The combination of church-as-temple with a heavenly location also accounts for Ephesians' strong emphasis on access: through Christ, both Jew and gentile "have access [προσαγωγήν] in one Spirit to the Father" (2:18), and in Christ "we have access to God in boldness and confidence [τὴν παρρησίαν καὶ προσαγωγὴν ἐν πεποιθήσει] through faith in him" (3:12). The cognate verb in the Pentateuch often describes approaching God in ritual.[10] While "access" is found elsewhere in Paul (e.g., Rom. 5:2), its combination with language of boldness mirrors believers' stance with regard to the heavenly tabernacle in Hebrews (3:6; 4:16; 10:19).

In another key passage, Ephesians quotes Ps. 68:

> "When he ascended on high he made captivity itself a captive;
>   he gave gifts to his people."
> (When it says, "He ascended," what does it mean but that he had also descended into the lower parts of the earth? He who descended is the same one who ascended far above all the heavens, so that he might fill all things.) (Eph. 4:8–10)

Ephesians 4:8 differs from the Greek text of Ps. 68:18 (67:19 LXX) by using third person rather than second person and giving rather than receiving gifts.[11] The psalm is a song for triumphal procession to the sanctuary, and the targum renders this verse as follows: "You have ascended to heaven, that is, Moses the prophet; you have taken captivity captive, you have learnt the words of the Torah; you have given it as gifts to men."[12] While Ephesians may not be evoking a full Moses typology, the analogy with Christ is clear: the ascent to Sinai was an ascent into a heavenly sanctuary, just as Christ has now gone into heaven. This ascent entails a corresponding descent, which Ephesians

---

7. As does Long, "Ἐκκλησία in Ephesians," 211.

8. Lincoln, "'Heavenlies' in Ephesians," 479. Bruce (*Epistles*, 287) highlights the doctrine of the Spirit. For the anti-imperial resonances, see Long, "Ἐκκλησία in Ephesians," 209–15.

9. Bruce (*Epistles*, 405–6) takes the powers in 1:21 and 3:10 to be neutral references; in 6:12 clearly hostile powers are in view.

10. Shauf, *Jesus the Sacrifice*, 131.

11. This may be explained by a base text that read חלק instead of לקח (Lincoln, *Paradise Now and Not Yet*, 156).

12. As cited in Lincoln, *Paradise Now and Not Yet*, 156.

introduces after the ascent because it is logically consequent to it, even though Christ's incarnation (descent) chronologically precedes his ascension.[13] Language of fullness is again present. In this light the presentation of the church using building imagery as well as organic imagery in the following verses (4:11–16, see above) makes greater sense.

Ephesians thus offers a distinctive perspective on heavenly temple: the church is the temple, as elsewhere in Paul and in other texts we will explore in this chapter. Yet in Christ the church has a heavenly status and identity, even a heavenly location. For the church, this results in blessing, the overcoming of internal hostility, access to God, and growth toward maturity in Christ. It also entails the revelation of God's mystery and the display of his wisdom to cosmic rulers and, ultimately, the defeat of the devil and cosmic forces of darkness.

The Shepherd of Hermas

The Shepherd of Hermas is an early second-century text with apocalyptic features, consisting of a lengthy series of visions, commands, and parables given to Hermas via an angelic mediator. The structural difficulties have led to various proposals for distinct sources, though current scholarship tends toward seeing the text as a unity, albeit one that may have been developed over a number of years.[14] In two places, it makes elusive reference to the heavenly altar: "The prayer of the man filled with grief never has the power to rise up upon the altar before God [τοῦ ἀναβῆναι ἐπὶ τὸ θυσιαστήριον τοῦ θεοῦ]" (Herm. Mand. 10.3.2).[15] And in the eighth parable, the angel of the Lord commands the shepherd to oversee the handing over of sticks, charging him to do his job diligently. However, if anyone escapes the shepherd's notice, "I will put him to the test on the altar [ἐπὶ τὸ θυσιαστήριον δοκιμάσω]" (Herm. Sim. 8.2.5). In the first case, the altar evokes fairly conventional imagery of prayer rising to heaven, like the smoke of incense or a burnt offering; in the second, the altar bears connotations of testing and judgment. The motif is "not sustained later in the narrative,"[16] but it is all

13. Other possibilities for the descent include into Hades and the descent of the Spirit at Pentecost. The former is unlikely given Ephesians' lack of interest in a three-tier cosmology, and the latter must be ruled out because the Spirit is not "the *same one* who ascended." For a summary of the options and arguments, see Mouton, "'Ascended Far Above.'"

14. So Verheyden, "Shepherd of Hermas," 398; for a case that oral composition accounts for the loose structure, see Osiek, "Shepherd of Hermas in Context."

15. Text and translation of this and other Apostolic Fathers is from Ehrman, *Apostolic Fathers* (LCL).

16. Osiek, *Shepherd of Hermas*, 202.

the more telling for that: because it is not the focus of attention and receives no further elaboration, it must be assumed to make sense to early Christian readers.

One motif that is developed extensively in the Shepherd is the church as a tower.[17] This appears in Herm. Vis. 3 and is explored at greater length in Herm. Sim. 9–10. The tower is founded on water (Herm. Vis. 3.2.4), which evokes ancient Near Eastern cosmology of a temple built over the primordial water source. This is later elaborated as baptism ("saved through water"; cf. Herm. Sim. 9.16) with the tower founded on "the word of the almighty" (Herm. Vis. 3.3.5). In the ninth parable, Hermas first sees twelve mountains (Herm. Sim. 9.1) and then a giant rock that is higher than the mountains and cubic; it has a gate chiseled into it, and the tower is built upon it (Herm. Sim. 9.2.1–2; 9.3.1–4.8). Echoes of the cosmic mountain, a foundation stone, and the most holy place seem to be at play here, with the rock later specified as the Son of God (Herm. Sim. 9.12.1–3) who supports the church. This is later connected with creation, which is also sustained by the Son of God (Herm. Sim. 9.14.5–6). Various kinds of stones are described and tested (Herm. Sim. 9.5–9), which represent believers at different stages of ethical purity (Herm. Sim. 9.12–16). The respective layers of the foundation stones are the first and second generations followed by the prophets, apostles, and teachers (Herm. Sim. 9.15.4; cf. Herm. Vis. 3.5.1). This is one among several points that indicate "large-scale conceptual similarities" with Ephesians (see esp. Eph. 2:20),[18] just as the notion of living stones is a point of connection with 1 Pet. 2:4–8. The existence of different grades of stone in Shepherd, however, reflects varying moral status and serves exhortatory ends in a context in which the church is probably growing and its members are increasingly comfortable and lax.[19]

While the tower in the Shepherd represents an extended allegorical development of the notion of church as building,[20] it is nowhere explicitly identified as a temple or described in cultic terms, despite carrying these connotations in other texts (see Sib. Or. 5.420–33; 1 En. 89.73). Despite the cosmic evocations we have seen, the overwhelming emphasis is on the tower as an image for the church in the present, serving the urgent moral exhortation to repentance and holy living within the limited (if unspecified) time before the end.[21]

17. This "is the central image of the book" (Osiek, *Shepherd of Hermas*, 64).

18. Muddiman, "Ephesians, 2 Clement, and Hermas," 118–19.

19. Osiek, "Genre and Function," 118; Grundeken, *Community Building*, 181.

20. On the structure of the Shepherd's allegories and their paraenetic function, see Tagliabue, "Book of Visions," and on the tower specifically, see 234–37.

21. "Connections with myths of the heavenly city or heavenly Jerusalem should not be pushed too far with regard to the tower; it is precisely its presence in time and history that is stressed in

The Letter of Barnabas

The pseudepigraphal Letter of Barnabas likely dates from the early second century, around AD 130, though earlier dates have been proposed.[22] It is characterized by a thoroughgoing typological exegesis of the old covenant, in which sacrificial rites and the temple are connected to their fulfillment in Christ and the church, while their physical and material instantiation in Israel is condemned. Barnabas 2.4–10 states that God "has no need of sacrifices" (2.4) and cites prophetic critiques of sacrifice as fulfilled in Christ: "He nullified [κατήργησεν] these things that the new law of our Lord Jesus Christ . . . should provide an offering [προσφοράν] not made by humans" (2.6). While this statement might suggest a sequential, salvation-historical approach where sacrifices cede to Christ's offering, in fact the rest of the letter bears out a more categorical criticism of literally practicing these rites. For example, the physical practice of circumcision (9.4–7) and the actual construction of the temple (16.1–2) are condemned (cf. Diogn. 4.1–5).[23] Instead, only the typological function and its fulfillment in Christ matter. In this vein, the Day of Atonement and red heifer rituals are related to him in Barn. 7 and 8, respectively.

The key passage for our purposes is the discussion of the temple in Barn. 16.[24] The chapter opens with condemnation of Israel: "Those wretches were misguided in hoping in the building rather than in their God who made them, as if the Temple were actually the house of God" (16.1). It goes on to approximate the Jerusalem cult to pagan worship, before paraphrasing Isa. 40:12 and 66:1 to demonstrate God's disapproval: "Who has measured the heaven with the span of his hand? . . . The heaven is my throne and the earth is the footstool for my feet. What sort of house will you build me, or where is the place I can rest?" (Barn. 16.2).[25] In the context of building language, Isa. 40:12 might imply measuring for the purpose of construction, and 66:1 as noted in chapter 1 designates the whole cosmos as God's temple. Nevertheless, the

the ensuing narrative" (Osiek, *Shepherd of Hermas*, 64). See also Osiek, "Genre and Function," 115; Osiek, "Shepherd of Hermas in Context," 126; Verheyden, "Shepherd of Hermas," 399.

22. For a date under Nerva (96–98), see Carleton Paget, *Barnabas*, 9–30. For a late Hadrianic date (130–132), see Hvalvik, *Struggle*, 17–27. Other proposals include under Vespasian (70s) or earlier in Hadrian's reign (ca. 118–120).

23. For Barnabas, "the command to sacrifice or the command to build a temple was a mistake, and from its inception should have been understood in another way" (Carleton Paget, *Barnabas*, 224).

24. Peter Richardson and Martin Shukster have argued in a couple of pieces that temple is the central theme of Barnabas: "Barnabas, Nerva, and the Yavnean Rabbis"; "Temple and Bet Ha-Midrash." See the critique by Henne, "Barnabé."

25. Ehrman, *Apostolic Fathers*, modified.

primary focus is on the inability of any human structure to contain God.[26] A similar point, without the Isaiah citations, is made in Diogn. 3.3–4: "They manifest their own foolishness, rather than the worship of God. . . . For the one who made heaven and earth and all that is in them . . . is himself in need of none of the things that he himself provides." The following two verses in Barnabas refer clearly to the destruction of the temple in AD 70 and much more opaquely to rebuilding: "The servants of the enemies will themselves rebuild it" (16.4). These verses attract much attention in discussions of the dating and setting of the letter. The rebuilding must refer either to hopes for reconstructing the Jewish temple or possibly to the construction of a temple to Jupiter as part of Hadrian's refounding of the city as Aelia Capitolina.[27] Either would, in Barnabas's eyes, be equally idolatrous.

The second half of Barn. 16 explores whether "a temple of God still exists," arguing that it does on the basis of an otherwise unknown citation that states a temple will be built "when the seventh day is finished" (16.6; cf. Dan. 9:24; 1 En. 91.13 for similar phrasing). This temple is the heart of the believer, previously "a temple built by hand" and "full of idolatry" (16.7) but created anew such that "God truly resides within our place of dwelling— within us" (ἐν τῷ κατοικητηρίῳ ἡμῶν ἀληθῶς ὁ θεὸς κατοικεῖ ἐν ἡμῖν, 16.8; cf. 6.15, "The dwelling place of our heart . . . is a temple holy to the Lord"). In the following verse, the mouth is described as the temple door, which God opens, but then the imagery shifts slightly: "He leads into the incorruptible temple" (16.9). The direct object of God's leading (εἰσάγει) is not specified, but it is most likely "us" or perhaps those who are to be saved (16.10 has in view the witness of those in whom God dwells to those who long to be saved). In either case, the temple has become the corporate church rather than the individual, much as Barn. 4.11 urges, "We should be [γενώμεθα] a perfect temple to God." This fluidity is not surprising, and we find something similar in Paul (albeit not within the same passage: 1 Cor. 3, community, and 1 Cor. 6, individual).

The more significant shift is the move from heavenly temple to church as temple, although as we have seen, such fluidity is neither impossible nor unprecedented.[28] While Barnabas may be supposing that heaven or the whole cre-

---

26. Barnabas 16.2 "seems to presuppose that the house of God is found in heaven. . . . However, the single point in the quotation may be that God is rejecting the house 'you build for me'" (Hvalvik, Struggle, 127).

27. For rumors of reconstruction of the Jewish temple under Hadrian, see Sheppard, "Barnabas and the Jerusalem Temple"; for Aelia Capitolina, see Hvalvik, Struggle, 18–23.

28. "If [heavenly temple] is what Barnabas has in mind [in 16.2], there is a certain tension in what follows (concerning the spiritual temple)" (Hvalvik, Struggle, 127).

ated order is God's temple, the author makes little of this. Earlier, in Barn. 11, baptism and the cross take on the cosmic significance of the primordial water source and the holy mountain of Sinai, respectively (Barn. 11.3, 6–7, 10). This characteristically typological and Christocentric move entirely bypasses exploitation of the cosmic temple imagery in the sources and reinforces the impression that Barnabas shows relatively little interest in cosmology and much more in Christology and the church.

Ignatius of Antioch and 2 Clement

It is worth giving brief mention to the letters of Ignatius of Antioch (early second century AD) and to 2 Clement (in reality a homily by an author different from 1 Clement, likely mid-second century AD). These texts make passing reference to temple language in relation to believers.

Ignatius exhorts the Magnesians to "run together, as into one temple of God, as upon one altar, upon one Jesus Christ" (Ign. *Magn.* 7.2). It is less than clear what exactly is meant by the temple, but the context emphasizes the importance of the church meeting all together with the bishop and presbyters.[29] The altar may be identified with Christ.

Ignatius writes to the Ephesian church in terms that echo 1 Pet. 2 and the Shepherd of Hermas: "You are stones of the Father's temple [λίθοι ναοῦ πατρός], prepared for the building [εἰς οἰκοδομήν] of God the Father. For you are being carried up to the heights [ἀναφερόμενοι εἰς τὰ ὕψη] by the crane of Jesus Christ, which is the cross, using as a cable the Holy Spirit; and your faith is your hoist, and love is the path that carries you up to God" (Ign. *Eph.* 9.1). Here, unlike in Hermas, the building is explicitly named a temple, and its present heavenly location (like in the canonical Ephesians) is implied by the hoisting, which emphasizes process rather than a static location. Believers are bearers of the temple and of holy things (ναοφόροι, ἁγιοφόροι), perhaps envisaged as cultic servants (9.2).[30] Later in *Ephesians*, Ignatius exhorts his addressees to "do everything knowing that he is dwelling within us [ὡς αὐτοῦ ἐν ἡμῖν κατοικοῦντος], that we may be his temples [αὐτοῦ ναοί] and he our God in us, as in fact he is" (15.3).[31] Here the imagery is closer to 1 Cor. 3:16–17 and particularly 6:19, where Paul identifies the body of the individual as a temple, though he never uses the plural "temples" (ναοί). A further ethical

29. For a detailed study of this text, emphasizing unity, see Lookadoo, *High Priest and the Temple*, 228–62.
30. Lookadoo, *High Priest and the Temple*, 143–90.
31. Lookadoo, *High Priest and the Temple*, 191–227.

use of temple language similar to 1 Corinthians is found in Ign. *Phld.* 7.2: "Keep your flesh as the temple of God [ὡς ναὸν θεοῦ]."

Second Clement makes a very similar statement: "We must guard the flesh like the temple of God [ὡς ναὸν θεοῦ]" (2 Clem. 9.3).[32] There is also an apparent allusion to the temple clearing in the citation of Jer. 7:11 in 2 Clem. 14.1: "If we do not do what the Lord wants, we will belong to the Scripture that says, 'My house has become a cave of thieves.'" If this is right, then the Jerusalem temple is contrasted with "the church of life [ἐκκλησία τῆς ζωῆς]," subsequently identified with the body of Christ, which is spiritual and received in the Holy Spirit (14.2–5). This in turn "may imply the positive affirmation that the first church . . . is God's true temple and house of prayer."[33] Nevertheless, there is no suggestion in 2 Clement that the church as temple has a heavenly location or status.

Heavenly Temple

The First Letter of Clement

The second half of this chapter explores depictions of heaven itself (rather than the church in relation to heaven) as a temple in early Christian texts. First Clement is an anonymous letter written from the church in Rome to the church in Corinth. It was from early times attributed to Clement, a church leader about whom we know little else, and was likely written at the end of the first century.[34] In response to an internal conflict that led to the deposing of some church leaders in Corinth, 1 Clement affirms the God-given nature of order.[35] Clement draws on various examples to underline this point, most of them biblical, including the temple cult. This is a model of divinely mandated order, covering rites, their times, and the personnel who carry them out (40.1–5). Sacrifices were offered in one place after proper inspection (41.2). After applying this to the apostles and their successors (42), Clement turns to the validation of Aaron when his staff budded in the tabernacle (43.2–5). Earlier he makes reference to "that which is most holy" coming forth from the nation of Israel (29.3). This phrase (ἅγια ἁγίων) could be a reference to the

---

32. Second Clement uses "guard" (φυλάσσω) and Ignatius the essentially synonymous "keep" (τηρέω).

33. Muddiman, "Ephesians, 2 Clement, and Hermas," 115.

34. Gregory, "Introduction," 223–25.

35. See Moriarty, "Ministerial Appointments."

"holy of holies,"[36] a suggestion made more plausible by the context, which exhorts to worship using a verb of approach that is used of priestly service in the Pentateuch (προσέρχομαι, 1 Clem. 29.1).

Clement reflects on the Gen. 1 account of God as creator of the heavens, separating earth from water and establishing it on a firm foundation (1 Clem. 33.3; cf. chaps. 27–28). In its continuation, the heavenly sphere is a model of order (20.1–3). God alone is "the highest among the highest, the holy one who rests among the holy" (σε τὸν μόνον ὕψιστον ἐν ὑψίστοις ἅγιον ἐν ἁγίοις ἀναπαυόμενον, 59.3). Language of rest here evokes the sanctuary (see comments on the "resting place" in relation to the ark in chap. 1). The affirmation that "not even heaven is pure [καθαρός] before him" (1 Clem. 39.5) reflects its created and lesser status with respect to God and may also reflect the notion that the heavenly sanctuary, like the earthly one, is defiled by sin (cf. Heb. 9:23). Heaven is also the location of Paul as martyr, who was "transported up to the holy place [τὸν ἅγιον τόπον]" (1 Clem. 5.7).[37] As with "holy of holies" in 29.3, it is unclear whether this phrase is used generically or more specifically to refer to a heavenly sanctuary (or even its outer chamber).

Jesus is explicitly named as "high priest and benefactor" (ἀρχιερεύς, προστάτης, 1 Clem. 64.1) and "high priest of our offerings" (τὸν ἀρχιερέα τῶν προσφορῶν ἡμῶν, 36.1). The latter reference comes in a chapter replete with allusions to Heb. 1,[38] and Clement goes on to specify Christ's location: "Through this one we gaze into the heights of the heavens [εἰς τὰ ὕψη τῶν οὐρανῶν]" (36.2). He is superior to angels and seated at the Master's right hand (36.2, 5).[39] This serves as an apposite summary of Hebrews' notion of an open heavenly tabernacle in which Jesus as high priest is seen (see above, chap. 4). Jesus's priestly and royal status is also affirmed in 1 Clem. 32.3, where he is placed among Jacob's offspring between "the priests and all the Levites who ministered at the altar of God," on the one hand, and "the kings, rulers, and leaders in the line of Judah," on the other. Christ is also specified as the location of the "gate of righteousness that opens up onto life" (1 Clem. 48.2–4),

36. The first part of the citation bears resemblances to Deut. 4:34; 14:2; Num. 18:27, but the last clause containing this phrase is unknown elsewhere.

37. Some manuscripts read "journeyed" (ἐπορεύθη) in place of "was taken up" (ἀνελήμφθη). The net result is the same, though the "upward" direction connoting heaven is lost.

38. See Gregory, "The Writings," esp. 152–53. More extensively, see Hentschel, "Lebendiges Gotteswort," 38–222.

39. For an extended treatment of 1 Clem. 36, emphasizing Christ's role as intermediary and his preexistence, see Henne, La christologie chez Clément et Hermas, 77–114. Bumpus (Christological Awareness of Clement of Rome) includes a word study of "high priest," but I have been unable to locate a copy. On the transformative nature of gazing at Christ, see Battaglia, "Vision in Clement's Christology."

a reference to Ps. 118:19–20, which is associated with temple worship. This seems likely to have a figurative sense here.

As for sacrifice, Clement references Jesus's blood, which "was given for us" (οὗ τὸ αἷμα ὑπὲρ ἡμῶν ἐδόθη, 1 Clem. 21.6), and the Ninevites appeasing God via their pleas (ἐξιλάσαντο τὸν θεὸν ἱκετεύσαντες, 7.7). Myriads of angels stand and minister before God (λειτουργοῦσιν, ἐλειτούργουν) and offer praise in the words of the Trisagion (cf. Isa. 6:3), a model for believers' praise (34.5–7). Drawing especially on Pss. 50 and 51, Christians offer a sacrifice of praise (θυσία αἰνέσεως) and the sacrifice of a crushed spirit (πνεῦμα συντετριμμένον, 1 Clem. 35.12; 52.3–4; cf. 18.16–17, which cites Ps. 51 in its entirety). Christian offerings (προσφοροί) are made through Christ (36.1).

First Clement thus reflects a Christian outlook in which the old covenant cult speaks eloquently of God's desire for order. The letter presents a model for order within the church. It also shares with Hebrews (which, along with a couple of Paul's letters, was undoubtedly known to the author)[40] the notion that Christ is the high priest of the heavenly sanctuary, enabling Christian worship and offering help and benefaction to believers on earth. The church below and angels above offer praise and cultic service, and through Christ believers can see into the very heights of heaven.

Martyrdom and Prayer as Sacrifices Ascending to a Heavenly Temple

A number of early Christian texts contain relatively fleeting references to heaven as a temple or as containing an altar, particularly in relation to the prayers of the saints, which are likened to sacrifice or incense. In terms reminiscent of 1 Clement and Ignatius's letters, Polycarp describes widows as "God's altar" (Polycarp, *Phil.* 4.3) and Christ as an "eternal priest" (*sempiternus pontifex*, 12.2). The Martyrdom of Polycarp, dating from the third quarter of the second century,[41] casts Polycarp's death in terms reminiscent of Jesus's and Stephen's: as he enters the stadium, a voice comes from heaven to strengthen him (Mart. Pol. 9.1). Before the fire is set to burn him at the stake, Polycarp is likened to a ram ready as a whole burnt offering (ὁλοκαύτωμα, 14.1). He looks into heaven and prays, "May I be received before you today as a sacrifice [ἐν θυσίᾳ] that is rich and acceptable. . . . I glorify you through the eternal and heavenly high priest Jesus Christ [διὰ τοῦ αἰωνίου καὶ ἐπουρανίου ἀρχιερέως

---

40. The author certainly had access to 1 Corinthians, and knowledge of Romans, like Hebrews, is highly likely; see Gregory, "The Writings."

41. Ehrman, *Apostolic Fathers*, 1:361–62.

'Ιησοῦ Χριστοῦ]" (14.2–3). The scent from his burning is "a particularly sweet aroma, like wafting incense [λιβανωτοῦ]" (15.2). While the martyrological tradition goes back some way, the explicit identification of martyrdom with sacrifice appears to emerge only in the late first century AD (see the depiction of the killing of a Jewish mother and her seven sons in 4 Macc. 16:20; 17:22, in contrast to the absence of sacrificial language in the earlier account of the same events in 2 Macc. 7).

The association of prayer with sacrifice and incense has long standing, and we have encountered various instances of this already. In Irenaeus of Lyons's treatise *Against Heresies*, written toward the end of the second century, this connection is briefly established from Scripture. First, Irenaeus demonstrates the priority of obedience, faith, righteousness, and mercy using prophetic critiques of sacrifice from the OT (*Haer.* 4.17.1–4). He then states that the Eucharist is the pure sacrifice offered in every place (see Mal. 1:11) and that incense is equivalent to the prayers of the saints, referencing Revelation (*Haer.* 4.17.5–6). Throughout 4.17 and 18, Irenaeus is at pains to emphasize that God does not need sacrifice; sacrifices are for our benefit, not his, and the OT sacrifices fulfilled a pedagogical function so that we might learn to produce godly fruit. After citing from Matt. 25, Irenaeus continues:

> Thus is it, therefore, also his will that we too [i.e., Christians] should offer a gift at the altar, frequently and without intermission. The altar, then, is in heaven (for towards that place are our prayers and oblations directed); the temple likewise is there, as John says in the Apocalypse, "And the temple of God was opened"; the tabernacle also, "For, behold," he says, "the tabernacle of God, in which he will dwell with people." (*Haer.* 4.18.6)[42]

The brevity of Irenaeus's comments suggests that he sees the direction of Christian prayer toward a heavenly altar and temple as relatively uncontroversial. At the same time, his citations could indicate that he feels the need to justify or at least reinforce this notion using explicit references to Revelation.

Writing a little later, at the turn of the third century, Clement of Alexandria offers comparable reflections. He is emphatic, both from OT citations and from quotations from Greek writers including Euripides, that God cannot be housed in any human-made edifice and has no need of sacrifice (*Strom.* 5.11; cf. 7.6). Christians, the "true gnostics," have access to God through our great high priest (7.3) and advance toward him via a life of virtue by which we approach "the Father's vestibule" and the great high priest (7.7). The church is fashioned into a temple (7.5), and the Christian altar is the earthly congregation devoted

42. Text from *ANF* 1:486, modified.

to prayer (7.6). Clement displays his attunement to Greek philosophical reflection in his avoidance of both anthropomorphism and physical cosmological explanations of how God receives prayer. Prayer is incense, but it does not rise upward to heaven; rather, it is instantly perceived and present to God:

> The instantaneous perception of the angels, and the power of conscience touching the soul—these recognize all things with the quickness of thought by means of some indescribable faculty apart from sensible hearing. Even if one should say that it was impossible for the voice, rolling in this lower air, to reach God, still the thoughts of the saints cleave, not the air alone, but the whole universe as well. And the divine power instantly penetrates the whole soul, like light. (*Strom.* 7.7.37)[43]

A similar idea can be noted in Origen's *Against Celsus* half a century later: responding to attacks on Christians for not joining in civic festivals, Origen affirms that the Christian's duty is to pray at all times, "offering up continually bloodless sacrifices in prayer to God" (*Cels.* 8.21; cf. 8.22 where he quotes Eph. 2:6 as evidence Christians always live in the season of Pentecost). The reference to "bloodless sacrifices" partly reflects the fact that these are oblations of prayer, not animal victims, but also implies their fitness for entering the heavenly realm (cf. the angels' "rational and bloodless oblation" in T. Levi 3.5–8).

Early Christians understood prayer and martyrdom to be closely related to heaven—one's petitions or oneself passing to the divine realm—and both were naturally and easily aligned with cultic motifs in light of earlier Jewish and Christian traditions.

The Martyrdom and Ascension of Isaiah and the Epistula Apostolorum

The Martyrdom and Ascension of Isaiah is an early second-century Christian text that recounts the martyrdom of Isaiah (1–5) and his ascent through the seven heavens (6–11), where he sees the Beloved and has a vision of his descent, incarnation, and ascension. Earlier scholarship discerned three sources: the Martyrdom (1–5), a Jewish text elaborating on the prediction and fulfillment of Isaiah's death at Manasseh's hands; a late first-century Christian insertion into the Martyrdom (3.13–4.22); and the Vision (6–11), a Christian composition from the second century.[44] More recently, scholars have been skeptical of

---

43. Text from Oulton and Chadwick, *Alexandrian Christianity*.
44. So, e.g., M. A. Knibb, "Introduction to Ascension of Isaiah," in *OTP* 2:143–55.

the need for or at least the possibility of discerning different sources behind the text and have made a variety of arguments for its unity, at least in its final form.[45] Our interest is in the ascent in the second half of the work.[46]

The vision is part of a broader exegetical tradition of reading Isa. 6.[47] A door is opened, and worship is offered to "the One who (dwells) in the upper world and who sits on high, the Holy One, the One who rests among the holy ones, and they ascribed glory to the one who had thus graciously given a door in an alien world, had graciously given it to a man" (Mart. Ascen. Isa. 6.8–9).[48] Isaiah ascends, though not bodily, with an angel who comes from the seventh heaven. As noted previously, seven is both a biblically auspicious figure and the number of planetary spheres in Aristotelian cosmology. Isaiah proceeds through five heavens, each more glorious than the previous one, and each containing a centrally located throne and angels offering praise to the left and right (e.g., 7.18–23). He is transformed in glory as he ascends (7.25). A shift occurs when he enters the "air of the sixth heaven" (8.1): here there are no angels on the left side and no throne in the middle, but instead their praise is directed "by the power of the seventh heaven, where the One who is not named dwells, and his Chosen One, whose name is unknown" (8.7). Isaiah joins in the angelic praise of the Father, the Beloved, and the angel of the Spirit. He dons a robe that, with the intervention of the Beloved, enables him to enter the seventh heaven (9.1–5). Here he finds innumerable angels and all the righteous "stripped of (their) robes of the flesh," awaiting their thrones and crowns, all of which they will receive after Christ has ascended (9.18). The hymns of praise from the six lower heavens all ascend into the highest heaven (10.1), where they are not just heard but *seen* (10.5), implying that they rise like incense or smoke.

There follows an account of Christ's descent through the heavens, changing his likeness in the fifth heaven and each subsequent one so that he is not recognized by the angels but instead appears as one of their own kind (10.7–31). Following his incarnation and infancy he ascends, but this time without changing form so that he is seen and praised by the angels in each heaven, who are surprised and sorrowful that they did not recognize him on his descent (11.23–33; cf. 1 Cor. 2:8). He returns to his place at the Father's

45. Knight, *Disciples of the Beloved One*; Hannah, "Ascension of Isaiah." Robert Hall ("Ascension of Isaiah") posits that the final author is responsible for 3:13–31 and chap. 6, bringing together two sources. Elsewhere, Hall ("Isaiah's Ascent") argues that there is nothing that is non-Jewish or non-Christian in the text and that it is unnecessary to posit a Jewish source.

46. The descent and ascent to the seventh heaven and robes for the righteous are pre-echoed in Mart. Ascen. Isa. 3.13–4.22.

47. Hannah, "Ascension of Isaiah."

48. Translation from Knibb in *OTP*.

right hand, with the Spirit sitting on the left hand (11.33). Isaiah then puts on his robe of flesh, and the vision ends (11.34–35).

The descent narrative of the Ascension of Isaiah is paralleled in the later Epistula Apostolorum (dated with some probability to the AD 170s),[49] albeit with certain differences. The Epistula does not contain a visionary ascent, and Christ's disguise is as an archangel in order to conceal his descent from the leading angels in the higher heavens as well as the powers in the lower ones (13.1–4).[50] He then appears to Mary in the form of Gabriel and enters her in order to become flesh (14.1–8). Although the Epistula is terse in describing the heavens, it contains details that supplement the picture offered in the Ascension of Isaiah. First, Christ is explicitly a priest. He is addressed as such in the closing words of the text by the angels, "Gather us, O priest, into the light of glory!" (Ep. Ap. 51.3), and he prepares the archangels to cover his own heavenly cultic duties at the altar in his absence (Ep. Ap. 13.5–6).[51] Second, the Epistula like the Ascension of Isaiah recognizes a distinction between the highest heavens (sixth and seventh, though these are not explicitly enumerated in the Epistula) and the lower heavens, such that "the fifth firmament marks the boundary."[52] This suggests a heaven-as-temple model with the seventh heaven equivalent to the most holy place, the sixth to the holy place, and the fifth to the courtyard or veil, with lower heavens as additional gradations of holy space.

This model fits the Ascension of Isaiah as well, a conclusion reinforced by several features: the absence of one entire class of angels (those on the left) from the sixth and seventh heavens, akin to the Levites' absence from the sanctuary proper; the absence of a throne in the sixth heaven, thus emphasizing the throne/ark in the seventh; visible praise rising into these spaces like the smoke of the incense; and the requirement for specific garments and intercession from the Beloved in order for Isaiah to enter the seventh heaven. The goal of this portrayal of heaven seems to be to engender greater desire for its glories and to offer reassurance in the heavenly destination of the righteous, who in the light of the Beloved's descent and ascent are assured of their own future entry to the seventh heaven to receive robes, thrones, and crowns (Mart. Ascen. Isa. 9.24–26; cf. Ep. Ap. 21.1; 28.4, using language of a prepared place that echoes John 14).[53] Such future access to the center of heaven is promised for

49. Elliott, *Apocryphal New Testament*, 556; Watson, *Apostolic Gospel*, 7–11. Text is from Watson's translation in the same volume.

50. For a detailed comparison of the two descent narratives, see Watson, *Apostolic Gospel*, 140–48.

51. Watson (*Apostolic Gospel*, 137) rightly notes that there is some tension between this and his disguise.

52. Watson, *Apostolic Gospel*, 145.

53. So also Hall, "Isaiah's Ascent," 475–83.

those who believe in the cross, and in the meantime vicarious and proleptic heavenly participation is enabled by the account of Isaiah's vision.

The Apocalypse of Paul

The Apocalypse of Paul (also known as the *Visio Pauli*), the last of the texts explored here, is also the latest. It dates in its origins from perhaps the mid-third century but in its fuller form from the late fourth century.[54] It takes its cue from the reference in 2 Cor. 12:2 to Paul's ascent to the third heaven.[55] As well as reflecting more developed church orders and eucharistic theology, it is responsible for some of the more gruesome depictions of hell's torments, which had such influence in later Christian preaching and art.[56] Our interest is happily in the other side of the coin—namely, Paul's tours of heaven. These are not so much a single tour as a journey encompassing a number of (by now familiar) motifs: third or seventh heaven, city, and paradise. The Apocalypse reflects notions of a heavenly liturgy, with the angels worshiping God at the hour when the sun sets, presenting mankind's works of the day before God (7–8). Paul is taken up to the third heaven, through a door of gold with "two columns of gold above it full of golden letters" (19).[57] There are also indications of a now-familiar basic cosmology: the foundation of the firmament is on the ocean, which surrounds the earth (21; 31).

Paul is then taken over the Acherusian Lake to the City of Christ, which has twelve walls, each greater and more glorious than the previous one (23; 29), serving to preserve the purity of the city.[58] In the midst of the city is a great altar, where David ministers with a harp: Christ sits at the Father's right hand, and David "sings psalms before him in the seventh heaven." This one reference to the seventh heaven is surprising because the Apocalypse elsewhere (like 2 Cor. 12) mentions only three heavens.[59] David's ministry is connected

54. The preface (found at the end of the Syriac version) gives a rationale for its rediscovery during the consulate of Theodosius and Cynegius, ca. AD 388.

55. On Paul's ascent, see Gooder, *Only the Third Heaven?*

56. Some of these derive from the earlier Apocalypse of Peter (mid-second century), which has Christ on a throne of glory (6) and an extended account of the transfiguration (15–17) but does not develop the cultic aspects of heaven.

57. Text from Elliott, *Apocryphal New Testament.*

58. David Frankfurter ("Legacy of Jewish Apocalypses," 195) notes that later Coptic martyrologies owe more to the Apocalypse of Paul than to Jewish apocalypses in their portrayal of the heavenly city.

59. There is also a short "Apocalypse of Paul" found among the Nag Hammadi library (Codex V), in which Paul ascends from the third to the tenth heaven. See Schneemelcher, *New Testament Apocrypha*, 2:695–700; Kaler, *Apocalypse of Paul* (translation on 1–11).

to the Eucharist: "A sacrifice may not be offered to God without David, but it is necessary that David should sing psalms in the hour of the oblation of the body and blood of Christ: as it is performed in heaven, so also on earth" (29). The archangel Michael also has a liturgical function, praying ceaselessly for humanity (43). In a scene clearly dependent on Revelation, there are twenty-four elders, four beasts, an altar and throne (with smoke rising near the throne), and angels and ministers interceding (44). Of note here is the presence of a veil, which is not mentioned in Revelation. The Coptic version ends with Paul being carried into the third heaven again, where he sees an altar with seven angels to its left and right, and thousands of angels singing praise to God. He is shown to a throne in a tabernacle of light and sees paradise with three walls around it, where the trees praise God thrice daily.[60]

It is striking that Christ is essentially passive, the recipient of worship along with the Father; he is neither priest nor sacrifice. While angels and David (and a number of other patriarchs and prophets) serve in priestly or intermediary roles, the overarching emphasis is on moral purity, which determines not only whether a soul goes to hell or heaven but how far within heaven that soul is able to advance. The imagery is fluid, but all of it points in the same direction: access is reserved for the purest of the pure, who can enter the innermost sphere of God's presence, and this is the grounds for moral exhortation. There is little interest in redemption or atonement, and indeed Michael's prayers seem to be entirely without effect.

Conclusion

This necessarily cursory survey of early Christian texts exhibits significant diversity but also a number of common threads. Ephesians focuses on the cosmic import of the church as temple, displaying and accomplishing God's sovereignty and victory in heavenly and not only earthly realms. Ephesians thus contrasts with 1 Corinthians and 1 Peter, where church-as-temple is developed in chiefly earthbound terms, and also with 2 Clement and Ignatius's letters, which largely follow in the same stream. For 1 Clement, the old covenant cult is a model of order for the church, and the church's worship continues through Christ as high priest. Worship, particularly in the form of prayer, is explicitly (and yet often only fleetingly) associated with a heavenly

---

60. This longer ending is summarized in Schneemelcher, *New Testament Apocrypha*, 2:741; Elliott, *Apocryphal New Testament*, 644.

temple, high priest, or altar, whether in Irenaeus, Clement of Alexandria, or Origen. The cultic associations of martyrdom are connected with a heavenly destination in the Martyrdom of Polycarp, as in Revelation and in Jesus's and Stephen's deaths. It is the promise of, and heightening of desire for, access to heaven that characterizes texts like Ephesians and the Ascension of Isaiah. The latter, when read with the help of the Epistula Apostolorum, offers a conceptualization of heaven as temple that rivals the portrayals in Hebrews and Revelation as among the most developed in early Christianity. In this regard, the moral concerns of texts like Shepherd of Hermas and the Apocalypse of Paul represent at best a desire for purity that is consonant with the temple imagery but at worst a moralizing reversal of the emphasis on access through Christ, which is a common theme in texts as diverse as John's Gospel, Hebrews, Ephesians, and the Ascension of Isaiah. What is perhaps most striking is the recurrent presence of the heavenly temple motif, often in brief and allusive terms and without any felt need for further elaboration. The Shepherd of Hermas and the Letter of Barnabas are good illustrations of this, in that both make cursory allusion to heavenly temple ideas but do not develop them, as they are not central to the interests and arguments of either text. This suggests that the idea of a heavenly temple—with corollaries such as Christ's high priesthood, the heavenly destination of Christian prayer and martyrs as sacrifices, and themes of access and assurance—has become part of the fabric of early Christian thought and practice.

Conclusion

Cosmos, Cultus, and Christ

The presence of the exalted Christ in the heavenly temple is a fundamental part of early Christian experience and confession. The gospel is, in part, temple-shaped, and the texts produced by early Christians reflect this. Their map of reality enabled them to plot in a cultic frame who Jesus was, what he had accomplished, and where he now is.[1] At the same time, Jesus's descent, earthly ministry, ascent, and ongoing heavenly presence transformed their cartography. This book has sought to describe both the map and its reconfiguration. In this conclusion, I revisit and synthesize my findings with these two points in mind. The map is the presence and extent of the idea of a heavenly temple across the NT. Its reconfiguration identifies the Christian transformations of the notion of heavenly temple in terms of personnel, process, and place. Before we get to this, I first summarize the findings of each chapter and then comment on the relationship of heavenly temple to other usage of temple imagery in early Christianity, offering some reflections on its relative neglect in biblical studies and biblical theology.

The Road Thus Far: Summary of the Argument

The linkage of heaven and temple was found almost everywhere in the ancient world, but it was not everywhere the same. In the ancient Near East, gods

---

1. Jonathan Z. Smith (*Map Is Not Territory*, 292) defines a cosmology as "a locative map of the world . . . which guarantees meaning and value through structures of congruity and conformity."

created the cosmos or its upper or lower tier as their dwelling, and earthly monarchs as their regents imitated them in building temples. The temple to a chief god was the bond of heaven and earth, the cosmic center, whether in Babylon or Delphi. Ancient Israel shared this concept, modeling its sanctuaries after Eden and the universe and describing heaven as God's temple. Developments from the basic notion of correspondence are seen already in exilic times in Ezekiel's visionary temple, and much fuller elaborations are found by the Second Temple period. Conceptualizations of the heaven-temple correspondence can be envisaged along a spectrum of possibilities ranging from blueprints in heaven (the likely original meaning of Moses's heavenly vision in Exod. 25), through a temple building in heaven and heaven as a temple, to temple-as-microcosm (or cosmos-as-macro-temple). This last idea is similar to the rather fleeting connection between temple and world made by Greek and Roman writers, but it is both more elaborate and thoroughly Jewish in writers such as Philo and Josephus.

In this context, it is unsurprising to find Revelation's visions revolving around the heavenly throne-room-sanctuary. This is the location of God and the exalted Lamb who was slain, who are at the center of worship offered by the whole of creation. The heavenly temple is the place of ultimate holiness, and its opening in the last days unleashes judgment toward unholiness and impurity on earth. It is also opened for revelation to John the Seer and as a place of refuge for saints and martyrs. These openings anticipate the fuller transformation in the new age, when the heavenly Jerusalem comes down to earth as an immense most holy place. It is a place of perfect purity with twelve open gates and has no temple building because it is itself a sanctuary, the place where God and the Lamb can dwell with their redeemed people.

Hebrews, in slight contrast, dwells at length on heaven as a *tabernacle*. This was, it seems, formed at creation and was the model for the wilderness tabernacle. Israel's tent-sanctuary in turn had a didactic function, teaching through its arrangements and rites how Jesus would fulfill the old covenant. It is through his death, resurrection, ascension, and session on the divine throne that he performs the ultimate Day of Atonement rite as both high priest and sacrificial victim. He also fulfills the *tamid* and continues in priestly intercession. As a result of Jesus's inauguration of the heavenly tabernacle, its two chambers have become one, and any impediment to believers' sight of him is removed.

As we turn to the Gospels, we are no longer dealing with texts that offer explicit visions or descriptions of the heavenly sanctuary. Yet a shared cultic cosmology informs the evangelists' writings as well. Mark sets up a careful structural connection between the tearing of the heavens and the temple veil.

Together with the theophany at the transfiguration, and amid echoes of the closing chapters of Isaiah, this establishes a sense of the anticipated eschatological sanctuary. In Jesus's trial, we glimpse the expectation that he will shortly take up his place in this sanctuary "not made by hands." For Matthew, the basic heaven-temple connection is a shared assumption revealed in numerous sayings of Jesus. Matthew highlights the sharp separation of heaven and earth and the crucial role of the holy mountain—and of the one "greater than the temple," whose ministry is frequently exercised from the mountain—in overcoming that separation.

For Luke, angels are not simply couriers and couriers. As cultic servants, they turn up in holy places and at sacred times. A series of visionary encounters leads up to the life and ministry of Jesus and then carries on his work on earth. Luke has his own take on the transfiguration and crucifixion, highlighting the cosmic breach that enables heaven to be a refuge for the Messiah, as it is later for his martyr Stephen. The ascension is pivotal to the two volumes, and the heavenly location and activity of Jesus proves instrumental for catalytic moments in Acts: the sending of the Spirit as divine presence into the disciples at Pentecost, Stephen's heavenly vision and death, Paul's transformation from persecutor to promoter of the Way through a vision of the glorified Jesus, and Cornelius's reception of the Spirit in response to his temple-timed piety. Decisive intervention from the heavenly temple drives forward the universal mission.

While Jesus and temple are related in Matthew and Luke, it is John's Gospel that is best known for developing an explicit temple Christology. The Wisdom traditions undergirding the Prologue suggest that the Word should be identified as a divine emanation like those that inhabited prior earthly sanctuaries. Thus, for the Word to become flesh and "tabernacle" among us is the culmination of a series of divine indwellings. The heavenly temple lies behind and is in turn reinforced by this temple Christology in a whole range of permutations embracing patriarchal holy place, tabernacle, and the second temple, including its courtyards. It finds its most overt expression in the conviction that Jesus's death and return constitute the preparing of the Father's house as a heavenly holy place with many rooms that will serve as the eschatological dwelling for God's people.

The idea of heavenly temple is also found in a range of other early Christian texts. Church-as-temple comes together with heaven-as-temple in Ephesians, which has a strong emphasis on the present heavenly location of the church. The Ascension of Isaiah shows numerous similarities with Jewish apocalypses and portrays the highest heavens as a two-part sanctuary in order to give believers a sense of the glory that awaits after death. A heavenly temple, altar, or high priest is a common point of reference in numerous texts, most often in connection with descriptions of or exhortations to worship. Martyrdom also takes on a sacrificial connotation by the start of the second century AD. The fact that many of these references are fleeting or allusive demonstrates that the notion of a heavenly temple has become part of the fabric of early Christian thought. It was to be further embedded by the particular constellation of texts that came to form the NT canon, not least (but also not only) Hebrews and Revelation. In this light, it is perhaps surprising that the concept of a heavenly temple has been relatively neglected in the modern period.

The Road Less Traveled: Heavenly Temple, Biblical Scholarship, and Biblical Theology

In his book *The New Temple: The Church in the New Testament*, R. J. McKelvey notes the theological problems arising from the shortcomings of the earthly temple and from doubts about human ability to construct a temple worthy of God and safe from the vicissitudes of history. In Jewish literature— whether Ezekiel, the Temple Scroll, or 4 Ezra—these problems gave rise to hopes for an eschatological, utopic temple, often of heavenly origin. For McKelvey, this "would suggest that one need not look for the conception of the heavenly temple in the NT. Were not such problems resolved in the incarnation and gift of the Spirit?" That is, temple Christology and temple ecclesiology should a priori obviate the need for temple cosmology. Jesus and church trump heaven. As a good reader of texts, McKelvey is quick to clarify: "Whatever the conclusions of the argument of logic would appear to be, the fact of the matter is that the conception of the heavenly temple is in the New Testament."[2] His comments are nevertheless insightful, for they reveal the kind of widely shared modern "logic" that, I contend, underlies the relative neglect in scholarship of the theme of heavenly temple. Temple imagery in relation to Jesus and church or community has received more attention than heavenly temple.[3]

There are at least four factors, I think, that help explain this neglect. Two relate to canon and two to cosmos. First, there is the bias of (largely Protestant) biblical scholarship of the last two centuries against priestly and cultic

2. McKelvey, *New Temple*, 139.

3. A raft of studies of part or all of the biblical canon have been concerned primarily or only with community-as-temple, both those that are historical (e.g., Gärtner, *Temple and the Community*; McKelvey, *New Temple*) and those that have a more overtly theological interest (e.g., Congar, *Mystère du Temple*; Beale, *Temple and the Church's Mission*).

material within Scripture. This has been well documented and rightly critiqued.[4] Yet in spite of this, there has been significant scholarly interest in Jesus-as-temple and community-as-temple. This interest is not in proportion to the biblical material. With the notable exception of John's Gospel, temple Christology is at best a marginal theme within the NT. One's judgment about the relative weighting of temple-as-community and temple-as-cosmos material is affected by decisions on a number of passages open to interpretation, and vice versa. Nevertheless, the extent of heavenly temple material is at least equal to and arguably much greater than the several prominent community-as-temple passages. We therefore need to attend to *where* such passages occur. This is the second factor. A bias in favor of the Pauline corpus and texts in its wider orbit (i.e., a canon-within-the-canon that favors documents such as the Corinthian letters, Ephesians, and 1 Peter) would partly account for this interest. Mining the rich seams in these texts may have fueled (and colored) the search for similar materials in other parts of the NT.

A third factor is the neglect of space in modern thought, which I referenced in the introduction. In biblical studies, this has meant a disregard for cosmology, often in favor of eschatology and/or ecclesiology. As we have seen at points in this book, even apparently straightforward cosmic temple language has often been explained in terms of the people of God. I do not want to suggest that people versus place is a zero-sum game. My concern is precisely that many studies have treated it as such, favoring people to the detriment of place. Rather, as Doreen Massey highlights, space is inherently relational. All our texts recognize this, and works like Revelation and Ephesians give particular attention to the relationality of space. They portray heaven as a place for the righteous to relate to God intimately and eternally (Revelation) and the church as enjoying a heavenly status and location even now (Ephesians).

The fourth factor, and perhaps the most significant obstacle to engaging with the idea of a heavenly temple, is the advent of modern scientific cosmology. The Copernican revolution of the sixteenth century shattered the prevailing Aristotelian cosmology by decentering the earth and dismantling the heavenly spheres around it in favor of planetary orbits around the sun. The empirical and mathematical advances of Greek thinkers, culminating in the work of Ptolemy in the second century AD, had simply qualified ancient (and therefore also biblical) cosmology. The work of Copernicus, Galileo, and Kepler, however, radically challenged it. In this light, where sacred Scripture

---

4. Julius Wellhausen is most prominently associated with this view. It has been countered by biblical scholars (see, e.g., the comments in Levenson, "Temple and the World") and also by anthropologists such as Mary Douglas (e.g., in *Purity and Danger*; *Leviticus as Literature*).

articulates a three-tiered cosmos, it looks at best charmingly naive and at worst "primitive" and wrong. With community-as-temple or Jesus-as-temple passages, the pastor might instinctively feel "that'll preach"; antiquated cosmology, on the other hand, definitely "won't preach."

One way of coping with this discrepancy is to assert that the authors of these texts did not, in fact, hold such a cosmology. N. T. Wright expresses this view:

> We must not caricature ancient Jews and Christians as though they were naïve cave-men, believing in a three-decker universe with "supernatural" upstairs, "natural" downstairs and something nasty down in the cellar. That shallow cosmological sketch is like the early maps that tried and failed to capture the globe on a sheet of paper. Perhaps some did "take it literally," but that is not the main point.[5]

This is partially correct in that some of the nuances of Aristotelian cosmology had by the turn of the eras trickled down to the level of common understanding[6] and in that philosophical and religious thought had long wrestled with the question of what heaven was really like, whether there could be water above the firmament, and so forth.[7]

Yet Wright is too quick to dismiss ancient cosmology (and early cartography, for that matter), and in this respect it is fair to ask who is doing the caricaturing. The NT authors and other early Christians believed that heaven was part of this creation and that it was in some sense "up there." Indeed, the idea that heaven and spiritual ascent involve upward spatial movement has proved remarkably difficult to shake, even in the centuries since Copernicus.[8] By plotting heaven within the universe and yet in a place that no human being can access apart from divine intervention or help, these writers affirm its reality as a firstspace region of the physical world, even as they acknowledge its essential otherness. In this they are doing something very similar to the early cartographers who included the garden of Eden on their world maps.[9] In our

5. Wright, *History and Eschatology*, 159. Similar comments are found in Wright, *Resurrection of the Son of God*, 655.

6. See, e.g., the naming of the seven "heavenly circles" in the account of creation in 2 En. 30.2–3, though with Jupiter (Zeus) and Venus (Aphrodite) swapped from Ptolemy's order (Greenwood, *Scripture and Cosmology*, 142).

7. In chap. 8, we noted Clement of Alexandria's disavowal of vertical spatial language in favor of temporal instantaneity in regard to prayer as incense.

8. On this, see Mix, "Decoupling." Eliade (*Sacred and the Profane*, 209–11) argues that nonreligious "modern man" remains indebted to and a product of religious mythologies.

9. For an exploration of this, see Bockmuehl, "Locating Paradise." He concludes that Jews and Christians in late antiquity "refused to take for granted what the Enlightenment world would

day, the language that readily suggests itself is that of another dimension or parallel universe, drawn from the intersection of contemporary philosophy, science, science fiction, and fantasy.[10] In a millennium or two, people may look back on our idiom as just as naive as language of a three-tiered cosmos. This does not matter. The point is that in every age we find ways to express the idea that heaven is a real place and at the same time somewhere other and ordinarily inaccessible. The concept of a temple encapsulates exactly this tension between the reality of localized divine presence and the challenges and obstacles to access. The notion of a heavenly temple thus merits the attention of biblical scholars and has a part to play within biblical theology.

The Road Ahead: A Map Reconfigured

The argument of this book has mapped early Christian understandings of the heavenly temple in their ancient and Second Temple contexts. In closing, I trace the map while articulating its early Christian reconfiguration. The notion that heaven is a temple is a common presupposition across the NT, one shared with the wider Second Temple Jewish world, and one that has left its mark even on texts that do not explicitly dwell on or explore it. Indeed, the idea of heaven as temple helps make sense of certain features or episodes of those texts. At the same time, we can note a gradation of increasing interest in the heavenly temple from Jesus's earthly life, through his ascension and the present life of the church, and on through to the eschaton. This gradation roughly follows the progression of the canonical arrangement from the Gospels, through Acts, toward Hebrews and Revelation. The degree to which such an idea is shared with many Second Temple Jewish texts is indicated by the overlapping and difficult-to-disentangle Jewish and Christian aspects of texts such as the Testaments of the Twelve Patriarchs and the Ascension of Isaiah. Yet it is reconfigured by the person and work of Jesus. Those reconfigurations can be traced under the cultic aspects of personnel, process, and place that I noted in the introduction.

In terms of cultic personnel, in addition to the expected angels, living creatures, and "faithful departed" encountered in heaven or sent from there, Jesus

---

refuse to question: the notion that spiritual and terrestrial truth belong in two incompatible spheres, which must be kept separate and not be allowed to 'contaminate' each other" (207).

10. E.g., Alexander ("Dualism of Heaven and Earth") uses language of a "parallel universe" to describe apocalyptic accounts of heaven. For philosophy of science, see Carr, *Universe or Multiverse?* Science fiction and fantasy references abound; I recently watched the Marvel Studios film *Doctor Strange in the Multiverse of Madness* with my son (purely for the purposes of research, of course).

is a (high) priest. He has offered sacrifice and continues to aid his people via his compassionate intercession and help for them and occasionally by theophanic appearance. His priesthood pertains primarily to heaven, in keeping with the fact that both the levitical priesthood and the new priesthood (the church) belong to the earthly sphere. These are not mutually exclusive domains, as all priesthood has a bridging or mediatorial function and thus must be concerned in some sense with both. Jesus's preparation for his priesthood incorporates his incarnation and earthly experience, but the major sphere of his priestly ministry lies in the heavenly realm. This in turn explains a lower level of interest in Jesus's priestly ministry in the Gospels, which increases in Acts, the letters, and Revelation.

With regard to cultic process, Jesus's death is likened to the Passover offering, effecting redemption on earth, but it has ongoing significance in his heavenly appearance as the slain Lamb in Revelation. This is likely a continuation of the identification with Passover but could also reflect the guilt, peace, or *tamid* offerings. Heavenly sacrifices include the prayers of the saints offered by the angels. Hebrews provides the most developed portrayal of sacrifice in heaven. Jesus offers himself there following the resurrection and ascension, and before his session, as the ultimate Yom Kippur sacrifice. He continues to pray in fulfillment of the function of the *tamid*, ensuring ongoing relationship between God and his people. In the terms of Sojan spatiality, explained in the introduction, Jesus's ascension into heaven as a priest to perform sacrificial work can be assessed as a thirdspatial interruption of the highest order.[11] The ascension and heavenly session of a human being are among the most explosive of the beliefs held by early Christians, not least because by these very acts Jesus shows himself to be more than human. Visions, heavenly openings, and theophanies during his ministry serve to prepare this transformation. The same phenomena after the ascension serve to implement its effects by catalyzing the secondspatial reconfiguration of early Christian understandings of place, purity, and relations.

As to cultic place, which has been the primary focus of this study, the structure of the heavenly temple as NT authors perceive it is underdetermined. This is certainly the case in the Gospels and Acts but is also true of Hebrews and Revelation, where, despite the greater evidence, the various indications within each text are equivocal or at times stand in tension with one another. I have nevertheless sought to demonstrate that both of these documents, despite their differences, portray a single-chambered sanctuary, where the most holy place

11. For an exploration of thirdspatial transformations in Luke-Acts, see Moore, "He Saw Heaven Opened," 48–50.

or throne room is the focus of interest to the exclusion—or incorporation—of other parts. Hebrews depicts a structural shift that unites the two tabernacle chambers into a single one. Neither Hebrews nor Revelation evinces the notion of temple-as-cosmos that we find in Philo and Josephus, at least not explicitly, as there is no indication that the earth and sea form outer chambers or courts to heaven. The lack of interest in outer chambers or courts, which largely served to reinforce the gradations of holiness in the earthly temple, is in keeping with an emphasis on greater access.

This is the fundamental spatial and structural transformation: the heavenly temple has been rendered accessible through Jesus's ministry.[12] Access is described through a variety of motifs: the tearing or opening of heaven, ascending a holy mountain, the opening of a door, the drawing aside or tearing of a curtain, or the New Jerusalem's twelve open gates. Temporary revelations come to individuals, including in the transfiguration, Stephen's and Peter's visions in Acts, and Paul's ascent. There is also asylum for martyrs in Revelation while they await the last day. All of these are in keeping with Second Temple vision and ascent traditions. Yet the direction of travel within the NT is toward a permanent opening by and through Christ, a democratization whereby heavenly access becomes the possession not only of elite figures such as patriarchs and prophets but also of every believer, both now and in the future. This is intimated in the gentile centurion's confession at the torn veil and exemplified in visual access to Jesus and the throne of grace in Hebrews. Such present access is a foretaste of the full and lasting availability of Revelation's New Jerusalem, which is God's most holy place. In short, heaven has become an open sanctuary.

12. Doreen Massey (*For Space*, 163–95) offers a helpful exploration of the openness and closure of different spaces, taking London's Isle of Dogs peninsula and scientists' laboratories and homes as examples. She emphasizes that what matters is not the *degree* of openness or closure—all spaces are both open and closed in some measure—but rather "the *terms* on which that openness/closure is established" (179, emphasis original). Revelation is most eloquent on this: heaven is open in judgment toward the impure and unrighteous, and the New Jerusalem is ultimately closed to them while at the same time emphatically open to the redeemed people of God.

Bibliography

Adams, Edward. *The Stars Will Fall from Heaven: Cosmic Catastrophe in the New Testament and Its World.* Library of New Testament Studies 347. London: T&T Clark, 2007.

Alexander, Philip S. "The Dualism of Heaven and Earth in Early Jewish Literature and Its Implications." In *Light against Darkness: Dualism in Ancient Mediterranean Religion and the Contemporary World*, edited by Armin Lange, Eric M. Meyers, Bergit Peters, and Bennie H. Reynolds, 169–85. Journal of Ancient Judaism Supplements 2. Göttingen: Vandenhoeck & Ruprecht, 2011.

———. *The Mystical Texts.* Library of Second Temple Studies 61. Companion to the Qumran Scrolls 7. London: T&T Clark, 2006.

Allen, Leslie C. *Psalms 101–50.* 2nd ed. Word Biblical Commentary. Nashville: Nelson, 2002.

Anderson, Charles. "Lukan Cosmology and the Ascension." In *Ascent into Heaven in Luke-Acts: New Explorations of Luke's Narrative Hinge*, edited by David K. Bryan and David W. Pao, 175–212. Minneapolis: Fortress, 2016.

Ashley, Timothy R. *The Book of Numbers.* New International Commentary on the Old Testament. Grand Rapids: Eerdmans, 1996.

Asumang, Annang, and Bill Domeris. "Ministering in the Tabernacle: Spatiality and the Christology of Hebrews." *Conspectus* 1 (2006): 1–25.

Attridge, Harold W. *The Epistle to the Hebrews: A Commentary on the Epistle to the Hebrews.* Hermeneia. Philadelphia: Fortress, 1989.

Aune, David E. *Revelation 1–5.* Word Biblical Commentary. Dallas: Word, 1997.

———. *Revelation 6–16.* Word Biblical Commentary. Nashville: Nelson, 1998.

———. *Revelation 17–22.* Word Biblical Commentary. Nashville: Nelson, 1998.

Bachmann, Michael. "Himmlisch: Der 'Tempel Gottes' von Apk 11.1." *New Testament Studies* 40 (1994): 474–80.

———. *Jerusalem und der Tempel: Die geographisch-theologischen Elemente in der lukanischen Sicht des jüdischen Kultzentrums*. Beiträge zur Wissenschaft vom Alten und Neuen Testament 109. Stuttgart: Kohlhammer, 1980.

Bammel, Ernst. "The Farewell Discourse of the Evangelist John and Its Jewish Heritage." *Tyndale Bulletin* 44 (1993): 103–16.

Barker, Margaret. *The Gate of Heaven: The History and Symbolism of the Temple in Jerusalem*. London: SPCK, 1991.

———. *Temple Mysticism: An Introduction*. London: SPCK, 2011.

Barnard, Jody A. *The Mysticism of Hebrews: Exploring the Role of Jewish Apocalyptic Mysticism in the Epistle to the Hebrews*. Wissenschaftliche Untersuchungen zum Neuen Testament 2/331. Tübingen: Mohr Siebeck, 2012.

Battaglia, Peter. "'Gazing toward Heaven' in Clement of Rome: The Function of Vision in Clement's Christology." Paper presented at the South Central Jurisdiction of the United Methodist Church Conference Meeting, 2019.

Bauckham, Richard. "James and the Jerusalem Church." In *The Book of Acts in Its Palestinian Setting*, edited by Richard Bauckham, 415–80. The Book of Acts in Its First Century Setting 4. Grand Rapids: Eerdmans, 1995.

———. *The Theology of the Book of Revelation*. New Testament Theology. Cambridge: Cambridge University Press, 1993.

Bauspieß, Martin. "Die Gegenwart des Heils und das Ende der Zeit: Überlegungen zur lukanischen Eschatologie im Anschluss an Lk 22,66–71 und Apg 7,54–60." In *Eschatologie—Eschatology: The Sixth Durham-Tübingen Research Symposium; Eschatology in Old Testament, Ancient Judaism and Early Christianity*, edited by Hans-Joachim Eckstein, Christof Landmesser, and Hermann Lichtenberger, 125–48. Wissenschaftliche Untersuchungen zum Neuen Testament 272. Tübingen: Mohr Siebeck, 2011.

Beale, G. K. "The Descent of the Eschatological Temple in the Form of the Spirit at Pentecost: Part 1: The Clearest Evidence." *Tyndale Bulletin* 56, no. 1 (2005): 73–102.

———. "The Descent of the Eschatological Temple in the Form of the Spirit at Pentecost: Part 2: Corroborating Evidence." *Tyndale Bulletin* 56, no. 2 (2005): 63–90.

———. "Eden, the Temple, and the Church's Mission in the New Creation." *Journal of the Evangelical Theological Society* 48 (2005): 5–31.

———. *The Temple and the Church's Mission: A Biblical Theology of the Dwelling Place of God*. New Studies in Biblical Theology 17. Leicester, UK: Apollos, 2004.

Beckwith, Roger T. "The Daily and Weekly Worship of the Primitive Church in Relation to Its Jewish Antecedents." *Evangelical Quarterly* 56 (1984): 65–80, 139–58.

Behr, John. *John the Theologian and His Paschal Gospel: A Prologue to Theology.* Oxford: Oxford University Press, 2019.

Ben-Eliyahu, Eyal. "'On That Day, His Feet Will Stand on the Mount of Olives': The Mount of Olives and Its Hero between Jews, Christians, and Muslims." *Jewish History* 30 (2016): 29–42.

Bénétreau, Samuel. *L'Épître aux Hébreux.* 2 vols. Commentaire Évangélique de la Bible. Vaux-sur-Seine: ÉDIFAC, 1988.

Blenkinsopp, Joseph. "The Structure of P." *Catholic Biblical Quarterly* 38 (1976): 275–92.

Block, Daniel I. "Eden: A Temple? A Reassessment of the Biblical Evidence." In *From Creation to New Creation: Biblical Theology and Exegesis: Essays in Honor of G. K. Beale*, edited by Daniel M. Gurtner and Benjamin L. Gladd, 3–29. Peabody, MA: Hendrickson, 2013.

Bloor, Joshua D. A. *Purifying the Consciousness in Hebrews: Cult, Defilement and the Perpetual Heavenly Blood of Jesus.* Library of New Testament Studies 675. London: Bloomsbury T&T Clark, 2023.

Blount, Brian K. *Revelation: A Commentary.* New Testament Library. Louisville: Westminster John Knox, 2009.

Bock, Darrell L. "The Son of Man Seated at God's Right Hand and the Debate over Jesus' 'Blasphemy.'" In *Jesus of Nazareth: Lord and Christ; Essays on the Historical Jesus and New Testament Christology*, edited by Joel B. Green and Max Turner, 181–91. Grand Rapids: Eerdmans, 1994.

Bockmuehl, Markus. "Being Emmanuel: Matthew's Ever-Present Jesus?" *New Testament Studies* 68 (2022): 1–12.

———. "Locating Paradise." In Bockmuehl and Stroumsa, *Paradise in Antiquity*, 192–209.

Bockmuehl, Markus, and Guy G. Stroumsa, eds. *Paradise in Antiquity: Jewish and Christian Views.* Cambridge: Cambridge University Press, 2010.

Boers, Hendrikus. *Neither on This Mountain nor in Jerusalem: A Study of John 4.* SBL Monograph Series 35. Atlanta: Scholars Press, 1988.

Botner, Max. "A Sanctuary in the Heavens and the Ascension of the Son of Man: Reassessing the Logic of Jesus' Trial in Mark 14.53–65." *Journal for the Study of the New Testament* 41 (2019): 310–34.

Boyarin, Daniel. *Border Lines: The Partition of Judaeo-Christianity.* Philadelphia: University of Pennsylvania Press, 2004.

Brant, Jo-Ann A. *John.* Paideia. Grand Rapids: Baker Academic, 2011.

Briggs, Robert A. *Jewish Temple Imagery in the Book of Revelation.* Studies in Biblical Literature 10. New York: Peter Lang, 1999.

Brooks, Walter Edward. "The Perpetuity of Christ's Sacrifice in the Epistle to the Hebrews." *Journal of Biblical Literature* 89 (1970): 205–14.

Brown, Raymond E. *The Death of the Messiah, from Gethsemane to the Grave: A Commentary on the Passion Narratives in the Four Gospels.* 2 vols. Anchor Bible Reference Library. New York: Doubleday, 1994.

———. *The Gospel according to John I–XII.* Anchor Bible. Garden City, NY: Doubleday, 1966.

Bruce, F. F. *The Book of the Acts.* New International Commentary on the New Testament. Grand Rapids: Eerdmans, 1988.

———. *The Epistles to the Colossians, to Philemon, and to the Ephesians.* New International Commentary on the New Testament. Grand Rapids: Eerdmans, 1984.

Brueggemann, Walter. *Genesis.* Interpretation. Atlanta: John Knox, 1982.

Bryan, Steven M. "The Eschatological Temple in John 14." *Bulletin for Biblical Research* 15 (2005): 187–98.

Bumpus, Harold Bertram. *The Christological Awareness of Clement of Rome and Its Sources.* Cambridge, MA: University Press of Cambridge, 1972.

Burge, Gary M. "Territorial Religion, Johannine Christology, and the Vineyard of John 15." In *Jesus of Nazareth: Lord and Christ; Essays on the Historical Jesus and New Testament Christology,* edited by Joel B. Green and Max Turner, 384–96. Grand Rapids: Eerdmans, 1994.

Burkert, Walter. "The Meaning and Function of the Temple in Classical Greece." In *Temple in Society,* edited by Michael V. Fox, 27–47. Winona Lake, IN: Eisenbrauns, 1988.

Burkett, Delbert. "The Transfiguration of Jesus (Mark 9:2–8): Epiphany or Apotheosis?" *Journal of Biblical Literature* 138 (2019): 413–32.

Burrows, Eric. "Some Cosmological Patterns in Babylonian Religion." In *Cult and Cosmos: Tilting toward a Temple-Centered Theology,* edited by L. Michael Morales, 27–47. Biblical Tools and Studies 18. Leuven: Peeters, 2014.

Butticaz, Simon David. *L'identité de l'Église dans les Actes des apôtres: De la restauration d'Israël à la conquête universelle.* Beihefte zur Zeitschrift für die neutestamentliche Wissenschaft und die Kunde der älteren Kirche 174. Berlin: de Gruyter, 2010.

Byers, Andrew J. *Ecclesiology and Theosis in the Gospel of John.* Society for New Testament Studies Monograph Series 166. Cambridge: Cambridge University Press, 2017.

Caird, George B. "Exegetical Method of the Epistle to the Hebrews." *Canadian Journal of Theology* 5 (1959): 44–51.

Calaway, Jaeda C. *The Sabbath and the Sanctuary: Access to God in the Letter to the Hebrews and Its Priestly Context.* Wissenschaftliche Untersuchungen zum Neuen Testament 2/349. Tübingen: Mohr Siebeck, 2013.

Caneday, Ardel B. "The Eschatological World Already Subjected to the Son: The Οἰκουμένη of Hebrews 1.6 and the Son's Enthronement." In *A Cloud of Witnesses:*

The Theology of Hebrews in Its Ancient Contexts, edited by Richard Bauckham, Trevor Hart, Nathan MacDonald, and Daniel Driver, 28–39. London: T&T Clark, 2008.

Carleton Paget, James. *The Epistle of Barnabas: Outlook and Background*. Wissenschaftliche Untersuchungen zum Neuen Testament 2/64. Tübingen: Mohr Siebeck, 1994.

Carr, Bernard, ed. *Universe or Multiverse?* Cambridge: Cambridge University Press, 2007.

Carter, Erica, James Donald, and Judith Squires. *Space and Place: Theories of Identity and Location*. London: Lawrence & Wishart, 1993.

Chalmers, Matthew. "Samaritans, Biblical Studies, and Ancient Judaism: Recent Trends." *Currents in Biblical Research* 20 (2021): 28–64.

Chance, J. Bradley. *Jerusalem, Temple and the New Age in Luke-Acts*. Macon, GA: Mercer University Press, 1988.

Charlesworth, James H., ed. *The Old Testament Pseudepigrapha*. 2 vols. Reprint ed. Peabody, MA: Hendrickson, 2009.

Chronis, Harry L. "The Torn Veil: Cultus and Christology in Mark 15:37–39." *Journal of Biblical Literature* 101 (1982): 97–114.

Church, Philip. *Hebrews and the Temple: Attitudes to the Temple in Second Temple Judaism and in Hebrews*. Supplements to Novum Testamentum 171. Leiden: Brill, 2017.

Cicero. *The Republic and the Laws*. Edited by Niall Rudd and Jonathan G. F. Powell. Oxford World's Classics. Oxford: Oxford University Press, 1998.

Clements, Ronald E. *God and Temple: The Idea of the Divine Presence in Ancient Israel*. Oxford: Blackwell, 1965.

Clifford, Richard J. "The Temple and the Holy Mountain." In *The Temple in Antiquity: Ancient Records and Modern Perspectives*, edited by Truman G. Madsen, 107–24. Salt Lake City: Brigham Young University, 1984.

Cockerill, Gareth Lee. *The Epistle to the Hebrews*. New International Commentary on the New Testament. Grand Rapids: Eerdmans, 2012.

Cocksworth, Hannah M. "Zechariah and Gabriel as Thematic Characters: A Narratological Reading of the Beginning of Luke's Gospel (Luke 1:8–20)." In *Characters and Characterization in Luke-Acts*, edited by Frank Dicken and Julia Snyder, 41–54. Library of New Testament Studies 548. London: Bloomsbury T&T Clark, 2016.

Cohen, Akiva. "Matthew and the Temple." In *Matthew within Judaism*, edited by Daniel M. Gurtner and Anders Runesson. Early Christianity and Its Literature 27. Atlanta: SBL Press, 2020.

Collins, Adela Yarbro. *Cosmology and Eschatology in Jewish and Christian Apocalypticism*. Supplements to the Journal for the Study of Judaism 50. Leiden: Brill, 1996.

Collins, John J., ed. *Apocalypse: Morphology of a Genre*. Semeia 14. Missoula, MT: Scholars Press, 1979.

Coloe, Mary L. *God Dwells with Us: Temple Symbolism in the Fourth Gospel*. Collegeville, MN: Liturgical Press, 2001.

———. "Temple Imagery in John." *Interpretation* 63 (2009): 368–81.

Congar, Yves. *Le Mystère du Temple: Ou l'économie de la présence de Dieu à sa créature, de la Genèse à l'Apocalypse*. Lectio Divina. Paris: Cerf, 1958.

Cook, Stephen L. *Ezekiel 38–48: A New Translation with Introduction and Commentary*. Anchor Bible. New Haven: Yale University Press, 2018.

Couprie, Dirk L. *Heaven and Earth in Ancient Greek Cosmology: From Thales to Heraclides Ponticus*. Astrophysics and Space Science Library 374. New York: Springer, 2011.

Craigie, Peter C. *Psalms 1–50*. 2nd ed. Word Biblical Commentary. Nashville: Nelson, 2004.

D'Angelo, Mary Rose. *Moses in the Letter to the Hebrews*. SBL Dissertation Series 42. Missoula, MT: Scholars Press, 1979.

Davidson, Richard M. "Christ's Entry 'Within the Veil' in Hebrews 6:19-20: The Old Testament Background." *Andrews University Seminary Studies* 39 (2001): 175–90.

Davies, W. D., and Dale C. Allison. *A Critical and Exegetical Commentary on the Gospel According to Saint Matthew*. 3 vols. International Critical Commentary. Edinburgh: T&T Clark, 1988.

Davis, Ellen F. *Proverbs, Ecclesiastes, and the Song of Songs*. Westminster Bible Companion. Louisville: Westminster John Knox, 2000.

Davis, R. Dean. *The Heavenly Court Judgment of Revelation 4-5*. Lanham, MD: University Press of America, 1992.

Deutsch, Celia. "Transformation of Symbols: The New Jerusalem in Rv 21:1–22:5." *Zeitschrift für die neutestamentliche Wissenschaft und die Kunde der älteren Kirche* 78 (1987): 106–26.

Dio Chrysostom. *Discourses 12–30*. Translated by J. W. Cohoon. Loeb Classical Library 339. Cambridge, MA: Harvard University Press, 1939.

Domeris, William. "The Enigma of Jesus' Temple Intervention: Four Essential Keys." *HTS Teologiese Studies/Theological Studies* 71 (2015): 1–8.

Donaldson, Terence L. *Jesus on the Mountain: A Study in Matthean Theology*. Journal for the Study of the New Testament Supplement Series 8. Sheffield: JSOT Press, 1987.

Douglas, Mary. *Leviticus as Literature*. Oxford: Oxford University Press, 1999.

———. *Purity and Danger: An Analysis of Concepts of Pollution and Taboo*. London: Routledge & Kegan Paul, 1966.

Draper, J. A. "Temple, Tabernacle and Mystical Experience in John." *Neotestamentica* 31 (1997): 263–88.

Du Toit, Philip La G. "Was Paul a Christian?" *Neotestamentica* 53 (2019): 1–29.

Eberhart, Christian. *Studien zur Bedeutung der Opfer im Alten Testament: Die Signifikanz von Blut- und Verbrennungsriten im kultischen Rahmen.* Wissenschaftliche Monographien zum Alten und Neuen Testament 94. Neukirchen-Vluyn: Neukirchener Verlag, 2002.

Edwards, J. R. "The Use of ΠΡΟΣΕΡΧΕΣΘΑΙ in the Gospel of Matthew." *Journal of Biblical Literature* 106 (1987): 65–74.

Ehrman, Bart D., ed. *The Apostolic Fathers.* 2 vols. Loeb Classical Library 24–25. Cambridge, MA: Harvard University Press, 2003.

Eisele, Wilfried. *Ein unerschütterliches Reich: Die mittelplatonische Umformung des Parusiegedankens im Hebräerbrief.* Beihefte zur Zeitschrift für die neutestamentliche Wissenschaft und die Kunde der älteren Kirche 116. Berlin: de Gruyter, 2003.

Electronic Text Corpus of Sumerian Literature. Oxford: University of Oxford, 2016. https://etcsl.orinst.ox.ac.uk/.

Eliade, Mircea. *The Myth of the Eternal Return: Cosmos and History.* Edited by Jonathan Z. Smith. Translated by Willard R. Trask. Princeton: Princeton University Press, 2005.

———. *The Sacred and the Profane: The Nature of Religion.* Translated by Willard R. Trask. New York: Harcourt Brace, 1959.

Elliott, J. K. *The Apocryphal New Testament: A Collection of Apocryphal Christian Literature in an English Translation.* Oxford: Clarendon, 1993.

Esler, Philip F. *Community and Gospel in Luke-Acts: The Social and Political Motivations of Lucan Theology.* Society for New Testament Studies Monograph Series 57. Cambridge: Cambridge University Press, 1987.

———. *God's Court and Courtiers in the Book of the Watchers: Re-Interpreting Heaven in 1 Enoch 1–36.* Eugene, OR: Wipf & Stock, 2017.

Etheridge, J. W. *The Targums of Onkelos and Jonathan Ben Uzziel on the Pentateuch, with the Fragments of the Jerusalem Targum, from the Chaldee.* 2 vols. London: Longman, Green, Longman & Roberts, 1862–65.

Falk, Daniel K. *Daily, Sabbath, and Festival Prayers in the Dead Sea Scrolls.* Studies on the Texts of the Desert of Judah 27. Leiden: Brill, 1998.

Fanning, Buist M. *Verbal Aspect in New Testament Greek.* Oxford Theological Monographs. Oxford: Clarendon, 1990.

Festugière, A. J. *Le Dieu cosmique.* Vol. 2 of *La révélation d'Hermès Trismégiste.* Paris: Les Belles Lettres, 2014.

Fischer, Günter. *Die himmlische Wohnung: Untersuchungen zu Joh 14,2f.* Europäische Hochschulschriften. Frankfurt: Peter Lang, 1975.

Fletcher-Louis, Crispin H. T. *All the Glory of Adam: Liturgical Anthropology in the Dead Sea Scrolls.* Studies on the Texts of the Desert of Judah 42. Leiden: Brill, 2002.

———. "The High Priest in Ben Sira 50: The High Priest Is an Incorporative Divine Messiah and At-One-Ment Takes Place through Worship in the Microcosm." In

Atonement: Jewish and Christian Origins, edited by Max Botner, Justin Harrison Duff, and Simon Dürr, 89–111. Grand Rapids: Eerdmans, 2020.

———. "On Angels, Men and Priests (Ben Sira, the Qumran Sabbath Songs and the Yom Kippur Avodah)." In *Gottesdienst und Engel im antiken Judentum und frühen Christentum*, edited by Jörg Frey and Michael R. Jost, 141–66. Wissenschaftliche Untersuchungen zum Neuen Testament 2/446. Tübingen: Mohr Siebeck, 2017.

Foster, Paul. *The Gospel of Peter: Critical Edition, Introduction, and Commentary*. Texts and Editions for New Testament Study 4. Leiden: Brill, 2010.

Foster, Robert L. "'A Temple in the Lord Filled to the Fullness of God': Context and Intertextuality (Eph. 3:19)." *Novum Testamentum* 49 (2007): 85–96.

France, R. T. *The Gospel of Mark: A Commentary on the Greek Text*. New International Greek Testament Commentary. Grand Rapids: Eerdmans, 2002.

———. *The Gospel of Matthew*. New International Commentary on the New Testament. Grand Rapids: Eerdmans, 2007.

Frankfurter, David. "The Legacy of Jewish Apocalypses in Early Christianity: Regional Trajectories." In *The Jewish Apocalyptic Heritage in Early Christianity*, edited by James C. VanderKam and William Adler, 129–200. Leiden: Brill, 1996.

Franklin, Eric. "The Ascension and the Eschatology of Luke-Acts." *Scottish Journal of Theology* 23 (1970): 191–200.

Fredriksen, Paula. "Paul the 'Convert'?" In *The Oxford Handbook of Pauline Studies*, edited by Matthew V. Novenson and R. Barry Matlock, 31–53. Oxford: Oxford University Press, 2014.

Fuglseth, Kåre. *Johannine Sectarianism in Perspective: A Sociological, Historical, and Comparative Analysis of Temple and Social Relationships in the Gospel of John, Philo, and Qumran*. Supplements to Novum Testamentum 119. Leiden: Brill, 2005.

Gäbel, Georg. *Die Kulttheologie des Hebräerbriefes: Eine exegetisch-religionsgeschichtliche Studie*. Wissenschaftliche Untersuchungen zum Neuen Testament 2/212. Tübingen: Mohr Siebeck, 2006.

———. "'You Don't Have Permission to Access This Site': The Tabernacle Description in Hebrews 9:1–5 and Its Function in Context." In *Son, Sacrifice, and Great Shepherd: Studies on the Epistle to the Hebrews*, edited by David M. Moffitt and Eric F. Mason, 135–74. Wissenschaftliche Untersuchungen zum Neuen Testament 2/510. Tübingen: Mohr Siebeck, 2020.

Gallusz, Laszlo. "The Ark of the Covenant in the Cosmic Conflict Vision of the Book of Revelation." *TheoRhema* 6 (2011): 103–22.

———. *The Throne Motif in the Book of Revelation*. Library of New Testament Studies 487. London: Bloomsbury T&T Clark, 2014.

Gärtner, Bertil E. *The Temple and the Community in Qumran and the New Testament: A Comparative Study in the Temple Symbolism of the Qumran Texts and the New Testament*. Society for New Testament Studies Monograph Series 1. Cambridge: Cambridge University Press, 1965.

Giambrone, Anthony. *The Bible and the Priesthood: Priestly Participation in the One Sacrifice for Sins*. A Catholic Biblical Theology of the Sacraments. Grand Rapids: Baker Academic, 2022.

———. "'Why Do the Scribes Say' (Mark 9:11): Scribal Expectations of an Eschatological High Priest and the Interpretation of Jesus' Transfiguration." *Revue Biblique* 128 (2021): 201–35.

Giblin, Charles Homer. "Revelation 11.1–13: Its Form, Function, and Contextual Integration." *New Testament Studies* 30 (1984): 433–59.

Gooder, Paula. *Only the Third Heaven? 2 Corinthians 12.1–10 and Heavenly Ascent*. Library of New Testament Studies 313. London: T&T Clark, 2006.

Goppelt, Leonhard. *Typos: The Typological Interpretation of the Old Testament in the New*. Grand Rapids: Eerdmans, 1982.

Grässer, Erich. *An die Hebräer*. 3 vols. Evangelisch-Katholischer Kommentar zum Neuen Testament. Zürich: Benziger/Neukirchener Verlag, 1990.

Gray, George Buchanan. *Sacrifice in the Old Testament: Its Theory and Practice*. Oxford: Clarendon, 1925.

Gray, Timothy C. *The Temple in the Gospel of Mark*. Wissenschaftliche Untersuchungen zum Neuen Testament 2/242. Tübingen: Mohr Siebeck, 2008.

Greene, Joseph R. "Jesus as the Heavenly Temple in the Fourth Gospel." *Bulletin for Biblical Research* 28 (2018): 425–46.

Greenfield, Jonas C., Michael Stone, and Esther Eshel. *The Aramaic Levi Document: Edition, Translation, Commentary*. Studia in Veteris Testamenti Pseudepigrapha 19. Leiden: Brill, 2021.

Greenwood, Kyle. *Scripture and Cosmology: Reading the Bible Between the Ancient World and Modern Science*. Downers Grove, IL: IVP Academic, 2015.

Gregory, Andrew F. "1 Clement and the Writings That Later Formed the New Testament." In *The Reception of the New Testament in the Apostolic Fathers*, edited by Andrew F. Gregory and Christopher M. Tuckett, 129–57. Oxford: Oxford University Press, 2005.

———. "1 Clement: An Introduction." *Expository Times* 117 (2006): 223–30.

Gregory, Andrew F., and C. Kavin Rowe, eds. *Rethinking the Unity and Reception of Luke and Acts*. Columbia: University of South Carolina Press, 2010.

Gruenwald, Ithamar. *Apocalyptic and Merkavah Mysticism*. Arbeiten zur Geschichte des antiken Judentums und des Urchristentums 14. Leiden: Brill, 1980.

Grundeken, Mark. *Community Building in the Shepherd of Hermas: A Critical Study of Some Key Aspects*. Vigiliae Christianae Supplements 131. Leiden: Brill, 2015.

Gundry, Robert H. "'In My Father's House are Many Μοναί' (John 14 2)." *Zeitschrift für die neutestamentliche Wissenschaft und die Kunde der älteren Kirche* 58 (1967): 68–72.

———. "The New Jerusalem: People as Place, Not Place for People." *Novum Testamentum* 29 (1987): 254–64.

Gurtner, Daniel M. "The Rending of the Veil and Markan Christology: 'Unveiling' the ΥΙΟΣ ΘΕΟΥ (Mark 15:38–39)." *Biblical Interpretation* 15 (2007): 292–306.

———. *The Torn Veil: Matthew's Exposition of the Death of Jesus*. Society for New Testament Studies Monograph Series 139. Cambridge: Cambridge University Press, 2006.

Guthrie, George H. "The Tree and the Temple: Echoes of a New Ingathering and Renewed Exile (Mark 11.12–21)." *New Testament Studies* 68 (2022): 26–37.

Hahn, Robert. *Anaximander and the Architects: The Contributions of Egyptian and Greek Architectural Technologies to the Origins of Greek Philosophy*. SUNY Series in Ancient Greek Philosophy. Albany: State University of New York Press, 2001.

———. "Architectural Technologies and the Origins of Greek Philosophy." *Archai* 29 (2020).

Hall, Robert G. "The Ascension of Isaiah: Community Situation, Date, and Place in Early Christianity." *Journal of Biblical Literature* 109 (1990): 289–306.

———. "Isaiah's Ascent to See the Beloved: An Ancient Jewish Source for the Ascension of Isaiah?" *Journal of Biblical Literature* 113 (1994): 463–84.

———. "Living Creatures in the Midst of the Throne: Another Look at Revelation 4.6." *New Testament Studies* 36 (1990): 609–13.

Hamm, Dennis. "Praying 'Regularly' (Not 'Constantly'): A Note on the Cultic Background of *Dia Pantos* at Luke 24:53, Acts 10:2 and Hebrews 9:6, 13:15." *Expository Times* 116 (2004): 50–52.

———. "The Tamid Service in Luke-Acts: The Cultic Background behind Luke's Theology of Worship (Luke 1:5–25; 18:9–14; 24:50–53; Acts 3:1; 10:3, 30)." *Catholic Biblical Quarterly* 65 (2003): 215–31.

Hannah, Darrell D. "Isaiah's Vision in the Ascension of Isaiah and the Early Church." *Journal of Theological Studies* 50 (1999): 80–101.

———. "Of Cherubim and the Divine Throne: Rev 5.6 in Context." *New Testament Studies* 49 (2003): 528–42.

Haran, Menahem. *Temples and Temple-Service in Ancient Israel: An Inquiry into the Character of Cult Phenomena and the Historical Setting of the Priestly School*. Oxford: Clarendon, 1978.

Harrington, Wilfrid J. *Revelation*. Sacra Pagina 16. Collegeville, MN: Liturgical Press, 1993.

Harvey, David. *The Condition of Postmodernity: An Enquiry into the Origins of Cultural Change*. Oxford: Blackwell, 1990.

Hay, Jared W. "'And Suddenly, Two Men . . .': Moses and Elijah in Lukan Perspective." *Expository Times* 134, no. 10 (2023): 435–44.

Haynes, Theresa Abell. "Voices of Fire: Sinai Imagery in Acts 2 and Rabbinic Midrash." *Nordisk Judaistik/Scandinavian Jewish Studies* 32 (2021): 30–45.

Hays, Richard B. *Echoes of Scripture in the Gospels*. Waco: Baylor University Press, 2016.

Hayward, C. T. R. *The Jewish Temple: A Non-biblical Sourcebook*. London: Routledge, 1996.

Heath-Whyte, George R. "The Uses of 'Bēlu' and 'Marduk' in Neo-Assyrian Royal Inscriptions and Other Sources from the First Millennium BC." PhD diss., University of Cambridge, 2021.

Heil, John Paul. "The Narrative Strategy and Pragmatics of the Temple Theme in Mark." *Catholic Biblical Quarterly* 59 (1997): 76–100.

Henne, Philippe. "Barnabé, le temple, et les pagano-chrétiens." *Revue Biblique* 103 (1996): 257–76.

———. *La christologie chez Clément de Rome et dans le Pasteur d'Hermas*. Paradosis 33. Fribourg: Éditions universitaires, 1992.

Hentschel, Christoph. "Lebendiges Gotteswort: Die Rezeption des Hebräerbriefs im Ersten Clemensbrief und im Hirten des Hermas." ThD diss., Ludwig-Maximilians-Universität, 2008.

Herodotus. *The Persian Wars*. Edited by A. D. Godley. 4 vols. Loeb Classical Library 117–120. London: Heinemann, 1920.

Himmelfarb, Martha. *Ascent to Heaven in Jewish and Christian Apocalypses*. Oxford: Oxford University Press, 1993.

———. "Temple and Priests in the Book of the Watchers, the Animal Apocalypse and the Apocalypse of Weeks." In *The Early Enoch Literature*, edited by Gabriele Boccaccini and John J. Collins, 219–36. Supplements to the Journal for the Study of Judaism 121. Leiden: Brill, 2007.

Hofius, Otfried. *Katapausis: Die Vorstellung vom endzeitlichen Ruheort im Hebräerbrief*. Wissenschaftliche Untersuchungen zum Neuen Testament 11. Tübingen: Mohr Siebeck, 1970.

Hørning Jensen, Morten. "The Temple 'before the Temple' in the Gospel of Mark." *Early Christianity* 12 (2021): 388–420.

Hoskins, Paul M. *Jesus as the Fulfillment of the Temple in the Gospel of John*. Paternoster Biblical Monographs. Carlisle: Paternoster, 2007.

Hubbard, David A. *Joel and Amos*. Tyndale Old Testament Commentaries. Nottingham: Inter-Varsity, 1989.

Hundley, Michael B. *Gods in Dwellings: Temples and Divine Presence in the Ancient Near East*. Writings from the Ancient World Supplement Series 3. Atlanta: Society of Biblical Literature, 2013.

Hurst, L. D. *The Epistle to the Hebrews: Its Background of Thought*. Society for New Testament Studies Monograph Series 65. Cambridge: Cambridge University Press, 1990.

———. "How 'Platonic' Are Heb 8:5 and Heb 9:23f.?" *Journal of Theological Studies* 34 (1983): 156–68.

Hutchens, Joshua C. "Christian Worship in Hebrews 12:28 as Ethical and Exclusive." *Journal of the Evangelical Theological Society* 59 (2016): 207–22.

Hvalvik, Reidar. *The Struggle for Scripture and Covenant: The Purpose of the Epistle of Barnabas and Jewish-Christian Competition in the Second Century.* Wissenschaftliche Untersuchungen zum Neuen Testament 2/82. Tübingen: Mohr Siebeck, 1996.

Jacobson, Howard. *A Commentary on Pseudo-Philo's Liber Antiquitatum Biblicarum, with Latin Text and English Translation.* Leiden: Brill, 1996.

Jamieson, R. B. "Hebrews 9.23: Cult Inauguration, Yom Kippur and the Cleansing of the Heavenly Tabernacle." *New Testament Studies* 62 (2016): 569–87.

———. *Jesus' Death and Heavenly Offering in Hebrews.* Society for New Testament Studies Monograph Series 172. Cambridge: Cambridge University Press, 2018.

Janowski, Bernd. "Tempel und Schöpfung: Schöpfungstheologische Aspekte der priesterschriftlichen Heiligtumskonzeption." *Jahrbuch für Biblische Theologie* 5 (1990): 37–69.

Jenson, Philip. "A Cosmic Temple? A Skeptical Assessment." Paper presented at the Tyndale Fellowship Biblical Theology Study Group, High Leigh, Broxbourne, 2022.

Johnson, Luke Timothy. *The Gospel of Luke.* Sacra Pagina 3. Collegeville, MN: Liturgical Press, 1991.

Jones, Larry Paul. *The Symbol of Water in the Gospel of John.* Journal for the Study of the New Testament Supplement Series 145. London: T&T Clark, 1997.

Jordaan, Gert J. C. "Cosmology in the Book of Revelation." *In Die Skriflig* 47 (2013): 1–8.

Joyce, Paul M. "Ezekiel 40–42: The Earliest 'Heavenly Ascent' Narrative?" In *The Book of Ezekiel and Its Influence*, edited by H. J. de Jonge and Johannes Tromp, 17–41. Aldershot: Ashgate, 2007.

———. "Temple and Worship in Ezekiel 40–48." In *Temple and Worship in Biblical Israel: Proceedings of the Oxford Old Testament Seminar*, edited by John Day, 145–63. London: T&T Clark, 2005.

Juel, Donald. *Messiah and Temple: The Trial of Jesus in the Gospel of Mark.* SBL Dissertation Series 31. Missoula, MT: Scholars Press, 1977.

Kaler, Michael. *Flora Tells a Story: The Apocalypse of Paul and Its Contexts.* Waterloo, ON: Wilfrid Laurier University Press, 2008.

Kanagaraj, Jey J. *"Mysticism" in the Gospel of John: An Inquiry into Its Background.* Journal for the Study of the New Testament Supplement Series 158. Sheffield: Sheffield Academic, 1998.

Kapelrud, Arvid S. "Temple Building: A Task for Gods and Kings." *Orientalia* 32 (1963): 56–62.

Käsemann, Ernst. *The Wandering People of God: An Investigation of the Letter to the Hebrews*. Translated by Roy A. Harrisville and Irving L. Sandberg. Minneapolis: Augsburg, 1984.

———. *Das wandernde Gottesvolk: Eine Untersuchung zum Hebräerbrief*. Göttingen: Vandenhoeck & Ruprecht, 1939.

Kearney, Peter J. "Creation and Liturgy: The P Redaction of Ex 25–40." *Zeitschrift für die alttestamentliche Wissenschaft* 89 (1977): 375–87.

Keener, Craig S. *Acts: An Exegetical Commentary*. 4 vols. Grand Rapids: Baker Academic, 2012.

Kerr, Alan R. *The Temple of Jesus' Body: The Temple Theme in the Gospel of John*. Journal for the Study of the New Testament Supplement Series 220. Sheffield: Sheffield Academic, 2002.

Kibbe, Michael. *Godly Fear or Ungodly Failure? Hebrews 12 and the Sinai Theophanies*. Beihefte zur Zeitschrift für die neutestamentliche Wissenschaft und die Kunde der älteren Kirche 216. Berlin: de Gruyter, 2016.

Kinzer, Mark. "Temple Christology in the Gospel of John." *SBL Seminar Papers* 37 (1998): 447–64.

Kistemaker, Simon J. "The Temple in the Apocalypse." *Journal of the Evangelical Theological Society* 43 (2000): 433–41.

Klauck, Hans-Josef. "Himmlisches Haus und irdische Bleibe: Eschatologische Metaphorik in Antike und Christentum." *New Testament Studies* 50 (2004): 5–35.

Klawans, Jonathan. *Purity, Sacrifice, and the Temple: Symbolism and Supersessionism in the Study of Ancient Judaism*. Oxford: Oxford University Press, 2006.

Kleinig, John W. *Hebrews*. Concordia Commentary. St. Louis: Concordia, 2017.

Knight, Jonathan. *Disciples of the Beloved One: The Christology, Social Setting and Theological Context of the Ascension of Isaiah*. Journal for the Study of the Pseudepigrapha Supplement Series 18. Sheffield: Sheffield Academic, 1996.

Koester, Craig R. *The Dwelling of God: The Tabernacle in the Old Testament, Intertestamental Jewish Literature, and the New Testament*. Catholic Biblical Quarterly Monograph Series 22. Washington, DC: Catholic Biblical Association of America, 1989.

———. *Hebrews: A New Translation with Introduction and Commentary*. Anchor Bible 36. New York: Doubleday, 2001.

Kramer, Samuel Noah. "The Temple in Sumerian Literature." In *Temple in Society*, edited by Michael V. Fox, 1–16. Winona Lake, IN: Eisenbrauns, 1988.

Kugler, Robert A. *From Patriarch to Priest: The Levi-Priestly Tradition from Aramaic Levi to Testament of Levi*. Early Judaism and Its Literature 9. Atlanta: Scholars Press, 1996.

Kupp, David D. *Matthew's Emmanuel: Divine Presence and God's People in the First Gospel*. Society for New Testament Studies Monograph Series 90. Cambridge: Cambridge University Press, 1996.

Kutsko, John F. *Between Heaven and Earth: Divine Presence and Absence in the Book of Ezekiel*. Biblical and Judaic Studies 7. Winona Lake, IN: Eisenbrauns, 1999.

Laansma, Jon. *"I Will Give You Rest": The "Rest" Motif in the New Testament with Special Reference to Mt 11 and Heb 3–4*. Wissenschaftliche Untersuchungen zum Neuen Testament 2/98. Tübingen: Mohr Siebeck, 1997.

Lanier, Gregory R. "Luke's Distinctive Use of the Temple: Portraying the Divine Visitation." *Journal of Theological Studies* 65 (2014): 433–62.

Larsen, Kevin W. "The Structure of Mark's Gospel: Current Proposals." *Currents in Biblical Research* 3 (2004): 140–60.

Larsson, Edvin. "Temple-Criticism and the Jewish Heritage: Some Reflexions on Acts 6–7." *New Testament Studies* 39 (1993): 379–95.

Lefebvre, Henri. *The Production of Space*. Translated by Donald Nicholson-Smith. Oxford: Blackwell, 1991.

Lentzen-Deis, Fritzleo. "Das Motiv der 'Himmelsöffnung' in verschiedenen Gattungen der Umweltliteratur des Neuen Testaments." *Biblica* 50 (1969): 301–27.

Leonhardt, Jutta. *Jewish Worship in Philo of Alexandria*. Texte und Studien zum antiken Judentum 84. Tübingen: Mohr Siebeck, 2001.

Levavi, Yuval. "The Sacred Bureaucracy of Neo-Babylonian Temples." In *Contextualizing Jewish Temples*, edited by Tova Ganzel and Shalom E. Holtz, 6–22. Leiden: Brill, 2020.

Levenson, Jon D. *Creation and the Persistence of Evil: The Jewish Drama of Divine Omnipotence*. San Francisco: Harper & Row, 1988.

———. *Sinai and Zion: An Entry into the Jewish Bible*. New Voices in Biblical Studies. San Francisco: HarperCollins, 1987.

———. "The Temple and the World." *The Journal of Religion* 64 (1984): 275–98.

———. *Theology of the Program of Restoration of Ezekiel 40–48*. Harvard Semitic Monographs 10. Cambridge, MA: Scholars Press, 1976.

Levine, Lee I. "Josephus' Description of the Jerusalem Temple: War, Antiquities, and Other Sources." In *Josephus and the History of the Greco-Roman Period: Essays in Memory of Morton Smith*, edited by Fausto Parente and Joseph Sievers, 233–46. Leiden: Brill, 1994.

Lilly, Ingrid E. "'Like the Vision': Temple Tours, Comparative Genre, and Scribal Composition in Ezekiel 43." In *Ezekiel: Current Debates and Future Directions*, edited by William A. Tooman and Penelope Barter, 210–32. Forschungen zum Alten Testament 112. Tübingen: Mohr Siebeck, 2017.

Lincoln, Andrew T. *Paradise Now and Not Yet: Studies in the Role of the Heavenly Dimension in Paul's Thought with Special Reference to His Eschatology*. Society for New Testament Studies Monograph Series 43. Cambridge: Cambridge University Press, 1981.

————. "A Re-examination of 'the Heavenlies' in Ephesians." *New Testament Studies* 19 (1973): 468–83.

Lioy, Dan. *Axis of Glory: A Biblical and Theological Analysis of the Temple Motif in Scripture.* Studies in Biblical Literature 138. Peter Lang, 2010.

Litwa, M. David. *How the Gospels Became History: Jesus and Mediterranean Myths.* Synkrisis. New Haven: Yale University Press, 2019.

Long, Fredrick J. "Ἐκκλησία in Ephesians as Godlike in the Heavens, in Temple, in γάμος, and in Armor: Ideology and Iconography in Ephesus and Its Environs." In *The First Urban Churches 3: Ephesus,* edited by James R. Harrison and L. L. Welborn, 193–234. Atlanta: SBL Press, 2018.

Lookadoo, Jonathon. *The High Priest and the Temple: Metaphorical Depictions of Jesus in the Letters of Ignatius of Antioch.* Wissenschaftliche Untersuchungen zum Neuen Testament 2/473. Tübingen: Mohr Siebeck, 2018.

Lundquist, John M. "The Common Temple Ideology of the Ancient Near East." In *The Temple in Antiquity: Ancient Records and Modern Perspectives,* edited by Truman G. Madsen, 53–76. Salt Lake City: Brigham Young University, 1984.

Macaskill, Grant. *Union with Christ in the New Testament.* Oxford: Oxford University Press, 2014.

Mackie, Scott D. "Ancient Jewish Mystical Motifs in Hebrews' Theology of Access and Entry Exhortations." *New Testament Studies* 58 (2012): 88–104.

————. "'Let Us Draw Near . . . but Not Too Near': A Critique of the Attempted Distinction between 'Drawing Near' and 'Entering' in Hebrews' Entry Exhortations." In *Listen, Understand, and Obey: Essays on Hebrews in Honor Gareth Lee Cockerill,* edited by Caleb T. Friedeman, 17–36. Eugene, OR: Pickwick, 2017.

Manning, Gary T. *Echoes of a Prophet: The Use of Ezekiel in the Gospel of John and in Literature of the Second Temple Period.* Journal for the Study of the New Testament Supplement Series 270. London: T&T Clark, 2004.

Marcus Manilius. *Astronomica.* Edited by G. P. Goold. Loeb Classical Library 469. Cambridge, MA: Harvard University Press, 1977.

Marguerat, Daniel. "Du temple à la maison suivant Luc-Actes." In *Quelle maison pour Dieu?,* edited by Camille Focant, 285–317. Lectio Divina, hors série. Paris: Cerf, 2003.

Marinatos, Nanno. "What Were Greek Sanctuaries? A Synthesis." In *Greek Sanctuaries: New Approaches,* edited by Nanno Marinatos and Robin Hägg, 228–33. London: Routledge, 1993.

Mason, Steve, ed. *Flavius Josephus, Translation and Commentary.* 10 vols. Leiden: Brill, 2000.

Massey, Doreen B. *For Space.* London: SAGE Publications, 2005.

Massyngberde Ford, J. *Revelation: A New Translation with Introduction and Commentary.* Anchor Bible. Garden City, NY: Doubleday, 1975.

McCaffrey, James. *The House with Many Rooms: The Temple Theme of Jn. 14,2–3.* Analecta Biblica 114. Rome: Editrice Pontificio Istituto Biblico, 1988.

McDonough, Sean. "Revelation: The Climax of Cosmology." In *Cosmology and New Testament Theology*, edited by Jonathan T. Pennington and Sean McDonough, 178–88. Library of New Testament Studies 355. London: T&T Clark, 2008.

McGrath, James F. "'Destroy This Temple': Issues of History in John 2:13–22." In *John, Jesus, and History.* Vol. 2, *Aspects of Historicity in the Fourth Gospel*, edited by Paul N. Anderson, Felix Just, and Tom Thatcher, 13–22. Atlanta: Society of Biblical Literature, 2009.

McKelvey, R. J. *The New Temple: The Church in the New Testament.* London: Oxford University Press, 1969.

Meeks, Wayne A. "The Man from Heaven in Johannine Sectarianism." *Journal of Biblical Literature* 91 (1972): 44–72.

Michaels, J. Ramsey. *The Gospel of John.* New International Commentary on the New Testament. Grand Rapids: Eerdmans, 2010.

Middleton, Paul. *The Violence of the Lamb: Martyrs as Agents of Divine Judgement in the Book of Revelation.* Library of New Testament Studies 586. New York: Bloomsbury T&T Clark, 2018.

Milgrom, Jacob. *Leviticus 1–16: A New Translation with Introduction and Commentary.* Anchor Bible. New York: Doubleday, 1991.

———. *Numbers.* The JPS Torah Commentary. Philadelphia: Jewish Publication Society, 1989.

Mix, Lucas John. "Decoupling Physical and Spiritual Ascent Narratives in Astronomy and Biology." In *The Institutions of Extraterrestrial Liberty*, edited by Charles S. Cockell, 233–53. Oxford: Oxford University Press, 2022.

Moffitt, David M. *Atonement and the Logic of Resurrection in the Epistle to the Hebrews.* Supplements to Novum Testamentum 141. Leiden: Brill, 2011.

———. "Atonement at the Right Hand: The Sacrificial Significance of Jesus' Exaltation in Acts." *New Testament Studies* 62 (2016): 549–68.

———. "Observations on Directional Features of the Incarnation and Jesus's Sacrifice in Hebrews." In *Rethinking the Atonement: New Perspectives on Jesus's Death, Resurrection, and Ascension*, 159–80. Grand Rapids: Baker Academic, 2022.

———. "Serving in the Tabernacle in Heaven: Sacred Space, Jesus's High-Priestly Sacrifice, and Hebrews' Analogical Theology." In *Hebrews in Contexts*, edited by Gabriella Gelardini and Harold W. Attridge, 259–79. Arbeiten zur Geschichte des antiken Judentums und des Urchristentums 91. Leiden: Brill, 2016.

———. "Wilderness Identity and Pentateuchal Narrative: Distinguishing between Jesus' Inauguration and Maintenance of the New Covenant in Hebrews." In *Muted Voices of the New Testament: Readings in the Catholic Epistles and Hebrews*, edited by Katherine M. Hockey, Madison N. Pierce, and Francis Watson, 153–71. Library of New Testament Studies 565. London: Bloomsbury T&T Clark, 2017.

Monier, Mina. *Temple and Empire: The Context of the Temple Piety of Luke-Acts.* Lanham, MD: Lexington Books/Fortress Academic, 2020.

Moore, Nicholas J. "'God's Sanctuary in Heaven Was Opened': Judgment, Salvation, and Cosmic Cultus in Revelation." *Neotestamentica* 55 (2021): 409–30.

———"Heaven and Temple in the Second Temple Period: A Taxonomy." *Journal for the Study of the Pseudepigrapha* 33, no. 1 (2023): 75–93.

———. "Heaven's Revolving Door? Cosmology, Entrance, and Approach in Hebrews." *Bulletin for Biblical Research* 29 (2019): 187–207.

———. "'He Saw Heaven Opened': Heavenly Temple and Universal Mission in Luke-Acts." *New Testament Studies* 68 (2022): 38–51.

———. "'In' or 'Near'? Heavenly Access and Christian Identity in Hebrews." In *Muted Voices of the New Testament: Readings in the Catholic Epistles and Hebrews*, edited by Katherine M. Hockey, Madison N. Pierce, and Francis Watson, 185–98. Library of New Testament Studies 565. London: Bloomsbury T&T Clark, 2017.

———. "Jesus as 'the One Who Entered His Rest': The Christological Reading of Hebrews 4.10." *Journal for the Study of the New Testament* 36 (2014): 383–400.

———. "'Once More unto the Breach': The Sanctuary Veil in the Synoptic Gospels and Hebrews." *Revue Biblique* 130, no. 2 (2023): 197–216.

———. *Repetition in Hebrews: Plurality and Singularity in the Letter to the Hebrews, Its Ancient Context, and the Early Church.* Wissenschaftliche Untersuchungen zum Neuen Testament 2/388. Tübingen: Mohr Siebeck, 2015.

———. "Sacrifice, Session, and Intercession: The End of Christ's Offering in Hebrews." *Journal for the Study of the New Testament* 42 (2020): 521–41.

———. "'The True Tabernacle' of Hebrews 8:2: Future Dwelling with People or Heavenly Dwelling Place?" *Tyndale Bulletin* 72 (2021): 49–71.

Morgen, Michèle. "La promesse de Jésus à Nathanaël (Jn 1,51) éclairée par la hagaddah de Jacob-Israël." *Revue des sciences religieuses* 67 (1993): 3–21.

Moriarty, W. "1 Clement's View of Ministerial Appointments in the Early Church." *Vigiliae Christianae* 66 (2012): 115–38.

Morray-Jones, Christopher R. A. "The Temple Within." In *Paradise Now: Essays on Early Jewish and Christian Mysticism*, edited by April D. DeConick, 145–78. SBL Symposium Series 11. Atlanta: Society of Biblical Literature, 2006.

Morris, Leon. *The Gospel according to John.* Rev. ed. New International Commentary on the New Testament. Grand Rapids: Eerdmans, 1995.

Moses, A. D. A. *Matthew's Transfiguration Story and Jewish-Christian Controversy.* Journal for the Study of the New Testament Supplement Series 122. Sheffield: Sheffield Academic, 1996.

Motyer, J. Alec. *The Prophecy of Isaiah: An Introduction and Commentary*. Downers Grove, IL: IVP Academic, 1993.

Motyer, Stephen. "The Rending of the Veil: A Markan Pentecost?" *New Testament Studies* 33 (1987): 155–57.

Mouton, Elna. "'Ascended Far above All the Heavens': Rhetorical Functioning of Psalm 68:18 in Ephesians 4:8–10?" *Hervormde Teologiese Studies* 70 (2014): 1–9.

Moxon, John R. L. *Peter's Halakhic Nightmare: The "Animal" Vision of Acts 10:9–16 in Jewish and Graeco-Roman Perspective*. Wissenschaftliche Untersuchungen zum Neuen Testament 2/432. Tübingen: Mohr Siebeck, 2017.

Moyise, Steve. "Ezekiel and the Book of Revelation." In *After Ezekiel: Essays on the Reception of a Difficult Prophet*, edited by Andrew Mein and Paul M. Joyce, 45–57. Library of Hebrew Bible/Old Testament Studies 535. London: T&T Clark, 2011.

Muddiman, John. "The Church in Ephesians, 2 Clement, and Hermas." In *Trajectories through the New Testament and the Apostolic Fathers*, edited by Andrew F. Gregory and C. M. Tuckett. Oxford: Oxford University Press, 2007.

Nelson, Richard D. "'He Offered Himself': Sacrifice in Hebrews." *Interpretation* 57 (2003): 251–65.

Newsom, Carol. *Songs of the Sabbath Sacrifice: A Critical Edition*. Harvard Semitic Studies 27. Atlanta: Scholars Press, 1985.

Neyrey, Jerome H. "The Jacob Allusions in John 1:51." *Catholic Biblical Quarterly* 44 (1982): 586–605.

———. "Jacob Traditions and the Interpretation of John 4:10-26." *Catholic Biblical Quarterly* 41 (1979): 419–37.

———. "Spaces and Places, Whence and Whither, Homes and Rooms: 'Territoriality' and the Fourth Gospel." *Biblical Theology Bulletin* 32 (2004): 60–75.

Nickelsburg, George W. E. "Enoch, Levi, and Peter: Recipients of Revelation in Upper Galilee." *Journal of Biblical Literature* 100 (1981): 575–600.

Niehaus, Jeffrey J. *God at Sinai: Covenant and Theophany in the Bible and Ancient Near East*. Studies in Old Testament Biblical Theology. Carlisle: Paternoster, 1995.

Orlin, Eric M. *Temples, Religion and Politics in the Roman Republic*. Mnemosyne Supplements 164. Leiden: Brill, 1997.

Orlov, Andrei. "Kavod on the River: Jesus's Baptism as Revelation of the Divine Glory." In *New Narratives for Old: The Historical Method of Reading Early Christian Theology*, edited by Anthony Briggman and Ellen Scully, 61–80. Washington, DC: Catholic University of America Press, 2022.

Osborne, Grant R. *Revelation*. Baker Exegetical Commentary on the New Testament. Grand Rapids: Baker Academic, 2002.

Osiek, Carolyn. "The Genre and Function of the Shepherd of Hermas." *Semeia* 36 (1986): 113–21.

———. *Shepherd of Hermas: A Commentary*. Hermeneia. Minneapolis: Fortress, 1999.

———. "The Shepherd of Hermas in Context." *Acta Patristica et Byzantina* 8 (1997): 115–34.

Oulton, J. E. L., and Henry Chadwick, eds. *Alexandrian Christianity: Selected Translations of Clement and Origen with Introductions and Notes*. The Library of Christian Classics 2. London: SCM, 1954.

Ounsworth, Richard J. *Joshua Typology in the New Testament*. Wissenschaftliche Untersuchungen zum Neuen Testament 2/328. Tübingen: Mohr Siebeck, 2012.

Park, Sejin. *Pentecost and Sinai: The Festival of Weeks as a Celebration of the Sinai Event*. Library of Hebrew Bible/Old Testament Studies 342. New York: T&T Clark, 2008.

Parry, Robin A. *The Biblical Cosmos: A Pilgrim's Guide to the Weird and Wonderful World of the Bible*. Eugene, OR: Cascade, 2014.

Parsons, Mikeal C. *The Departure of Jesus in Luke-Acts: The Ascension Narratives in Context*. Journal for the Study of the New Testament Supplement Series 21. Sheffield: JSOT Press, 1987.

Parsons, Mikeal C., and Richard I. Pervo. *Rethinking the Unity of Luke and Acts*. Minneapolis: Fortress, 1993.

Paul, Ian. *Revelation: An Introduction and Commentary*. Tyndale New Testament Commentaries. London: Inter-Varsity, 2018.

Paulien, Jon. "The Role of the Hebrew Cultus, Sanctuary, and Temple in the Plot and Structure of the Book of Revelation." *Andrews University Seminary Studies* 33 (1995): 245–64.

Pelletier, André. "La tradition synoptique du 'voile déchiré' à la lumière des réalités archéologiques." *Recherches de science religieuse* 46 (1958): 161–80.

Pena, Joabson Xavier. "Wearing the Cosmos: The High Priestly Attire in Josephus' Judean Antiquities." *Journal for the Study of Judaism* 52 (2021): 359–87.

Pennington, Jonathan T. *Heaven and Earth in the Gospel of Matthew*. Supplements to Novum Testamentum 126. Leiden: Brill, 2007.

Peterson, David G. *The Acts of the Apostles*. Pillar New Testament Commentary. Grand Rapids: Eerdmans, 2009.

Plutarch. *Moralia, Volume VI*. Edited by W. C. Helmbold. Loeb Classical Library 337. Cambridge, MA: Harvard University Press, 1939.

Porter, Stanley E. *Verbal Aspect in the Greek of the New Testament, with Reference to Tense and Mood*. Studies in Biblical Greek 1. New York: Peter Lang, 1989.

Price, S. R. F. *Rituals and Power: The Roman Imperial Cult in Asia Minor*. Cambridge: Cambridge University Press, 1984.

Pritchard, James B., ed. *Ancient Near Eastern Texts Relating to the Old Testament*. 3rd ed. Princeton: Princeton University Press, 1969.

Rab, Sebastian. "Christ and Church as Temple in John 14.2–3: And Implications for Eschatology and Funeral Ministry." *Theology and Ministry* 8 (2022): 3–16.

Regev, Eyal. *The Temple in Early Christianity: Experiencing the Sacred.* Anchor Yale Bible Reference Library. New Haven: Yale University Press, 2019.

Reynolds, Benjamin E. *The Apocalyptic Son of Man in the Gospel of John.* Wissenschaftliche Untersuchungen zum Neuen Testament 2/249. Tübingen: Mohr Siebeck, 2008.

Ribbens, Benjamin J. *Levitical Sacrifice and Heavenly Cult in Hebrews.* Beihefte zur Zeitschrift für die neutestamentliche Wissenschaft und die Kunde der älteren Kirche 222. Berlin: de Gruyter, 2016.

Richardson, Christopher A. *Pioneer and Perfecter of Faith: Jesus' Faith as the Climax of Israel's History in the Epistle to the Hebrews.* Wissenschaftliche Untersuchungen zum Neuen Testament 2/338. Tübingen: Mohr Siebeck, 2012.

Richardson, Peter, and Martin B. Shukster. "Barnabas, Nerva, and the Yavnean Rabbis." *Journal of Theological Studies* 34 (1983): 31–55.

———. "Temple and Bet Ha-Midrash in the Epistle of Barnabas." In *Anti-Judaism in Early Christianity.* Vol. 2, *Separation and Polemic*, edited by Stephen G. Wilson, 17–32. Waterloo, ON: Wilfrid Laurier University Press, 1986.

Richir, David. "Jacob à Cana? Échos à Jacob/Israël en Jn 2,1–11." *Hokhma* 118 (2020): 69–86.

Rojas-Flores, Gonzalo. "From John 2.19 to Mark 15.29: The History of a Misunderstanding." *New Testament Studies* 56 (2010): 22–43.

Root, Margaret Cool. "Palace to Temple—King to Cosmos: Achaemenid Foundation Texts in Iran." In *From the Foundations to the Crenellations: Essays on Temple Building in the Ancient Near East and Hebrew Bible*, edited by Mark J. Boda and Jamie R. Novotny, 165–210. Alter Orient und Altes Testament 366. Münster: Ugarit, 2010.

Rowland, Christopher. "John 1.51, Jewish Apocalyptic and Targumic Tradition." *New Testament Studies* 30 (1984): 498–507.

———. *The Open Heaven: A Study of Apocalyptic in Judaism and Early Christianity.* London: SPCK, 1982.

———. "The Second Temple: Focus of Ideological Struggle?" In *Templum Amicitiae: Essays on the Second Temple Presented to Ernst Bammel*, edited by William Horbury, 175–98. Journal for the Study of the New Testament Supplement Series 48. Sheffield: JSOT Press, 1991.

Rucker, Timothy M. *The Temple Keys of Isaiah 22:22, Revelation 3:7, and Matthew 16:19: The Isaianic Temple Background and Its Spatial Significance for the Mission of Early Christ Followers.* Wissenschaftliche Untersuchungen zum Neuen Testament 2/559. Tübingen: Mohr Siebeck, 2021.

Runia, David T. "Ancient Philosophy and the New Testament: 'Exemplar' as Example." In *Method and Meaning: Essays on New Testament Interpretation in*

Honor of Harold W. Attridge, edited by Andrew B. MacGowan and Kent Richards, 347–61. SBL Resources for Biblical Study 67. Atlanta: Society of Biblical Literature, 2011.

Safrai, Shmuel. "The Heavenly Jerusalem." *Ariel* 23 (1969): 11–16.

Salier, Bill. "The Temple in the Gospel according to John." In *Heaven on Earth: The Temple in Biblical Theology*, edited by T. Desmond Alexander and Simon J. Gathercole, 121–34. Carlisle: Paternoster, 2004.

Sanders, Jack T. "Hymnic Elements in Ephesians 1–3." *Zeitschrift für die neutestamentliche Wissenschaft und die Kunde der älteren Kirche* 56 (1965): 214–32.

Sarna, Nahum M. *Exodus*. The JPS Torah Commentary. Philadelphia: Jewish Publication Society, 1991.

Schenck, Kenneth L. "An Archaeology of Hebrews' Tabernacle Imagery." In *Hebrews in Contexts*, edited by Gabriella Gelardini and Harold W. Attridge, 238–58. Arbeiten zur Geschichte des antiken Judentums und des Urchristentums 91. Leiden: Brill, 2016.

———. *Cosmology and Eschatology in Hebrews: The Settings of the Sacrifice*. Society for New Testament Studies Monograph Series 143. Cambridge: Cambridge University Press, 2007.

Schiffman, Lawrence H. "Descriptions of the Jerusalem Temple in Josephus and the Temple Scroll." In *The Courtyards of the House of the Lord: Studies on the Temple Scroll*, edited by Florentino García Martínez. 175–87. Studies on the Texts of the Desert of Judah 75. Leiden: Brill, 2008.

Schimanowski, Gottfried. *Die himmlische Liturgie in der Apokalypse des Johannes: Die frühjüdischen Traditionen in Offenbarung 4–5 unter Einschluß der Hekhalotliteratur*. Wissenschaftliche Untersuchungen zum Neuen Testament 2/154. Tübingen: Mohr Siebeck, 2002.

Schneemelcher, Wilhelm. *New Testament Apocrypha*. Translated by Robert McLachlan Wilson. Rev. ed. 2 vols. Cambridge: Clarke, 1991.

Scholer, John M. *Proleptic Priests: Priesthood in the Epistle to the Hebrews*. Journal for the Study of the New Testament Supplement Series 49. Sheffield: JSOT Press, 1991.

Schreiner, Patrick. "Space, Place and Biblical Studies: A Survey of Recent Research in Light of Developing Trends." *Currents in Biblical Research* 14 (2016): 340–71.

Schumacher, Rob W. M. "Three Related Sanctuaries of Poseidon: Geraistos, Kalaureia and Tainaron." In *Greek Sanctuaries: New Approaches*, edited by Nanno Marinatos and Robin Hägg, 62–87. London: Routledge, 1993.

Scott, James M. *Geography in Early Judaism and Christianity: The Book of Jubilees*. Society for New Testament Studies Monograph Series 113. Cambridge: Cambridge University Press, 2002.

———. *On Earth as in Heaven: The Restoration of Sacred Time and Sacred Space in the Book of Jubilees*. Supplements to the Journal for the Study of Judaism 91. Leiden: Brill, 2005.

Scott, M. Philip. "Chiastic Structure: A Key to the Interpretation of Mark's Gospel." *Biblical Theology Bulletin* 15 (1985): 17–26.

Seneca. *Natural Questions*. Translated by Harry M. Hine. The Complete Works of Lucius Annaeus Seneca. Chicago: University of Chicago Press, 2010.

Shauf, Scott. *Jesus the Sacrifice: A Historical and Theological Study*. Lanham, MD: Lexington Books/Fortress Academic, 2022.

Sheppard, Anthony. "The Letter of Barnabas and the Jerusalem Temple." *Journal for the Study of Judaism in the Persian, Hellenistic, and Roman Period* 48 (2017): 531–50.

Sinn, Ulrich. "Greek Sanctuaries as Places of Refuge." In *Greek Sanctuaries: New Approaches*, edited by Nanno Marinatos and Robin Hägg, 88–109. London: Routledge, 1993.

Sleeman, Matthew. "Critical Spatial Theory 2.0." In *Constructions of Space*. Vol. 5, *Place, Space and Identity in the Ancient Mediterranean World*, edited by Gert T. M. Prinsloo and Christl M. Maier, 49–66. Library of Hebrew Bible/Old Testament Studies 576. London: Bloomsbury T&T Clark, 2013.

———. *Geography and the Ascension Narrative in Acts*. Society for New Testament Studies Monograph Series 146. Cambridge: Cambridge University Press, 2009.

Smith, Jonathan Z. *Map Is Not Territory: Studies in the History of Religions*. Studies in Judaism in Late Antiquity 23. Leiden: Brill, 1978.

Smith, Murray J., and Ian J. Vaillancourt. "Enthroned and Coming to Reign: Jesus's Eschatological Use of Psalm 110:1 in Mark 14:62." *Journal of Biblical Literature* 141 (2022): 513–31.

Smith, Steve. *The Fate of the Jerusalem Temple in Luke-Acts: An Intertextual Approach to Jesus' Laments over Jerusalem and Stephen's Speech*. Library of New Testament Studies 553. London: Bloomsbury T&T Clark, 2017.

Snyder, Barbara W. "Combat Myth in the Apocalypse: The Liturgy of the Day of the Lord and the Dedication of the Heavenly Temple." PhD diss., University of California, Berkeley, 1991.

Soja, Edward W. *Postmodern Geographies: The Reassertion of Space in Critical Social Theory*. London: Verso, 1989.

———. "Thirdspace: Expanding the Scope of the Geographical Imagination." In *Human Geography Today*, edited by Doreen Massey, John Allen, and Philip Sarre, 260–77. Oxford: Polity, 1999.

———. *Thirdspace: Journeys to Los Angeles and Other Real-and-Imagined Places*. Cambridge, MA: Wiley-Blackwell, 1996.

Spatafora, Andrea. *From the Temple of God to God as the Temple: A Biblical Theological Study of the Temple in the Book of Revelation*. Rome: Gregorian University Press, 1997.

Stambaugh, John E. "The Functions of Roman Temples." In *Aufstieg und Niedergang der römischen Welt*, part 2, *Prinzipat*, edited by Wolfgang Haase, 16.1:554–608. Berlin: de Gruyter, 1978.

Stanley, Steve. "Hebrews 9:6–10: The 'Parable' of the Tabernacle." *Novum Testamentum* 37 (1995): 385–99.

Stanton, Graham N. "Stephen in Lucan Perspective." In *Studia Biblica 1978*. Vol. 3, *Papers on Paul and Other New Testament Authors*, 345–60. Journal for the Study of the New Testament Supplement Series 3. Sheffield: JSOT Press, 1980.

Stavrakopoulou, Francesca. *God: An Anatomy*. London: Picador, 2021.

Stevenson, Gregory. *Power and Place: Temple and Identity in the Book of Revelation*. Beihefte zur Zeitschrift für die neutestamentliche Wissenschaft und die Kunde der älteren Kirche 107. Berlin: de Gruyter, 2001.

Stewart, Eric C. "New Testament Space/Spatiality." *Biblical Theology Bulletin* 42 (2012): 139–50.

Stolz, Lukas. "Das Einführen des Erstgeborenen in die οἰκουμένη (Hebr 1,6a)." *Biblica* 95 (2014): 405–23.

Strelan, Rick. "The Ascension as a Cultic Experience in Acts." In *Ascent into Heaven in Luke-Acts: New Explorations of Luke's Narrative Hinge*, edited by David K. Bryan and David W. Pao, 213–32. Minneapolis: Fortress, 2016.

Strong, John T. "Cosmic Re-creation and Ezekiel's Vocabulary." In *Ezekiel: Current Debates and Future Directions*, edited by William A. Tooman and Penelope Barter, 245–84. Forschungen zum Alten Testament 112. Tübingen: Mohr Siebeck, 2017.

———. "Grounding Ezekiel's Heavenly Ascent: A Defense of Ezek 40–48 as a Program for Restoration." *Scandinavian Journal of the Old Testament* 26 (2012): 192–211.

Stuart, Douglas K. *Hosea-Jonah*. Word Biblical Commentary. Waco: Word Books, 1987.

Suter, David W. "Temples and the Temple in the Early Enoch Tradition: Memory, Vision, and Expectation." In *The Early Enoch Literature*, edited by Gabriele Boccaccini and J. J. Collins, 195–218. Supplements to the Journal for the Study of Judaism 121. Leiden: Brill, 2007.

Sweeney, Marvin A. *The Twelve Prophets*. 2 vols. Berit Olam: Studies in Hebrew Narrative and Poetry. Collegeville, MN: Liturgical Press, 2000.

Sylva, Dennis D. "The Meaning and Function of Acts 7:46–50." *Journal of Biblical Literature* 106 (1987): 261–75.

———. "The Temple Curtain and Jesus' Death in the Gospel of Luke." *Journal of Biblical Literature* 105 (1986): 239–50.

Tagliabue, Aldo. "Learning from Allegorical Images in the Book of Visions of The Shepherd of Hermas." *Arethusa* 50 (2017): 221–55.

Tate, Marvin E. *Psalms 51–100*. Word Biblical Commentary. Dallas: Word, 1990.

Telford, William. *The Barren Temple and the Withered Tree: A Redaction-Critical Analysis of the Cursing of the Fig Tree Pericope in Mark's Gospel and Its Relation to the Cleansing of the Temple Tradition.* Journal for the Study of the New Testament Supplement Series 1. Sheffield: JSOT Press, 1980.

Theophilos, Michael. *The Abomination of Desolation in Matthew 24.15.* Library of New Testament Studies 437. London: Bloomsbury T&T Clark, 2013.

Thiessen, Matthew. "Luke 2:22, Leviticus 12, and Parturient Impurity." *Novum Testamentum* 54 (2012): 16–29.

Thompson, James W. *The Beginnings of Christian Philosophy: The Epistle to the Hebrews.* Catholic Biblical Quarterly Monograph Series 13. Washington, DC: Catholic Biblical Association of America, 1982.

———. "EPHAPAX: The One and the Many in Hebrews." *New Testament Studies* 53 (2007): 566–81.

———. *Hebrews.* Paideia. Grand Rapids: Baker Academic, 2008.

———. "What Has Middle Platonism to Do with Hebrews?" In *Reading the Epistle to the Hebrews: A Resource for Students*, edited by Eric F. Mason and Kevin B. McCruden, 31–52. SBL Resources for Biblical Study 66. Atlanta: Society of Biblical Literature, 2011.

Tóth, Franz. *Der himmlische Kult: Wirklichkeitskonstruktion und Sinnbildung in der Johannesoffenbarung.* Arbeiten zur Bibel und ihrer Geschichte 22. Leipzig: Evangelische Verlagsanstalt, 2006.

Tuell, Steven Shawn. *The Law of the Temple in Ezekiel 40–48.* Harvard Semitic Monographs 49. Atlanta: Scholars Press, 1992.

Ulansey, David. "The Heavenly Veil Torn: Mark's Cosmic Inclusio." *Journal of Biblical Literature* 110 (1991): 123–25.

———. "Heavens Torn Open: Mark's Powerful Metaphor Explained." *Bible Review* 7 (1991): 32–37.

Ullucci, Daniel C. *The Christian Rejection of Animal Sacrifice.* Oxford: Oxford University Press, 2012.

Um, Stephen T. *The Theme of Temple Christology in John's Gospel.* Library of New Testament Studies 312. London: T&T Clark, 2006.

VanderKam, James C., and William Adler, eds. *The Jewish Apocalyptic Heritage in Early Christianity.* Compendia rerum iudaicarum ad Novum Testamentum 3.4. Minneapolis: Fortress, 1996.

Vanhoye, Albert. "Esprit éternel et feu du sacrifice en He 9,14." *Biblica* 64 (1983): 263–74.

———. "Par la tente plus grande et plus parfaite (He 9,11)." *Biblica* 46 (1965): 1–28.

———. *A Perfect Priest: Studies in the Letter to the Hebrews.* Edited and translated by Nicholas J. Moore and Richard J. Ounsworth. Wissenschaftliche Untersuchungen zum Neuen Testament 2/477. Tübingen: Mohr Siebeck, 2018.

————. "Sanctuaire terrestre, sanctuaire céleste dans l'épître aux Hébreux." In *Quelle maison pour Dieu?*, edited by Camille Focant, 351–94. Lectio Divina, hors série. Paris: Cerf, 2003.

Van Leeuwen, Raymond C. "Cosmos, Temple, House: Building and Wisdom in Ancient Mesopotamia and Israel." In *From the Foundations to the Crenellations: Essays on Temple Building in the Ancient Near East and Hebrew Bible*, edited by Mark J. Boda and Jamie R. Novotny, 399–421. Alter Orient und Altes Testament 366. Münster: Ugarit, 2010.

van Unnik, Willem Cornelis. "Die 'geöffneten Himmel' in der Offenbarungsvision des Apokryphons des Johannes." In *Apophoreta: Festschrift für Ernst Haenchen*, edited by Walther Eltester and Franz H. Kettler, 269–80. Beihefte zur Zeitschrift für die neutestamentliche Wissenschaft und die Kunde der älteren Kirche 30. Berlin: de Gruyter, 1964.

Verheyden, Joseph. "The Shepherd of Hermas." *Expository Times* 117 (2006): 397–401.

Vermès, Géza. *The Complete Dead Sea Scrolls in English*. London: Penguin, 2011.

Verseput, Donald J. "Jesus' Pilgrimage to Jerusalem and Encounter in the Temple: A Geographical Motif in Matthew's Gospel." *Novum Testamentum* 36 (1994): 105–21.

Wacquant, Loïc. "Rethinking the City with Bourdieu's Trialectic." *City* 26 (2022): 820–30.

Wahlen, Clinton. "The Temple in Mark and Contested Authority." *Biblical Interpretation* 15 (2007): 248–67.

Walker, P. W. L. *Jesus and the Holy City: New Testament Perspectives on Jerusalem*. Grand Rapids: Eerdmans, 1996.

Walton, John H. "Creation in Genesis 1:1–2:3 and the Ancient Near East: Order out of Disorder after Chaoskampf." *Calvin Theological Journal* 43 (2008): 48–63.

————. *Genesis 1 as Ancient Cosmology*. Winona Lake, IN: Eisenbrauns, 2011.

————. *The Lost World of Genesis One: Ancient Cosmology and the Origins Debate*. Downers Grove, IL: IVP Academic, 2009.

Walton, Steve. "'The Heavens Opened': Cosmological and Theological Transformation in Luke and Acts." In *Cosmology and New Testament Theology*, edited by Jonathan T. Pennington and Sean McDonough, 60–73. Library of New Testament Studies 355. London: T&T Clark, 2008.

————. "Jesus, Present and/or Absent? The Presence and Presentation of Jesus as a Character in the Book of Acts." In *Characters and Characterization in Luke-Acts*, edited by Frank Dicken and Julia Snyder, 123–40. Library of New Testament Studies 548. London: T&T Clark, 2016.

Waters, Kenneth L. "Matthew 27:52–53 as Apocalyptic Apostrophe: Temporal-Spatial Collapse in the Gospel of Matthew." *Journal of Biblical Literature* 122 (2003): 489–515.

Watson, Francis. *An Apostolic Gospel: The "Epistula Apostolorum" in Literary Context*. Society for New Testament Studies Monograph Series 179. Cambridge: Cambridge University Press, 2020.

Watts, John D. W. *Isaiah 1–33*. 2nd ed. Word Biblical Commentary. Nashville: Nelson, 2005.

Wedderburn, A. J. M. "Sawing Off the Branches: Theologizing Dangerously *Ad Hebraeos*." *Journal of Theological Studies* 56 (2005): 393–414.

Weiß, Hans-Friedrich. *Der Brief an die Hebräer*. Kritisch-exegetischer Kommentar über das Neue Testament 13. Göttingen: Vandenhoeck & Ruprecht, 1991.

Wenham, Gordon J. *Genesis 1–15*. Word Biblical Commentary. Waco: Word, 1987.

———. "Sanctuary Symbolism in the Garden of Eden Story." *Proceedings of the World Congress of Jewish Studies* 9 (1985): 19–25.

Wilcox, Max. "'According to the Pattern (TBNYT) . . .': Exodus 25,40 in the New Testament and Early Jewish Thought." *Revue de Qumran* 13 (1988): 647–56.

Wilson, Brittany E. *The Embodied God: Seeing the Divine in Luke-Acts and the Early Church*. New York: Oxford University Press, 2021.

Winston, David. *The Wisdom of Solomon: A New Translation with Introduction and Commentary*. Anchor Bible. Garden City, NY: Doubleday, 1979.

Witherington, Ben, III. *The Acts of the Apostles: A Socio-Rhetorical Commentary*. Grand Rapids: Eerdmans, 1998.

Witherup, Ronald D. "Functional Redundancy in the Acts of the Apostles: A Case Study." *Journal for the Study of the New Testament* 48 (1992): 67–86.

Wray, Judith Hoch. *Rest as a Theological Metaphor in the Epistle to the Hebrews and the Gospel of Truth: Early Christian Homiletics of Rest*. SBL Dissertation Series 166. Atlanta: Scholars Press, 1998.

Wright, N. T. *History and Eschatology: Jesus and the Promise of Natural Theology*. London: SPCK, 2019.

———. *Jesus and the Victory of God*. Christian Origins and the Question of God. London: SPCK, 1996.

———. *The Resurrection of the Son of God*. Christian Origins and the Question of God. London: SPCK, 2003.

Young, Norman H. "The Gospel according to Hebrews 9." *New Testament Studies* 27 (1981): 198–210.

Zumstein, Jean. *L'Évangile selon Saint Jean (1–12)*. Commentaire du Nouveau Testament. Geneva: Labor et Fides, 2014.

———. *L'Évangile selon Saint Jean (13–21)*. Commentaire du Nouveau Testament. Geneva: Labor et Fides, 2007.

Index of Authors

Index of Scripture and Other Ancient Sources

227

Apostolic Fathers

Barnabas

2.4 173
2.4–10 173
2.6 173
4.11 174
6.15 174
7 173
8 173
9.4–7 173
11 175
11.3 175
11.6–7 175
11.10 175
16 173–74
16.1 173
16.1–2 173
16.2 173, 174n26, 174n28
16.4 174
16.6 174
16.7 174
16.8 174
16.9 174
16.10 174

1 Clement

5.7 177
7.7 178
18.16–17 178
20.1–3 177
21.6 178
27–28 177
29.1 177
29.3 176–77
32.3 177
33.3 177
34.5–7 178
35.12 178
36 177n39
36.1 177–78
36.2 xi, 177
36.5 177
39.5 177
40.1–5 176
41.2 176
42 176
43.2–5 176
48.2–4 177
52.3–4 178
59.3 177
64.1 177

2 Clement

9.3 176
14.1 176
14.2–5 176

Diognetus

3.3–4 174
4.1–5 173

Ignatius

To the Ephesians
9.1 175
9.2 175
15.3 155n30, 175

To the Magnesians
7.2 175

To the Philadelphians
7.2 176

Martyrdom of Polycarp

9.1 178
14.1 178
14.2–3 179
15.2 179

Polycarp

To the Philippians
4.3 178
12.2 178

Shepherd of Hermas

Mandates
10.3.2 171

Similitudes
8.2.5 171
9–10 172
9.1 172
9.2.1–2 172
9.3.1–4.8 172
9.5–9 172

9.12–16 172
9.12.1–3 172
9.14.5–6 172
9.15.4 172
9.16 172

Visions
3 172
3.2.4 172
3.3.5 172
3.5.1 172

Classical and Patristic Sources

Aëtius

De placitis philosophorum
1.7.4 80n7
2.6 83

Cicero

Laws
2.26 29

Republic
6.15 28–29
6.16 29

Clement of Alexandria

Stromateis
5.11 179
5.11.77 45n37
7.3 179
7.5 179
7.6 179–80
7.7 179
7.7.37 180

Dio Chrysostom

Olympic Discourse
12.24 28
12.33 28

Diodorus Siculus

Library of History
34.1.4 112n29

Diogenes Laertius

Lives
3.71 80n7

Epiphanius

Panarion
2.11 134n43

Euripides

Hippolytus
422 100n77

Herodotus

Persian Wars
1.131 29n72
1.183 64n36
2.86 83n21
6.16 64n36
8.37 68n51
9.21 90n42

Irenaeus

Against Heresies
4.17 179
4.17.1–4 179
4.17.5–6 179
4.18 179
4.18.6 179

Livy

History of Rome
6.33.4–6 68n51

Marcus Manilius

Astronomica
1.20–24 28

Origen

Against Celsus
8.21 180
8.22 180

Plato

Republic
514a–20a 80n6
515a 80n6

Timaeus
29a6–b1 39
29b 80
48e–49a 80

Plutarch

Isis and Osiris
368D 90n42

Moralia
477C 28

Pseudo-Heraclitus

Epistle
4 29n72

Seneca

Natural Questions
7.30.1 28

Ancient Near Eastern Text

Enuma Elish

1.69–77 14
5.113–30 14
6.47–72 15
6.113 15, 19

Index of Subjects